Awards Received for
Eger's ballet trilogy
84 Ribbons – *When The Music Stops*

2014 Moonbeam Book Award	Eric Hoffer Award, Young Adult
Hollywood Book Festival	Eric Hoffer, Montaigne Medal
Beach Book Festival	Reader's Views Reviewers Choice
New York Book Festival	Great Northwest Book Festival
Eric Hoffer Award, Young Adult	London Book Festival
Los Angeles Book Festival	San Francisco Book Festival
The San Francisco Book Festival	Beach Book Festival
Great Northwest Book Festival	Hollywood Book Festival
Feathered Quill	

Other Accolades for 84 Ribbons

Indie Excellence Awards—finalist, Book Interior Design—Fiction and Young Adult Fiction

Dance Spirit Magazine 'Pick of the Month' for April 2014.

YA ForeSight, ForeWord Magazine. *84 Ribbons* selected for showcase article. One of five young adult novels showcased for Spring 2014 in *The Risky Business of Growing Up.*

Praises for 84 Ribbons

Author Paddy Eger realistically portrays the daily life of a professional ballet dancer in this wonderful coming of age novel. The setting of 1950's America adds to the appeal of the story.

—**Cheryl Schubert** (Librarian)

It's a realistic look into the struggle of making it dancing professionally, including the pain, blood, sweat, and tears required, as well as the devotion to perfection. Marta doesn't have an easy ride at the Intermountain Ballet Company, but she's determined to prove herself and succeed. ...it's more than just a ballet book.

—**Leeanna Chetsko** (Net Galley Reviewer)

I loved this short book's quiet, deceptively simple voice; its strong sense of time and place (Billings, Montana in 1957); and the timelessness of its topics and themes, which include moving away from home, making friends and enemies, and dealing with first love, loneliness, temptations, and career decisions. It is squeaky clean in terms of language and content yet also candid about things like eating disorders.

—**Hope Baugh** (Librarian)

As a former bunhead who grew up in Washington, I thought this book was both credible and enjoyable.

—**Amy Anderson** (Librarian)

...Overall, this book was a pleasant surprise. It is the best ballet book I have read in a long, long time and I'm excited to see that Paddy Eger has a follow up planned as I'm keen to see what happens next.

—**Trish Hartigan** (Net Galley Reviewer)

I could see the whole thing unfold in front of me like a movie. ...I will continue to think about this story for a good while, it's just one of those books. ...Thank you, thank you, for the opportunity to read this beautiful story!

—**Holly Harkins** (Net Galley Reviewer)

Praises for
When the Music Stops

★ ★ ★ ★ ★ *A Great Sequel. I really enjoyed this book and would recommend it to those who love the world of dance or love to read about the world of dance.*
—**Sandra K. Stiles,** (Teacher, Reviewer)

★ ★ ★ ★ *...a beautifully written sequel to the enchanting first book, 84 Ribbons. ...The array of characters are complex, well developed, and the writing flows gracefully across the pages, easily captivating readers.*
—**Stacie Theis** (Beach Bound Books)

Eger's characters are entirely believable, the pace of the story is perfect, alternating in an almost ballet-like way between poses and bourrés, and the questions in Marta's heart are resolved beautifully.
—**Katie Johnson,** Author of *Red Flags for Elementary Teachers*

[The story] provides a wry look at ballet, while the beauty and passion of Marta's dancing demonstrates why people want to learn the craft.
—**Clare O'Beara,** *(Fresh Review)*

Author Paddy Eger has created a wonderful story for readers who love ballet and the dance. Part love story and part coming-of-age, readers will enjoy the story as the characters learn to overcome tragedy.
—**Kristi Bernard,** (Reviewer)

I would describe this book as gentle. It has a heart-warming theme of family and neighbors and friends all looking out for one another. But it still has a lot of depth.
—**Trish,** (Reviewer)

I found When the Music Stops-Dance On *to be an easy to read standalone novel, though it did inspire me to put* 84 Ribbons *on my reading list. The characters are realistic and believable, especially for the times. [late 1950s]*
—**Arianna Violante,** *(Reader's Views)*

Praises for Letters to Follow

★ ★ ★ ★ ★ ...a great plot with themes that fit very well inside the trilogy. The characters are very well-developed and the book is constantly taking off on a spin that I didn't see coming. ...These situations could happen in real life, which makes the book that much more interesting to read.

—LitPick Student Book Reviews

★ ★ ★ ★ Eger is masterful at letting people create places rather than letting long visual descriptions take over—we are there, in Paris, with the people, kind and mentoring or greedy and mean, who make it a world.... The ballet details were all new and interesting to me, and the weaving of the whole ballet story with the several plot lines was well done. I'll re-read the Paris section!

—Kay in Seattle

★ ★ ★ ★ ★...brilliantly-written conclusion to Paddy Eger's ballet trilogy. What a great book, and what a wonderful way to learn about the true life of ballerinas behind the stage curtain.

—Nancy Jo Jenkins
Grateful Reader

★ ★ ★ ★ ★ Eger's heroines just get better and better. Letters to Follow, A Dancer's Adventure,...flows as nimbly as the feet of her dancers through adventures, adversity, and accolades across a year of dancing and maturing on two continents. As a coming-of-age novel it could stand alone just fine; as the finale to the dance trilogy it is very satisfying, leaving the reader hoping for another sequel "to follow."

—Katie Johnson
Author, speaker, and advocate for change

★ ★ ★ ★ ★ Letters to Follow will appeal to dance lovers and to anyone who likes a good story well told. The narrative flow shares life itself, with all its expectations and disappointments... The story will break your heart and mend it at the same time.

—Gretchen Houser

★ ★ ★ ★ ★ If you like to read about talented young women who show amazing inner strength, you'll love Letters to Follow by Paddy Eger. And if you share my interest in ballet, you'll enjoy it even more.

—Gail Everett

TASMAN

An Innocent Convict's Struggle for Freedom

Paddy Eger

Tendril Press
AURORA, COLORADO

Enjoy the adventure!

TASMAN—An Innocent Convict's Struggle for Freedom

Published by Tendril Press™
www.tendrilpress.com
Denver, CO
303•696•9227

ISBN 978-0-9841543-4-0

Library of Congress Control Number: 2017947069

First Publishing: March 14, 2018
Printed in the United States of America

Author Photo by: Yuen Lui
www.YuenLuiStudio.com
Lynnwood, WA
425•771•3423

Cover Design by Karin Hoffman, AJBDPC, Inc.

Cover Image Tasmanian Archive and Heritage Office
The quay, Hobart Town J.J. Crew— SD_ILS:686388

Map (Original) © GraphicStock

Art Direction, Book Design and Cover Design
© 2017. All Rights Reserved by
A. J. Business Design & Publishing Center Inc.
www.AJImagesinc.com — 303•696•9227
Info@AJImagesInc.com

*Dedicated to those who seek
new understandings.*

Laws reflect the interests of those who frame them.

—Unknown

Author Notes

Some books move quickly from idea to finished novel. This one did not. The story began more than a decade ago after a trip to Australia. The museum at Port Arthur drew visitors in with convict playing cards and the suggestion we follow one convict's journey. My young exile fascinated me. The poem I wrote grew to a short story and eventually into this novel. If you want more information and can't travel to Tasmania, consult the suggested reading list at the back of the book.

FACTS vs. FICTION

The places, forms of work, and harsh conditions in the penal colony are based on recorded facts. The people are fictional, but all incidents could have happened. In a few instances the historical times and events were condensed or expanded to accommodate the story.

The ROUTE from England to Port Arthur, Tasmania

While not all ships sailed a route from England to North Africa to Rio and on to South Africa on their way to Tasmania, many did. The prevailing winds played a part in their decision on a route. Many carried legal and illegal cargo from port to port, which further accounts for the longer voyage used in this story.

THANK YOUs

A book is created with the support of a large number of people who believe in an author and the project. My thanks for my early readers: Marilyn Melville-Irvine, Gretchen Houser, Emily Hill, and my husband, Rich.

The Eggs, my early editors in my critique group: Kirby Larson, Dusty Cavaliere, Gail Everett, Karen Meissner, Bill Segger, Chris Kiehl, Sue Burrus, Dick Holmes, Susan King, and Ann Gonzales brought their reader-eyes and writer-suggestions to help me stay focused.

My editor, Linda Lane, and Karin Hoffman, my creative designer and CEO/publisher at Tendril Press, brought Ean's story to final form so you can follow his adventures. I thank each of you for taking the journey with Ean and me.

*** *I look forward to hearing from you once you've completed reading Ean's adventure.*

Chat, Comment, and Connect
at PaddyEger.com

A Brief GLOSSARY

Usually, a glossary follows a story. Since this is an adventure, I want you to have details *before* you encounter them so you'll not need to break away from the story once you begin reading.

aboriginal - native/indigenous people (in this story they are in Tasmania and Australia)

clark - British spelling of clerk, a person who records information

echidna - an ant-eating Tasmanian animal that looks like a porcupine with a long snout

gaol - British spelling of jail

Guy Fawkes - a captured Catholic dissident who tried to blow up British Parliament in 1605, later celebrated with fireworks (Remember, remember, the fifth of November.)

holystone - sandstone used to scrub the wooden deck of a ship to clean away debris and sea water salt

hulk - old British ships with their masts sawed down and used as prison ships in the 1850s

Johnny Raw - term for a new prisoner who doesn't know the procedures

pillory - a wooden framework that locked around a prisoner's neck and wrists

reticule - a 19th century woman's drawstring purse

scrimshaw - designs carved into bones (especially whale bones) and ivory such as walrus tusks

transport - 18th and 19th century term for moving prisoners to work in outposts/penal colonies

Tyburn Faire - the gallows near Newgate Gaol in London

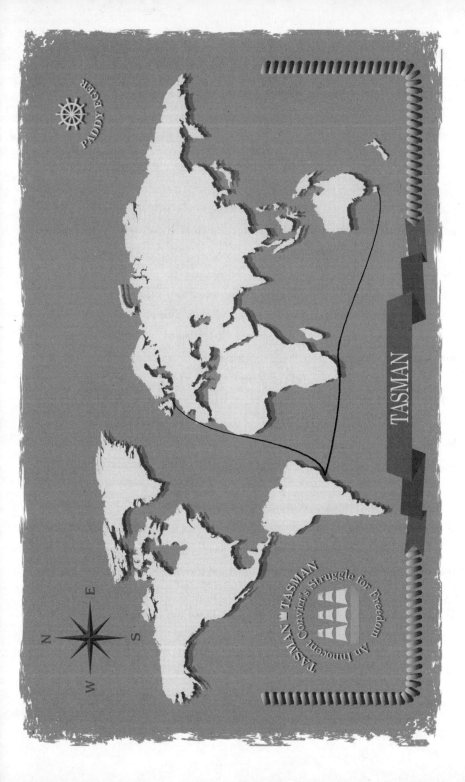

TASMAN

1850

Wham!

Strong arms yanked me from my cot and dragged me to standing. My eyes popped open. I shook my head to get my wits about me and tried to twist myself free. The Langstone constable pulled my arms behind my back, tied them with a rope, and shoved me roughly out the door of the print shop.

Fear clutched like a raven claw. "What's happening? Where are you taking me? I've done nothing wrong!"

"Silence!" The constable whacked my head as he forced me along Master John's path and out to the dusty lane. "Yer crimes will be listed in due time."

"But I've done nothing! I—"

He whacked my head again. "Silence!"

I stumbled along the village road, still trying to rouse myself. Moments before he'd arrived, I'd been listening to the wintry wind howling outside my window, waking slowly with thoughts of my lovely Fiona. Why had the constable nabbed me?

We passed farmers and their helpers off to their fields or to market. None spoke or met my glance. As the constable loaded me into the back of his wagon, the village clergy approached. "Where are you taking Ean McClaud, sir?"

"To London Town, Your Grace. Lord Colridge has spoken against him and demands his transport."

The clergy crossed himself and stared at me. "What crime?"

"Ask his Lordship, Your Grace." The constable tightened the rope around my wrists and shoved me into the back of the wagon, securing the rope to a rusty ring. "Good day, sir."

The constable flicked the reins. I tumbled and smashed into the side of the wagon when we lurched forward. "Tell Fiona Laren of my arrest."

The clergy raised his hand as if to say he'd grant my request. I prayed that to be so.

The wagon rumbled through the village and around a bend in the road. A blast of icy wind whipped the damp air through my tunic. I shivered. None of this made sense, but I had no power to stop the constable from taking me when and where he wished.

At the outskirts of London Town, we pulled up to a smithy's shop. The constable disappeared inside. Within minutes he pulled me from the back of the wagon and shoved me along the roadway, still bound and now tethered by the neck like a stray goat. If I remembered correctly, we remained a two-hour walk from any building of import in London Town. Perhaps we planned to stop long before reaching the city.

Morning light lifted slowly, promising another frosty day at the manor. By now Fiona would be up and working for Lady Colridge. She'd not learn of my arrest for many hours to come. I'd probably be back to Master John's, working on the press, before she heard any news. We'd laugh together over this mistake that took me to London Town.

As we entered the edge of city, the workers extinguished the gas lights; street sweeps and gawkers laughed at me and spit at my feet. Lavender ladies whispered behind their hands while they strolled to their rooms to rest up for the night's return to their corners, where they stood to entice men into their beds.

The jumble shops stood open, their bric-a-brac crowding onto the sidewalks to tempt early passersby. Outside a bakery a handful of muffin boys carried overflowing baskets of fresh buns to sell along the streets. My stomach growled as the aroma of breakfast breads trailed behind each lad.

The sun climbed through the cloud-laden sky at midday as we entered London Town proper. I attempted to stop walking when Newgate Gaol loomed directly ahead. My heart plummeted when the constable forced me inside its walls. Only serious criminals dwelt in the infamous filth of Newgate's dungeons.

Last year, when I accompanied Master John to town, we walked along this same cobbled street. I remember seeing prisoners stretching their hands out the narrow windows, begging for coins. I shuddered. Why was I here?

The constable spoke to a guard. Moments later, the three of us descended a spiral stairway, passing through iron-spiked wooden doors where turnkeys dressed in black jiggled their heavy ring of keys in my face and grinned. I fought the urge to gag at the smell of stale food, splashed ale, and unwashed bodies. The further we descended, the more the stench settled on my skin like dried sea salt.

We moved deeper and deeper into the gaol, passing iron-gated rooms overflowing with drunken men and dirty-skirted doxies whistling and hooting at my misfortune. Many reached out to grab my tunic. I pushed past them, pretending not to notice.

The stone passages narrowed, the light dimmed, the air cooled. The constable removed a torch from the stone wall as we approached yet another door. He yanked the rope around my neck, forcing me to an abrupt stop. The turnkey opened the iron bars, pushing me inside once the rope was removed. The lock clicked. Both men turned to leave.

I stumbled forward, smashing my face into the dank stone floor. Stars flashed before my eyes, and my head throbbed; my skin became slick as if I'd spent a day at the presses. I righted myself and crawled to the door. "Let me out! I can't breathe!"

I heard shifting and scuffling. A stout prisoner approached. "Can't handle the dim light, huh? Get used to it." He shoved his foot against my chest to pin me to the floor. Just as suddenly, he moved his foot away, grabbed me with both hands, and hauled me to my feet. "What's yer crime, lad?"

"Nothing!" I twisted, but he kept me pinned against the cell door.

Shuffling sounded in the dark corners. Men with clanking leg irons emerged from the shadows to encircle me. Their fists opened and closed.

The stout prisoner bellowed, "Liar!" He banged me against the door again and again. "Whose purse did ya lift, or was it the skirt of a pretty lass?"

"Neither. I did nothing wrong, I swear!"

My tormentor loosened his grip. I sank to the floor and curled up like a newborn, shivering, wishing I had my woolen jacket to block out the cold.

Every part of my body ached. I inhaled and focused on the hall torch spreading flickers of light along the passageway, praying the man would soon tire of having his sport with me.

Long minutes later, when the prison gaoler returned, the men backed into the shadows. The gaoler pulled himself tall and cleared his throat. "Ean McClaud, y'ur accused of stealing a silk handkerchief and three silver spoons from Lord Colridge of Langstone. Yer trial will commence in one week's time."

The words slapped like a hand against my face. "I have taken no handkerchief or silver spoons, sir!"

The gaoler ignored me. He removed my wrist chains, double-ironed my ankles, and glanced at his handiwork. "For three shillings each, I'll remove these irons."

"I have no money!"

He laughed, backed out the door, and slammed it shut. The only sounds that lingered were the restless men and a slow, irregular drip from a dark corner.

I sat on the floor, rubbing my ankles where the shackles dug into my skin. I couldn't believe the charges. The handkerchief was a gift from Lady Colridge for Fiona, my sweetheart. And silver spoons? I'd never been inside the manor. Did they think I stole spoons or did they blame Fiona? Was she in gaol as well? No. Her Ladyship gifted the maids with dresses she tired of wearing. Those hand-me-downs ensured their continued faithfulness. None would steal from her.

The stout prisoner approached again, his stench arriving ahead of him. "Oh, now I see, lad. Y'ur a thief like the rest of us. I suppose the lady *gave* ya a token. What else did she give ya?"

"Lady Colridge is Fiona's mistress."

"So, ya *know* Lady Colridge, and she gave ya a token for Fiona? I imagine she told her husband about her generosity. Rich women tend to brag and prattle."

Several prisoners stepped closer, their demon-like shadows elongating across the ceiling and the back wall. I scooted away. The dampness of the cell wall seeped through my tunic and mingled with the cold sweat running down my sides. I brushed my hands over my face and my hair. I couldn't catch my breath or gather a clear thought.

A voice from the shadows laughed. "Just look at him, Robb. He's thin enough to sneak in a skinny window, but his hands are stained black. His clothes fit too tight to hide any thievery. Bet he can't tell a believable lie."

My cellmates hooted and howled from their pallets. Robb, my stout tormentor, walked away, shoved a prisoner off a pallet, and flopped down.

Another voice spoke from the shadows. "Ah, this *fine* young man doesn't belong here, now does he, lads? Thinks he's better than the likes of us. He sounds to be an Irishman. He's lucky the lord didn't kill him on the spot."

Anger rose through me like a fever. I leapt up and lashed out, dragging my leg irons toward their pallets, swinging my arms and yelling. "You're all drunken thieves."

Within seconds they rushed me, pinning me to the wall. "Did ya plan to escape with the lovely, snaggle-toothed Fiona to a fine castle in Ireland?" shouted one man as he rammed my head against the iron bars and ranted. "What did ya tell her, lad? Speak up."

My head throbbed worse than the time Master John slammed me into the press for talking back. I twisted loose and banged my fists on the iron bars. "I'm innocent."

Robb approached again, smacking his fists together, taking a swipe at my head as I ducked away. "A touching tale. The poor innocent. All he did was love a lass. We'll see whose shilling removes the irons from this root-grubbing Irishman."

A deep voice from the darkened pallets spoke. "Give it a rest, man. Remember your first time in Newgate?"

The tallest man I'd ever seen stepped forward. His narrow face looked comical on top of his gigantic body. My skin burned with a rage I could not tamp down. I clenched my fists and started to get up, but the giant's strong hand interceded. "Easy, lad. No use going after him. He'll kick and beat ya with no better excuse than he doesn't like the color of yer tunic."

I backed down, but kept my fists ready.

While I sat panting, the giant's laughter echoed off the walls. "You believed that flouncing Brit, Lady Colridge? Yer stupidity brought ya here." He lowered himself onto his haunches and looked me in the eye. "What's yer name?"

"Ean McClaud, born of County Cork, Langstone printer's apprentice. I'll be out of here before any trial. You'll see."

The giant pushed my shoulder down as he rose to his feet. "Hope 'tis true, Ean."

All night I lay on the floor and shivered while listening to wheezing, snoring, and groaning of a dozen men sleeping two to a pallet or lying against the stone walls. When I closed my eyes, the space swayed, so I kept them open, focusing on my sweet Fiona's smile as she twisted her auburn-colored hair around her little finger. I pictured our secret bower deep in the woods of Lord Colridge's manor and sought to remember the smell of summer grasses when we kissed and shared brief caresses. Each time we met, it became more difficult to break apart.

A week ago, Fiona and I stood with our arms entwined, hidden behind the laurel hedge. She ran her fingers through my hair and tucked herself inside my woolen jacket. "I love the way your hair curls up on your shoulders. It's so—"

"Fiona, stop your teasing. I must leave."

She nestled against me; the smell of her hair and the touch of her lips warmed every inch of my body. "I so enjoyed our afternoon walk in the forest," she said. "Can you return before next Sabbath?"

I kissed her cheek and held her away for one last look at her sparkling green eyes. "I'll try, but I make no promises. Now I must go. It's almost dusk, and the printer will have my hide if I'm late another evening."

She stretched on tiptoe and kissed my cheek. Before I could return her kiss, she ran up the steps, glanced back to blow a kiss, then slipped inside the kitchen door.

As I left by the back gate, I touched my cheek where the warmth of her kiss lingered. My life in Langstone was good. I had food, a bed, and soon I'd finish my apprenticeship and earn wages from Master John.

Everyone knew Fiona belonged with me. We planned to announce our betrothal in six months' time, if I could convince her thus. I hungered to make her my wife.

When I entered the printer's cottage, the mistress stood with her hands on her hips pretending to look stern, but I saw the smile at the corners of her mouth. She shouted, "Ean McClaud! The master is yelling for you. Be quick about it."

I rushed past her to the print shop and grabbed my apron from the hook. Master John's muscular back bent over the press. His grumbles ricocheted off the walls as he banged gears with a wooden mallet. He straightened as I entered.

"Where have you been, lad?" His blue eyes flared with anger. "This gear is stuck again. I told you to fix it last week."

"I fixed it early this morning. We need to purchase—"

"Purchase? I have no money to replace it again. Fix the gear or find a new apprenticeship. We have adverts, handbills, and the penny paper to run at first light tomorrow." He turned away from the press, threw his mallet across the room, and walked out past the type table, leaving me to repair the contrary machine.

All night while I worked on the gear, I passed the time thinking of my beautiful Fiona running to the river, her auburn hair covering her face as she stooped to pluck a stray bird's feather from the frozen ground. I pictured her watching clouds drift overhead and remembered her impish smile when she sidled up to me and ran her fingers through my hair.

I kissed her forehead. "When will we wed, Fiona? You've sewn our linens and made a lovely gown to wear."

She brushed back my hair and kissed me. "You must set aside wages before we wed. We have no place to live."

"We can live in the game warden's cottage. I'll ask Lord Colridge."

She pushed me away and puffed up like a guinea hen. "Don't talk to him, promise me, Ean. I doubt he'd give us so much as a twist of lavender. He'll want more money for the cottage than you'll ever earn for food, clothing, and other necessaries. We must wait."

Her seriousness silenced me for a moment. Then I laughed and pulled her along the path to the herb garden. "Don't worry, Fiona, my love, we'll find a way." I kissed her and held her against me. She whispered sweet words until I forgot everything but her loveliness.

Night eased into morning; I'd repaired the press. By now she'd have her face turned up to enjoy any hint of sunlight as she aired out her mistress' clothes for the day. Did she dream of me, or did she dream of owning another of Lady Colridge's discarded gowns? I doubted I could wait a week to see her.

Each morning I ate breakfast in the master's cottage. His wife loved me like a son and expected me to act as a gentleman: polite, respectful, and clean-shaven. To insure her continued faith in me, I'd adjust my clothing to their best appearance; but, much as I scrubbed my hands, they remained black with ink, the tips of my nails mimicking the shadow side of a sliver moon. In less than one year's time, if his wife had her say, Master John would take me on as a pressman. Then Fiona and I would be together forever.

The day Master John and I finished early, I gulped down supper and walked the three miles to Lord Colridge's manor to see Fiona. Sunlight faded as I crossed through the fields, saving time off walking 'round to the road. The February coolness rippled at my coat, mirroring the beat of my heart.

My feet knew the route without thinking: up the hill, through the manor gate, along the worn dirt path, and beneath the grape arbor. I entered the last gate and paced by the kitchen door, waiting for a maid to exit. When the door opened, Lady Colridge herself stepped out. I doffed my cap and looked to the ground before facing her.

She fluttered her eyelids and smiled. "You're Fiona's young man, I believe?"

"Yes, My Lady."

"She's mending just now. I expect she'll finish within the hour. Will you wait?"

I nodded, looking back toward the ground. Hearing no voice or movement, I looked up.

She stared at me. "What's your name?"

"Ean McClaud, My Lady. I'm Master John's print devil." Her stare made me nervous. I fidgeted with my cap.

She tilted her head. "Do you have good intentions with Fiona?"

"Yes, My Lady."

She laughed, her voice as musical as small bells. "Do you gift her and bring her treasures?"

"No, Mistress. I have no coins for such things."

Lady Colridge walked down the steps; her wide skirt swished against the wooden treads. "Every lady deserves a treasure." She opened the draw string on her reticule and removed a white silk handkerchief. She placed it on my inky hand and laughed. "Tomorrow is my day in London Town. I'll purchase another."

Before I found words to answer, she turned, moved up the steps, and disappeared inside. I hesitated to close my inky fingers around the handkerchief, but I lifted it to my face; it held the scent of lavender. Why was the mistress generous to my sweet Fiona?

The twilight chilled me. I paced faster. Where was Fiona? When she finally emerged, the last of the sun's rays glanced off her auburn hair, creating a burnished halo. She rushed to me, enveloping me in her smell of soap and dampness.

"I didn't expect to see you again so soon, Ean."

I folded my arms around her. "I know. I couldn't wait 'til next Sabbath afternoon." I handed her the handkerchief and smiled. "Lady Colridge has gifted you."

Fiona took the silk and pressed it to her heart. "It's lovely." Dropping her chin, she kept her gaze on me and smiled. "Should I kiss her or you, Ean?"

"Don't tease, Fiona. I want you to save your kisses for me."

We moved behind the laurel hedge until a cold breeze reminded us it was late. As I turned to leave, the upstairs drape closed. Lady Colridge had watched to see how her silk handkerchief was received. My life felt bonnie good.

❖

A swift kick to my side jangled my thoughts back to the damp gaol floor. I groaned.

"You! Move yer boney arse out of the way!"

I scooted away, pressed myself against the wall, and sat with my head on my knees, reasoning through my plight. Did I misunderstand Lady Colridge? Why did her husband have me arrested? I remembered hearing the maids say that Lord Colridge brushed past them on the stairs, trying to grab them and kiss them. Did he do the same with Fiona? She never mentioned it. I shuddered, unable to erase the picture of him touching her.

The turnkey approached; opened the door; and set bowls of dry bread, meat scraps, and a pitcher of ale in our cell. Before he'd exited and locked the door, hungry prisoners grabbed every morsel.

My hunger overpowered my tiredness, but I feigned sleep to give my tormentors no cause to continue their attacks. Through squinting eyes, I watched them fight for the tiniest crumb and slap the pitcher away from the weaker cellmates' hands. Their meanness frightened me.

After the food was consumed, the shouting, fighting, and grumbling in the cell grew louder. A passing prisoner kicked whatever part of my body lay closest to his foot. I held myself quiet, knowing my skinny strength could never overpower their numbers.

The giant sat down beside me.

"What happens now?" I asked.

"Keep yer distance from Robb, yer tormentor. He's killed three men. Headed for solitary next week and on to Tyburn Faire. He'll put on a fine show dangling from the gallows. They can't hang him twice, so he's got nothin' to lose if he kills ya."

His words sent a cold chill down my spine.

❖

Day after day, hour by hour, prisoners were carted away to Old Bailey court to hear their charges. A fat, bearded man returned and sneered, "Well, lads, I'm off to the hulks for six months. Got me some barnacles to scrape, but at least I'll have fresh air and space from the likes of you."

"What are hulks?" I asked the giant.

"They're old military ships with their masts sawed down to stumps. The gov'ner turned 'em into prisons. Men sleep and eat there, but spend the rest of their days scraping barnacles for The Crown. Ladies and gents stand around making wagers. When the prisoners rest, the folks throw food at 'em ta urge 'em to fight hard enough to win the good bits."

I thought about the hulks. If I were there, Fiona might visit me. What was I thinking? She'd not know where I'd been sent. Perhaps she'd been taken to gaol as well. I'd die if that happened.

A scrawny young lad returned to the cell, shaking like a woman who'd seen a snake in her garden. "Got four years for stealing a dented silver pocket watch and two candlesticks. They're transporting me to Macquarie Harbor."

The cell hushed like a cemetery at midnight.

Robb shook his head. "Lord, man. That's a horrible place on the other side of the world. They chain ya up dusk to dawn and work ya like slaves. Death is better than that place."

The scrawny lad flopped on a pallet, turned his back, and curled up.

Robb passed my space on the floor. He kicked but missed, banging his foot against the cell bars. "Lucky ya only stole a hanky and silver. Otherwise, ya could end up transported—gone forever."

"What does transported mean?" I asked the giant.

Robb passed by again and answered. "It means ya never see yer home again. Y'll be in a land of savages and strange, wild beasts with two heads and claws like lions. The guards value nothing and no one. 'Tis not a place I'd want to visit."

Time lost meaning in the dusky light as guards took men away one by one. Several gained releases by their innocence; others bought off their gaol time with pouches of coins. Unfortunate men returned with a gallows sentence.

To pass the time, I focused on avoiding Robb and finding any small flicker of light to keep the darkness at bay. I hoped for the best, but each day I sat in the gaol meant a smaller chance I'd soon be freed.

I turned away from the others and fingered the crown Fiona had sewn into my waist band. She'd made me promise to use it only in case of need. It wasn't enough to buy my release, but it might remove my heavy, skin-rubbing leg irons.

But that afternoon when a scribe offered his services for hire to write letters, I knew what I wanted to do. "Sir, may I buy paper, ink, and a pen to write my own letter?"

He smirked and studied my face. "Two shillings fer paper and two more fer ink and a nib."

"Four shillings! That's tenfold their value!"

He shrugged and awaited my decision.

I handed him the crown. My cell mates saw the exchange. I waited until I could turn away to hide leftover coins, praying I could hang on to them until my release.

As I wrote to Fiona, I gave a prayer of thanks to Ma. She'd forced me to learn numbers and letters from our village clergy. Once I reached England, my skill allowed me to become a printer's devil. I wrote:

Dearest Fiona,

I humbly beseech you to speak with Master John on my behalf. Tell him I am innocent. I pray you are not in gaol for keeping the handkerchief.

I think of you every moment and await your reply. Your love sustains me.

Ean

The scribe returned and took my letter, promising to deliver it within a week's time.

"A week? I'll be free and back in the print shop by then."

"For five shillings I'll deliver it tomorrow."

I started to protest, but stopped and shook my head. What a mean soul. He knew I had less than that after buying paper and a pen.

The turnkey arrived and opened the cell door. He stood with his palm outstretched toward the scribe. Coins clinked as he closed his hand and locked the cell.

❖

Yesterday, the giant left Newgate. His friends brought a bag of coins, and he walked free. Before he left, he whispered and pointed into the shadows. "The fat man, there on the last pallet, may protect you from the ruffians if you give him your shillings."

"I have but two left."

"That may be enough."

I watched the giant's shadow disappear along the hallway. Loneliness sucked away my energy. Unless two shillings interested the fat man, I'd be unprotected until my turn at court.

The next evening, I grabbed a portion of the food, but not enough to satisfy my hunger. The rough-edged irons rubbed my ankles raw, but I kept my own counsel and my shillings. I saw myself buying a raw turnip or a bun slathered in butter to eat as I returned home.

Mid-day. No word arrived from Fiona, Master John, or Lady Colridge. No one visited me in the press yard, so I spent my brief time outside walking in circles. Back inside, my cellmates continued to taunt me. Knowing I'd soon be free, I swallowed my rage and feigned sleep most of my time in the cell.

"McClaud!" the gaoler said. "Step to the door!" I stepped forward. He removed my leg irons and bound my wrists behind my back. My ankles throbbed and my stomach grumbled with emptiness, but I straightened and allowed a smile to crowd the corners of my mouth as I walked from the cell.

At the street, the first glimpse of sunlight blinded me. The gaoler released me to a constable and pocketed a handful of coins. The constable tethered my waist with a stout rope. I stumbled as he pushed me along.

The salt-tinged London Town air filled my nostrils, replacing the stench from the cell. This time tomorrow, I'd be back to work. In the evening I'd walk to visit Fiona. Newgate Gaol would fade like a bad dream.

I couldn't suppress a small smile of triumph until I noticed where we walked. "This isn't the way to court. Where are you taking me?"

"Quiet, lad. Takin' a little side trip, that's all."

2

We walked along narrow, twisting streets. The smell of wood and tar mingled with that of stale ale and rotting vegetables. A sea of barefoot men dressed in rough jackets and canvas breeches steered past, hauling boxes and crates on their rickety carts. The constable yanked my tether and used the loose end of the rope to whip my back and head. He smiled as the sailors jeered and spit on me.

Overhead, gulls wheeled in descending circles near tall masts that crowded the sky. We'd arrived at the sailing docks next to Blackstone Bridge on the Thames River.

A two-masted brig lay tied to the closest pier, its name hidden by draped rigging and sagging sails. The constable pushed me up the gangplank and handed papers to an officer in a blue cutaway coat. In return he received a bag that jangled with coins. The papers passed to a soldier, who grabbed me by the neck and shoved me down worn, wooden steps. I crashed into a pole and fell onto the floor.

"Ah-h!" I shook my head to clear away my confusion and the pain shooting through my shoulder. "This is a mistake. I'm to be freed! Ask Lady Colridge!"

A burly soldier clamored down the steps. He shoved me against the wooden planks, laughed, and shook papers in front of my face. "And who do ya think signed these? Your savior's husband, Lord Colridge, he did. Ya belong to the government for the next three years."

I rose to my knees. "What? Three years? This isn't right. I stole nothing! Lady Colridge gifted Fiona."

My secreted coins fell from my waistband and rolled across the splintered wooden deck as men scrambled to grab them. I didn't bother trying to recover them. "No matter," I whispered to myself, "I'm to be freed."

A second young soldier clomped down the steps and secured my ankles with rusty leg irons. He yanked them to check the tightness. I screamed. He slapped my head hard with his open palm. "Silence! You're on your way to Van Diemen's Land, where all thieves, murderers, and luckless Irish belong. Pulled me a rotten duty this, watching over the likes of you!"

Knife-like pain zig-zagged through my shoulder as I pulled myself upright. I inhaled and shook my head, trying to understand why I'd been kidnapped and brought here. Lord Colridge must have wanted me away from Langstone. Why?

A small, dark-skinned man scooted from the shadows and leaned in to speak to me. The light from the open hatch allowed me to see the long scar that bisected his right cheek and disappeared into the haphazard whiskers around his chin. "Don't do no good to talk back."

"But this is a mistake. Three years for a piece of silk, I…"

"Don't matter. You've been sold, and now y'ur a slave to the gov'ner."

I leaned against a post. Pain and wintry cold penetrated my body like a spear of ice. "What? Where are we going? To the hulks?"

"Didn't ya listen?" The dark-skinned man coughed and cleared his throat. "We're on our way to the other side of the world."

Was that the place the young prisoner in Newgate moaned about— the place where men were chained like animals? It couldn't be. I was no forger or embezzler, not a thief or a murderer. How will I get word to Fiona? Is there even a way to get back from the other side of the world?

❖

After my eyes adjusted to the dusky light, I focused on the sights and sounds around me. The space smelled of unwashed bodies like the stale air of the Newgate gaol cell. I noticed the clanking of leg irons and bodies shifting. My Lord! The ship must have dozens of men crowded cheek to jowl around me.

I sidled over to the dark-skinned man. "Where are these men from? Surely the gaol notices when men go missing."

"Most were filled with spirits and stolen from pubs," he said. "Some from prisons 'n reported as escaped. Doesn't matter; once y'ur on a ship, yer future changes forever."

"How is it these men stay so quiet?"

The dark-skinned man snorted. "If we make noise, our rations and our time on deck are cut. Now, move away! I don't want to give the soldiers any reason to punish me further."

I stayed upright, leaning against a post in the center next to huge barrels draped in ropes and padlocks. Mice and other crawly things skittered across the floor and over my legs. I batted them away. All too soon, I felt stings on my legs as bugs began biting me. I itched more than the time Fiona and I rolled in the hay.

After an additional handful of prisoners clanked down the steps, the hatch cover slammed shut and a heavy chain rattled across it, locking us below the deck. Only a sliver of light seeped in around the cover. I inhaled the stagnant air and waited for whatever came next.

Overhead, feet hurried across the deck like animals scurrying for food. A loud, grinding noise scraped inside the hull, shuddered, followed by a swoosh of water. The ship pitched and rolled. We'd set sail. All was lost.

The ship rocked and vibrated, causing the barrels to shift and graze my fingers. I pulled back my hand and clutched the post. I closed my eyes. Bile filled my mouth with each swaying motion of the ship.

Heavy footsteps and muted voices continued above our heads. Water splashed against the outer walls as if trying to break through. Would the boards withstand the constant pounding? I prayed so.

The hatch cover scraped aside. Two soldiers clomped down the steps, carrying buckets with dippers. They set them down, grabbed up a set of smelly buckets, and left. Another soldier threw two buckets down the steps.

Grumblings surrounded me. "Pass those privy buckets and be quick about it!"

"Send the food buckets and don't mix them up." Anger circled as buckets filled and emptied.

The smell of porridge made me heave; death hovered nearby. I moaned, "I think I'm dying."

"No, you're sick from the ship's rocking," the dark-skinned man said. "Wait 'til we reach the open sea. Then y'll feel true waves." He scooted closer and whispered, "Why are ya here?"

I explained and asked after his reason for being on the ship.

"I'm judged a traitor by the Crown for the times I spoke out against the King."

"Did you speak thus against him?"

The dark-skinned man snickered. "Too late to matter now."

Within the hour, the heavy anchor chain rattled beyond the wall of our space. We no longer moved forward. Soldiers opened the cover and descended the steps with bayoneted muskets pointed at us. "Get up!

Cap'n wants ya on deck. Now!"

They herded us against the sides of the ship to stand beneath the limp sails. We'd anchored in the middle of the Thames River, far from any settlements. The biting wind sucked away my energy; I wobbled with dizziness from the rocking of the ship but managed to stay on my feet. Two dozen soldiers flanked us with their guns pointed to our heads as we stood crowded together like a herd of dumb sheep, blinking in the frigid yet bright wintry sunlight.

A wall of a man with his sword strapped to his belt paced a raised section of the deck. He drew the sword from its scabbard, holding it like an extension of his hand, and waved it over our heads as he spoke. "I am Captain Jonas Woodwright. This is His Majesty's ship the *Sara Jane*. For the next five or six months, you exiles belong to me."

I gasped. We'd be on this ship for six months?

The captain strutted across the deck. "My word is law. Do as y'ur told, and y'll live to feel dry land 'neath yer feet. Disobey my rules —and y'll be fitted with extra leg irons, flogged, or cast overboard to feed the hungry sharks.

"All one hundred fifty of you will *not* interfere with the crew's tasks of sailing this ship. Remain along the sides, behind the ropes on port and starboard, when y'ur on deck. Y'll remain 'tween decks in the hold until we leave the Channel for the open sea. Every man and woman who cooperates will receive extra time on deck."

I replayed Captain Woodwright words. Women on the ship? I scanned the deck and saw them standing forward. Was Fiona one of them? I didn't see her. Thank heaven.

Many of the women wore frowns meaner than the cooper's wife when she bellowed the fire. Some looked to be lasses Fiona's age, but none shared her beauty.

The captain resheathed his sword, turned, and walked to the front of the ship. Another man jumped onto the raised deck. "I'm Mister Meed. When the captain is not on deck, I'm in charge. You *will* do as I say."

I held my arm against my chest and closed my eyes to lessen my pain and to keep my focus on his words.

Mister Meed continued. "Do not engage the soldiers in conversation. Keep clear of the crew as they work the sheets. You'll receive two meals a day and—"

I awoke thinking of Fiona with her body pressed close to mine, her hand nudging me. Instead of her sweet face, a man stood over me with his hand pressed against my shoulder. "Ready?"

I blinked and moved my head from side to side to clear my sleepy haze. Was I dreaming? The man stared down at me. "Hold yer breath."

The vision of Fiona faded, replaced by searing pain. I screamed and tried to sit up, but I couldn't move; I was tied to a wooden table.

The man patted my arm and untied the ropes holding me down. "Yer shoulder is back in place." He tore a long rag from an old tunic and strapped my arm against my body. "Wear this."

I swallowed hard, gulping down mouthfuls of salty air.

"Guard!" he called out. A soldier arrived and pulled me to standing. He pushed me ahead of him until I descended into the darkness of the hold at the base of the steps. I slumped against the post and tried to figure out what had happened. I must have fainted. I needed to speak with the dark-skinned man, I thought, but he didn't appear to be in his place.

For the rest of the day, I listened as footsteps crossed the deck. I kept my eyes on the seam of light that entered around the hatch. To distract myself from my pain, I thought about the swish of Fiona's skirt when she ran with me to the river. Why did she not come to Newgate to visit me?

I pictured Master John banging the press to submission. I wondered why he allowed the constable to take me away? Did he not believe my innocence? He'd not wait three years' time for my return; my apprenticeship was gone. What would be left for me, for my future?

Muffled shouts seeped down from the deck. Exiles whispered and passed the buckets. The dark-skinned man was missing.

Soon the hatch opened. He stumbled down the steps, falling against my feet. Blood streamed down his face. His shirt hung in shreds; his hands were bound behind his back, and his ankles wore double chains.

"Are you alright?" I said.

"Do I look alright? They think because I'm called a traitor, I've secrets they c'n sell to the gov'ner. They c'n flog me every day, but I have nothing to tell them. Now, let me rest." He spat on the floor and turned away.

Day and night, bells rang in a pattern I didn't understand. People scuttled up and down the stairs on the other side of our prison wall. Each roused me; my heaving continued making our space smell worse than a slacker's barn on a blistering summer's day. Men chained near me scooted as far away as possible, leaving only their curses behind.

When the soldiers discovered my vomit, they lowered down a bucket of water and a broom and watched me clean up the mess, much less punishment than I anticipated. It didn't matter; I knew I'd soon be dead in the darkness that whirled around me.

Minutes stretched to hours and hours to days that bumped into each other in a blur of sameness. Through snatches of conversation, I learned it was a new month, March, with its short days and long nights away from Fiona and Langstone.

From our brief moments on the deck, I saw that our ship remained anchored in the Thames. Would we sail away, or was this a cruel trick to weaken us before we were set free or sent to work on the hulks?

I dreaded returning to the darkness below, where I was forced to lie on the bottom tier of sleeping shelves lining the outer edges of the narrow lower deck. I couldn't sit up for fear of bumping my head. I couldn't easily turn over without bumping the man on either side of me. I felt like a stored slab of meat rather than a human. But even a slab of meat didn't have the disgrace of wearing leg irons.

I busied my thinking with images of Master John working. He'd have finished the most recent village newspaper and made hundreds of handbills without me. Maybe he'd hired the scrawny boy from the next village who begged for a job every time he collected his master's adverts.

My thoughts always wandered from the print shop to Fiona. Was she safe or in prison? Did she keep her job with Lady Colridge, or had my situation caused her to be sent away? Why was this happening to me, to us?

On the morrow's dawn, the hatch creaked opened and four crew men tossed it aside. Two soldiers clamored down the steps. "On deck. Stay within the roped areas and no talking!"

Captain Woodwright paced a raised platform on the main deck. His deep blue uniform jacket refused to meet in front. His white shirt and breeches carried heavy food stains and grime. He swaggered and swayed like an unhappy man with an appetite for spirits.

"We're about to set sail. When we reach the open sea, the likes of you will be allowed above deck during daylight hours. Just now, we'll be recording each prisoner's name and crimes and assigning yer prison number. If you read and write, take three steps forward, now."

I stepped forward. Dozens of angry eyes glowered at me and the others who formed a scrawny line.

Woodwright pointed his finger at me and two others. "Follow Mr. Meed. The rest of ya stay where ya are. If these three fail, ya may be called to take their place."

Mister Meed handed out log books, pens, and ink pots. He watched us to determine if we truly knew how to write. Soon he set us to inventorying the prisoners. Each exile stepped forward to have his name and crime recorded: thieves, burglars, counterfeiters, murderers. Most professed their innocence.

Meed ordered each man's leg irons removed so he could strip off his clothing. I blushed at seeing grown men stand naked before me and averted my eyes from their private parts. Meed handed out coarsely-woven canvas tunics and breeches. He took a narrow brush, dipped it in hot tar, and marked each tunic with a set of numbers front and back. After we recorded tunic numbers, leg irons were reattached and each exile sent below deck.

Most of the convicts were commoners wearing worker clothes. A few were gentlemen who wore fine, yet soiled velvet and silk coats, lace collars, and knee breeches. They received no special treatment, only heckles from the ship's crew as they removed their finery. I imagine their flabby skin felt the coarseness of the canvas in ways we commoners failed to notice.

The women arrived next from their separate prison area. I recorded their crimes: theft, bribery, and birthing children without husbands. They were all ages: old hags, mothers, and young girls like Fiona. Most wore homespun clothing like the maids at Langstone; only a few wore finery with silk petticoats.

Embarrassment crept along my skin as each woman removed her clothing. I intended to look away; instead I stared at their naked bodies, wondering if Fiona's body resembled theirs. Her hips felt ample and her breasts swelled to rounds when we touched. Would she have cowered, feeling the eyes of strangers scan her body, or would she have stared back in defiance as many of these women did?

The discarded clothing pile grew higher and higher. Silk and lace turned a lady's head in London Town; here the crew donned the finery, splitting seams to accommodate their muscular bodies. They resembled clusters of drunken folk, dancing toward heaven as they climbed the rigging in their newly-claimed finery.

I wrote as fast as possible to match Mister Meed's pace. My shoulder throbbed, my hand and back cramped, but I held back my words, fearing a promised flogging if I lagged.

As it was, yesterday I'd witnessed my first flogging. I shuddered when I replayed the images.

Mid-day, Yeoman Marcus rang the bell. "All assemble, all assemble!"

When the scraping and dragging sounds of chains ended, Marcus nodded to the soldiers. "Bring the men forward!"

Three convicts soon stood before Yeoman Marcus, who held his cat-o-nine whip above his head. He snapped it. The thin leather tails of the whip whistled above our heads, causing me to duck down in surprise.

"These men were caught fighting," Marcus said. "We don't tolerate such behavior. Each will receive ten lashes with you as their witnesses. Strip away their shirts!"

Soldiers removed each man's tunic. They selected one man, yanked his arms around the mast, and tied them securely, as if he might attempt an escape.

Yeoman Marcus strutted behind the man, flicking his long leather cat-o-nine tails around his body. He smiled and raised his arm. With one quick motion, he slashed the man's back open, leaving nine, thin, bloody lines.

The convict screamed. I convulsed at his outcry when I saw how the lead balls attached to the end of each leather thong dug into the man's back and drew blood.

Again and again, Marcus lay the cat across the man's back. Again and again, the man cried out. By the time Marcus finished, he'd created a cross-hatch pattern of bleeding slashes.

Before cutting down the prisoner, two crew members threw sea water onto the open wounds. The man screamed and sucked in air as the icy water splashed onto his back and stung the raw flesh. The soldiers cut him down, shackled him, and pushed him below deck before stringing up the next man.

The third man tied to the mast whimpered before the first lash crossed his back. From the back of the exiles, I heard, "Be an iron man, not a crawler. Wear yer blood-red skin in silence."

Marcus stopped midway through a stroke and stared out across his audience of exiles. "Who's so brave to shout?"

No exiles responded.

"Not brave enough to show yerself, uh?" Marcus waited with the whip dangling at his side. "Very well, we'll let this man take an extra five lashes for the exile who hides like a woman."

Satisfied, Marcus resumed the lashing. I shuddered. Bile filled my mouth. I knew I'd be a crawler, crying out with each lash across my back. At that moment I swore a silent vow to never find myself guilty of a crime that merited a flogging and disgraced the McClaud name.

"You! There on the far end," shouted Mr. Meed. "Why have you stopped writing?"

I looked up. He was talking to me. Being caught thus, I felt as sick to my stomach as I did remembering the smell of blood from the flogging. I pressed my pen into the page. "Sorry, sir. My nib broke."

Mr. Meed handed me a new nib, and I returned to recording names and crimes.

❖

I received my convict clothes. I held my breath as Mister Meed dipped his brush into the tar. The heat of the tar seeped through my tunic, burning my skin, but I held back any sounds and reactions as he painted the numbers 57457 onto my tunic and my life. This nightmare was real. If I wanted to clear my family name and reclaim Fiona as my bride, I'd need to survive each day one at a time.

Meed disappeared below deck. In his absence we scribes acquainted ourselves in whispers. "I'm Ean McClaud of County Cork and Langstone."

The tall lad fidgeted and looked at his feet. "Edward Maddox of Fleet Gaol."

"Fleet? That's debtors prison."

"I was born there."

I eyed him. Edward looked no more than a young lad and thin as a fence rail. His sandy hair, many shades lighter than mine, hung on his neck in unwashed, stringy clumps. Edward shivered like a frightened animal. If I'd shouted, he would have jumped like a grasshopper.

The third scribe, a small, wiry lad, leaned closer, "What's your crime, Edward?"

Edward shrugged, "I have none."

The third scribe shook his head. "At least I wasn't nicked for as long as I expected. Worked the streets of London Town where the swells lived, I did. Had a good run liftin' their gold pocket watches with a quick brush." He reached out his hand. "Name's Charley Stern."

"I have three years," I said and turned to Edward. "How many years for you?"

Edward shrugged. "They say when I'm eighteen, they'll release me. That's more than three years' time."

Charley stuffed his hands in his pockets and bounced up and down on the balls of his feet. "Two years for me. Got my urchins trained to keep liftin' watches while I'm away."

Edward asked, "How do you know they'll wait for you?"

Charley scowled, then half-smiled. "The lads better wait. They're mostly my brothers, 'n blood kin stays true. Besides, what else c'n they do? They need to eat. Most of these sailor blokes think they're goin' to get rich sailin'. They're as dumb as a fencepost. I c'n make more in a day than they make in a month. 'Course, I got caught this time."

"You'll be in trouble if you keep talking to the crew," Edward said.

Charley laughed. "Ed, ya worry too much. Be a man. Take a chance! This ship is too busy for them to watch us all the time. Besides, what's the worst that c'n happen?"

"Flogging," Edward replied.

3

Mister Meed returned and gave us small portions of salted meat, hard tack, and a half pint of ale. "Every time you work for the captain, you'll receive extra portions. He's a fair man *if* you do as you're told."

Last month at the printer's dinner table, I might have fed such scraps to the stray dogs in the lane. But since I'd eaten no more than a few morsels this past week, the food tasted better than the last village feast.

We returned below deck in time for the counting of feet. Soldiers crawled over us and around beams, checking the shackle links. Two-hundred-sixty dirty, stinking feet. One-hundred-thirty men crowded onto two tiers of narrow bunks. Do the women experience a similar count and discomfort? Charley would know. He gathers information like the printer gathers typeset to build words.

After leaving the Thames, we crossed the English Channel astride a brisk wind. My sickness continued, changing over several days to a feeling of unease and shakiness and back to feeling like I was about to die. Many others joined me at the railings, heaving every bit of food into the sea as we sailed to the Canaries, off the coast of Africa.

While most exiles remained shackled below deck while in port, Meed called us three scribes to record the exchange of cargo and the addition of more convicts. It allowed us to see Tenerife and the mountain that loomed over the harbor and pierced the sky. I'd never seen such a tall mound of land. Had I not been a prisoner of the ship, I'd have climbed its cliffs and walked its trails to stare down on the island like an unfettered bird.

The barrels where I'd earlier slept apart from the others were now removed, replaced by chained crates. I remained on the lower tier next to the dark-skinned man. Since his flogging, he'd become silent, refusing all my attempts at conversation.

In two days' time, the reloaded ship left the calm, green harbor water to reenter the foamy blue ocean. Waves rushed against the side of the ship, then toppled, allowing their white edges to disappear much like us disappearing from our homeland, perhaps forever.

Charley and I stared across the unending ocean.

"I get dizzy watching the waves," I said. "The stale air and the darkness below deck make me sweat so I can't sleep more than a couple hours at a time."

Charley chuckled and shook his head. "I've watched you, Ean. Y'ur afraid of the dark, and y'ur still seasick."

"No. I don't like it, that's all."

"Y'ur afraid, Ean, and..." Charley leaned into me and pointed out to sea, "Look! What's that?"

I followed the angle of his finger. A shiny, dark mound rose from the sea before it rolled back under the water. "Looks like a sea monster."

"Whale to starboard!" a sailor shouted down from the crow's nest. "Whale!"

Mister Meed turned his spy glass to scan the sea off the right side of the ship as the whale glided past. "Hard to port!"

The helmsman spun the giant wheel, turning the ship away from the whale. We grabbed for anything to keep on our feet. Soldiers raced to the bow and stern with their weapons ready.

"Aim for his head," Meed yelled. "He'll capsize us if we run into him."

Exiles pushed to the rails pointing, shouting. The whale resurfaced, sending a huge spray of water into the sky before it disappeared.

From the crow's nest a sailor yelled, "Clear!"

Edward pushed between us. "That beast had to be half as long as this ship. Do you think there are more that size out here?"

"Probably," Charley said.

Edward stared after the whale. "I'd like to be free like the whale, moving where I wished with no one telling me what to do minute by minute."

Charley stretched. "Take each day, Ed. The sun's warm; we've got a steady breeze. It's a holiday away from the soot and grime back in London Town."

I stared at Charley. "We're prisoners. This isn't a holiday."

He shrugged and looked out across the ocean. "Maybe not, but we've seen a new beast and new lands. I might never return to England if it weren't for the lads waitin' for me."

I huffed. "Not me. I plan to return to Fiona and my printing job. My whole life is back in Langstone."

Edward's shoulders dropped. He bit his lip to stop its quivering. "I have no reason to go back. No family. I—" The words that followed blew away as huge waves slapped against the ship.

I held tight to my thoughts of Fiona and wondered what Edward had to think or dream about that gave him hope.

❖

Days rolled together as the *Sara Jane* bucked the waves and caught pockets of wind. The ship's bells no longer woke me, nor did the yelling and feet running overhead. My life fell into a pattern of staring at the sea, eating porridge, and watching the rain barrels on deck capture drinking water off the sails.

One morning, the soldiers herded us onto the deck earlier than usual, our chains still attached from overnight. The crew hung on the ropes and masts, wearing our discarded clothing and nasty grins. A short, thin soldier stood on the raised platform. He wore a ruffled gentlemen's shirt and satin breeches. Over that he'd draped a woman's dress, mocking the King's robe. Instead of a crown, a bucket covered his head.

"Today, I'm in charge. Listen to me. I'm Mister Meedy Weedy Tweedy." The soldiers laughed.

"Today, y'll dance for yer porridge," he shouted over the wind.

Everyone laughed at his comic outfit and his absurd comment.

I shifted from foot to foot, watching the soldiers for a clue, nervous about their intentions. The soldiers lifted their bayonets and beat a steady rhythm on the ship's metal fittings and alternately tapped the deck with their gun butts.

Mr. Meedy Weedy Tweedy waved his arms. "Dance if ya want ta eat." We stood motionless.

He raised his pistol and shot it into the air, drilling a hole in a sail. We started moving our feet.

"Step lively! Rattle those chains. We only cross the equator once on this trip!"

We danced jig steps, jangling our chains, turning and twisting, trying not to get tangled with others. The soldiers and crew laughed, tapping and clapping faster and faster.

Bang, bang, bang. Sweat ran down my arms and legs; if they didn't stop soon, I feared I'd drop to the deck and be trampled. Bang, bang, bang, faster and faster.

Another pistol shot rang out. Captain Woodwright stood aft. "Enough! Get these men below and fed."

I continued to pant as I scooped out a dipper of porridge. A shudder ran through me; we lived under the control of madmen who could make us do whatever they wished. What if I'd refused to dance? Would I be lashed? At least they hadn't made me sing for my porridge. Fiona knew I couldn't carry a tune in a bucket.

Charley chatted up two soldiers to learn what had happened. "It's tradition. When a ship crosses the equator, all must honor Neptune, the god of the sea. Transport ships seldom bother, but Woodwright allows the crew and soldiers to force our dancing for their entertainment."

"I'll be ready for that on my return trip," I said.

Soldiers rousted us early another morrow and took us above deck in small groups. They removed our chains. I bent to rub my chaffed ankles, careful to avoid the raw patches.

The captain oversaw us from the forecastle, the raised platform where he often stood to make announcements. "Y'll no longer wear chains unless we encounter problems, foul weather, or treasonous acts. Should ya choose to work on deck, y'll earn bits of meat, extra hard tack, dried peas, and a dram of ale. Mister Meed will hand out duties to all who step forward."

I'd work with a handful of other convicts to holystone the deck. Three crewmen uncovered large sandstone rocks, worn flat on one side. They scattered sand on the deck, slid the stones toward us, and stepped back.

Yeoman Marcus explained the duty. "These stones remove sea salt and other grime that settles on the deck. They must be used weekly while we are at sea. Scour small circles on top of the sand and rinse with sea water. Y'll know this deck well by the time we reach Port Arthur."

Relying on my stronger arm, I worked the heavy stone in small circles across the boards, trying to keep it from sliding under the sailor's feet. Ka-whoosh, ka-whoosh, ka-whoosh. Each scrape reminded me of a giant pestle crushing seeds in a cook's mortar.

The soldiers' rants were unending. They jeered and jabbed at us if we stopped for more than a moment. "Work faster, lads. You've the entire deck to stone or it's half rations. Cap'n 'spects a safe deck before dusk."

That first evening, pain radiated through my body like a hot knife from kneeling on gritty sand and from forcing my injured arm to circle the heavy stone. For all the monotonous circling motion, I received quarter rations. The overseeing soldier decided my holystoning covered too small an area to warrant a full portion of food.

Edward sat down next to me. He sniffed the air. "The soldiers' cheese smells tasty. I've never eaten fresh cheese. 'N this bristly lump of bread is worse than the bread in gaol."

I gnawed loose a piece of dry bread. "Last spring, Fiona and I strolled through the Langstone festival. We bought rolls just from the oven, smothered in butter, and drank cool, fresh milk from a tin cup. You'd have had a grand day, Edward."

He swallowed his measure of ale and stared out to sea. "I've never been to a festival. What else would I have seen?"

I closed my eyes, thinking back to that sunny day. "The stalls smelled of tarts and jam, live poultry, herbs, leather harnesses, and dried seeds for next planting season. Minstrels played and dancers followed them around the field. A man with a pet monkey begged for coins. For a ha' penny the monkey would dance or sit on your shoulder."

Edward took a bite of his bread. "Must've been grand."

"'Twas. We walked down to the grist mill. Fiona dared me to enter a race around the lake. I promised to win a yellow hair ribbon for her, but the other lads ran like the wind. I shoved one to the side, and he shoved back. That's when I stumbled and fell into the lake. Fiona laughed until tears filled her eyes."

I bit into my dry bread, letting the remembrance fade.

A sad expression crossed Edward's face. "One day, I'll have a sweetheart and go to a fair. I'll live in a small cottage by a lake where I can sit and watch the land. There'll be shade trees and fresh fish I'll catch from the lake."

Charley sat next to Edward. "A lake? Haven't ya seen enough water?"

Edward shrugged. "Having my own home by a lake would be grand."

"And how could ya afford a cottage?" Charley asked. "What job will ya know?"

"I'm not sure," Edward said. "It's just my dream, but maybe 'twill come true." He stood, set his bowl aside, and turned back to his work repairing sails.

A small boy, no more than eight, stood near me on the deck while I holystoned. I'd seen him but never spoken to him. "Who are you?"

"Scotty."

I watched him fidget and twitch under my gaze. "Are you an exile?"

Scotty puffed himself up. "I most certainly am not. I'm Cap'n Woodwright's cabin boy."

"What do you do, Scotty?"

"Whatever the cap'n wants. I polish his boots, pour his rum, and sing if he wants me to."

I sat back on my heels to rest and studied his face. He reminded me of the youngest lads working around Langstone. "What do you sing?"

Scotty jumped up on the forecastle and sang out,

> The cap'n is a handsome man who sails the seven seas, oh.
> He carries riches for the King and never saves a pence, oh.

A crowd gathered to listen until the captain appeared on deck. His nod sent Scotty forward toward the captain's cabin. I put my head down and returned to holystoning. This time none of us were flogged or yelled after for our moments of idleness.

My injured arm ached day and night from long hours working on the deck, but if I wanted more than porridge, I had to work harder and faster. My clothes began to hang loose; I used a scrap of rope I found on the deck to hold up my breeches.

The equator's sun and surprising heat lightened my hair. It burned my arms and my face where a beard refused to grow. No one in Langstone would recognize me looking thus—not even Fiona.

Most days Scotty roamed nearby, watching me push the stone in small circles. He'd braid ropes or coil lines and ask questions. "Can ya truly read and write?"

"Yes."

"Will ya teach me?"

I stretched my arms and twisted my back side to side to loosen the knots in my shoulders. "Why do you want to learn?"

"I want to be a cap'n," Scotty said.

I leaned back on my heels and shielded my eyes from the sun. "A ship's captain? Why?"

Scotty jumped onto the forecastle. "I'll travel the world and get lots of gold and become a fine gent."

In a split second, Scotty grabbed up his ropes, leaped onto a yardarm, and disappeared. I returned to holystoning and wondered about my own life. The Crown said I owe them three years' time. Once I correct that misunderstanding, I'll sail back, become a fine printer, marry Fiona, and buy a cottage. We'll birth two fine lads and a girl. The lads would work for me; the girl would keep Fiona company. I'll earn enough money so my family would never need to hire out and work for others. It's a dream I knew I wanted to make real.

A boot kicked my backside and the butt of a gun pounded the deck next to my head. "Back to work!"

Startled, I stared up at the face.

"Now! Time's wastin'," the soldier shouted.

Time. We had too much ahead of us. I picked up the holystone and returned to the tiring and endless scouring.

4

The ship flew across the water, catching hearty winds thanks to the crew adjusting the sails day and night. Little distracted me from facing the holystone and the salty deck during my shift except my watching the sails ripple and vibrate with wind as we sailed further and further from England.

After the Sabbath service, Woodwright spoke of our route. "We'll continue across the Great Ocean to catch the trades and, with luck, we'll sail swiftly through the horse latitude to our next port stop, Rio de Janeiro."

But the next day, as if to dispute the captain, the gusty winds stopped. The sails hung limp. Two sailors straddled the mainsail beam mending ropes above my head. I listened to their conversation as I holystoned.

"Tol' ya we left too late. Curse those last exiles Woodwright waited for. Wanted every last pence, he did."

"Ah. It's not them's the problem. He's too drunk to demand we raise full sails when we've got fast winds. Now we're stuck. Goin' be tol' how we're the ones that's lazy."

And so it began. Woodwright yelled and screamed from morning to evening. He sent out rowers in small boats to search for a breeze to fill the sails. None was found.

The sun softened the tar 'tween the ship's boards; it oozed out, making the wooden deck as hot as the crew's tempers. Our bodies reeked from weeks without washing since all water had to be conserved. I remained on deck as much as possible, holystoning, jigging for fish, or repairing sails, knowing each time I went below, I'd gag in the fetid air.

Charley stood next to me and shielded his eyes to scan the sea. "There must be a breeze out there. It's a big ocean."

I followed his glance to the small boats sent to the horizon. "Doesn't look like it. But if they do find wind, how will the ship get to the wind?"

"Scotty tol' me they'd pull the ship with small boats."

I shook my head. "Can't be."

Charley shrugged. "Believe what ya will. Scotty says 'tis true."

"Bet the captain wishes he'd set sail on time."

Charley clapped me on the back. "Yes, but he'd not have the coins for so many of us. Wonder how much he gets paid for our delivery."

"Must be enough." I said. "Scotty told me it's his fifth voyage."

Charley laughed. "Maybe I should consider doin' this. Make more money sailin' convicts than liftin' rich men's watches."

I stared at him. His face looked serious. "Could you do this? I mean, would you sail exiles half way around the world for money?"

"Depends on how much I'd make," Charley said.

I shook my head and moved away.

Each Sabbath the captain read from the Bible while we stood in silent, ragged rows. "Lord, grant us a robust wind. Give us strength to survive this heat and strength to row. Pray for our wretched souls. Amen."

I prayed silently for Fiona's safety and my own, that I'd survive this ordeal and return to the life we'd planned. Would God bother to listen to a house servant and a printer's devil? I prayed so.

The next day, a gust of wind crossed the deck. The captain shouted to the sailors, "Adjust the sheets!" Before they could hoist a single sail, the wind died.

Two exiles mumbled. The captain turned their direction. "You, there! Who tol' ya to speak?"

The men lowered their heads.

"Chain them to the deck overnight," the captain shouted to nearby soldiers. "No food or water."

No other exiles spoke or stopped their tasks to watch the chaining up of the men. The captain made angry orders every day.

Staying on deck at night sounded like a great escape from the stagnant air below. Breaking a minor rule might be worth going without food or water. I thought more about it as I holystoned.

The next afternoon, I watched an exile sidle up to a sailor's Bible left on the deck. He kicked it to one side, allowing a group of men to circle it and tear out pages. They fashioned crude playing cards and occupied themselves for hours until…

"You there!" Woodwright pointed to the group. "What are ya doin'?"

The men separated, melding into other groups, and allowed the pages of the Bible to flutter to the deck.

Woodwright's face reddened. "Who desecrates a Bible? Step forward!"

No man twitched or turned his head.

The captain drew his cutlass. "Double rations for any man turnin' in the gamblin' exiles." He waited. We waited. Finally, two exiles gave up the six men, who were immediately flogged while we were commanded to watch; it replaced our mealtime.

❖

Crew and exiles alike sought the shadows to escape the blistering sun. With all sails repaired and all ropes coiled and ready for use, idleness tested the crew's tempers. Exiles picked fights to amuse themselves. The strong ruled above and below decks.

At mealtime three barrel-chested exiles stepped closer, shadowing me from the sun. With a quick move, they covered my mouth and pulled me down the steps out of sight from the crew and threw me to the boards.

Fear raced through me. I struggled but could not get free.

"Scribe. Where've ya hidden yer special ration?" a voice asked.

I flailed and bit the hand over my mouth. The man screamed. A large hand pounded my face into the deck. I shook off his blow. "I have no extra food."

"Check his tunic. He hides his good fortune for later."

When they found nothing, a short, chubby man pulled a sliver of metal from his breeches' waistband. Two men sat on me and covered my mouth while he made quick stabs into my arm above my wrist, then smeared it with liquid.

I prayed to lose consciousness as they jabbed and pricked my skin. When they finished, they left me on the boards, exhausted from my struggles and breathing hard.

Edward pushed through the crowd that gathered. "Ean. What happened?"

"They cut me."

Charley pulled me upright.

I flinched as he brushed away blood and a black, inky mess.

"Hm-m. They've given ya a jagged "f" tattoo. Must've heard yer cries to Fiona. Wash it off in salt water. Y'll be fine."

"Fine? How can I be fine? I have a tattoo like a common sailor. The printer and most especially his wife will shun me when they see it."

Charley helped me to my feet. "It could be worse, Ean. They could've killed ya and dumped ya overboard."

I yanked myself free from Charley and paced the deck rubbing my arm. Many exiles smirked; others whispered as I passed. I longed to dip my wrist in the rain barrel, but I'd receive a lashing for muddying the water. I closed my eyes to stem the anger that threatened to erupt from inside me.

Would Fiona marry a man with a tattoo? Perhaps, but she'd more likely marry the butcher's fat-fingered son or the smithy's spindly cousin. Why had the men singled me out? When or if I ever received extra rations in the future, I'd always gobble them down long before I reached the hold to make certain any hint of a crumb had vanished.

Charley's hand on my shoulder brought my attention back to my situation. "Heared many men got tattooed this week, not of their choosing; one nearly died when he struggled against the attackers. What's strange is that the crew and soldiers let the attacks happen. Must amuse 'em."

As a faint breeze crossed the deck, sailors scurried up the ropes and set the sails. Before they dropped back down to the deck, the breeze faded. Our ship lay motionless on a sea so calm when we gazed over the railing, we viewed a perfect reflection of the Sara Jane.

Later that day, Charley and I watched an exile scraping a beef bone. "What's he doing?" I asked.

"Scrimshaw. The sailors been loaning exiles knives to carve ships, fish, and birds into meat bones. They earn extra rations or better clothes; the sailors sell the scrimshaw in port."

"But they could make weapons as well, couldn't they?"

Charley wiped sweat from his forehead. "True, but the sailors count the bones and collect the knives every afternoon. Must figger the risk is worth the coins they'll pocket in port."

Over the next days, I noticed more exiles on deck; each sat carving bones instead of tattoos. Days later, they wore new breeches or chewed on pieces of meat. Did any exiles make sharp-pointed tools instead of scrimshaw? Doubtful. Such weapons against guns and swords would be a lopsided battle.

Illness, jail fever, spread around the ship. Five exiles swayed and dropped onto the deck. Within an hour's time all exiles who were not working were confined below deck, where the heat and stench remained unbearable. I remembered the recent exile chained to the deck overnight as punishment. To escape the fetid air from dozens upon dozens of dirty, sleeping men, it would be worth spending a cold night on deck, I thought. I initiated my plan: I stopped working, sat back, and crossed my arms.

Mister Meed hurried across the deck and kicked my backside. "What are you doing?"

I shielded my eyes to look up at him. "I'm not holystoning any longer."

Meed yanked me to standing and rang the bell. Crew members and soldiers gathered around. "This exile refuses to work. His punishment shall be ten lashes."

"What?" My stomach knotted when I heard his decree.

"Silence!" yelled Meed.

Two crew men pulled away my shirt and the rag supporting my left arm. I shouted as they forcibly stretched my arm fully open and dislocated my shoulder once again.

The exiles on deck hushed. Yeoman Marcus strode toward me. He dipped his long, leather-tailed whip into the rain barrel and quickly raised his arm.

Slash! Fire greater than the smithy's furnace sliced across my back. I flinched; my breath escaped, followed by a scream I could not hold back. Over and over, the end of the whip cut my skin. Over and over, screams escaped my lips.

When he completed the ten, I slumped against the mast. I felt liquid, my blood, seep into my breeches and trickle down my legs like a heavy sweat. I gasped for air, then held my breath for the bucket of salt water I knew would follow.

The first splashes refreshed for a moment, followed by the sharp pain of salt sinking into my wounds. Another scream escaped my lips.

After they cut me down, they threw my shirt to my feet. I couldn't bend to retrieve it. Soldiers hauled me below deck, where Edward repositioned my shoulder and wrapped my arm in a rag sling. "How's this, Ean?"

I shook my head, gasping for air.

"I was forward when they strung you up. What happened?"

"I thought if I refused to work, I'd spend the night on deck and sleep in fresh air rather than another night in this stench."

"Both the captain and Mister Meed are meaner since we lost the wind," Edward said. "Best not try to figger their thinking. Both may have lost their minds."

My holystoning the deck continued daily if I wanted to eat. For many days, the touch of my shirt or an arm brushing against my back made me wince. Though scabs appeared over the slashes, many also reopened and oozed from using my arms as I worked. At times exiles suffered twenty or more lashes thrown across their backs. I don't think I could live through that much pain. I certainly never wanted to find out.

Jail sickness continued to pass through the ship. Several exiles died below deck. We did not call out for the removal of the dead, knowing our rations would be cut once the deaths were discovered.

Within two days' time however, the captain summoned us on deck. "Sailors removed the dead exiles ya failed to report. As punishment, all convict rations will be cut until I say otherwise."

His declaration didn't surprise me, but how could he cut our rations and expect us to continue to work with less food than we already received?

The captain paced the forecastle with his hands behind his back. "Two crew members died from the fever. I c'n offer a reduced sentence to any men with skills enough to work the sails and climb the rigging. Y'll receive crew rations, but y'll continue to live below deck."

No hands went up. I wished I'd the skills and strength to work the sails. Extra rations would help sustain me for the rest of the voyage.

Woodwright waited. We waited. Four convicts raised their hands. Mister Meed took them aside. The rest of us watched as they hauled the ropes and returned to the deck.

Meed heated a pot of tar and drew a box around each man's convict numbers to show they were now helping the crew. Then he sent them to stand with us during the burials.

Eight dead bodies lay sewn in cocoons of torn sail. Mister Meed held a Bible and bowed his head. "Dear Lord, we commend these souls to your keeping."

A sailor opened a gunwale doorway. Each body was pitched into the sea, much like the stale loaves of bread we pitched to the swans in the lake near Langstone. Within minutes, life on the ship resumed its daily routine as the crew continued to row out in search of wind.

Charley was summoned to the captain's cabin. When he returned, he drew Edward and me aside. "That was no jail fever. It was typhus. I overheard the doctor scold the cap'n for forcing us ta stay shackled below deck when we weren't working. Says we should have been on deck in fresh air ta rid the ship of the illness. Cap'n tol' him to bugger off."

"We're lucky we lived through that," Edward said. "Hope it's the last big problem on this rotten ship."

When a breeze blew up in two days' time, the four exiles were rousted from below deck to haul sails. The breeze strengthened; the sails fluttered and filled with air. The ship returned to its familiar roll and pitch.

Our journey to Van Diemen's Land continued along the Southern Americas as the next month arrived. Listening through the hatch after dark, I heard crew members talking about the route.

"Looks to be out of the way, but the trades work against us if we try to round the cape from here."

A second voice grumbled. "Aye, and we won't meet up with those cannibals I heared about. They'd make us slaves 'n treat us like animals."

"How do ya know?"

"A bloke who survived tol' me. Scared 'im so bad he never went to sea again."

"I don't believe you."

"But 'tis true."

I tied additional knots in the rope that held up my breeches, thus making it a calendar of the journey. Counting from boarding the ship in London Town to now, my rope suggested near sixty days. Add on my stay in Newgate and I'd been away from Langstone for seventy days. If I believed the crew's comments, we weren't yet half way.

After days of sailing through high winds and rough seas followed by no wind and fierce tempers, we'd made up time, and now we entered a calm harbor at midday. Mister Meed brought us on deck. We scanned the surrounding gigantic rocky mounds and mountains with steep sides, where sea birds circled and dove on the fruity breezes, swooping 'round our sails. Lush green forests filled the space between sea and sky around the uplifts.

"Tomorrow, we'll dock in Rio to exchange cargo. You'll remain chained below deck except for the scribes. Keep yourselves quiet if you want to avoid lashings. Scribes, follow me."

We sat before three battered ledgers much like Master John's log books. Mister Meed handed out pens and ink pots and took down a small journal that had been tucked in a cranny behind his desk. He opened it and scanned several pages before he looked up and barked, "Write what I tell you and only what I tell you."

I penned lists of goods, Charley recorded the reports on the voyage weather and conditions of the sails, and Edward wrote death certificates. Mister Meed paced in jerky movements, his face tight, daring us to question his dictates. I feared his wrath should I ask after the untrue numbers we wrote in the logs.

During a second four-hour shift, crew members came in. We wrote their letters, edited supply lists, and composed a new roster of exiles. By the end of the second dog watch, my hand cramped so I could barely hold the pen. Outside, daylight faded to dusk.

We received an extra ration of dried beef and a half pint of ale, then worked until midnight bells rang, when we returned below deck.

A nearby bunkmate awoke as I lay down. "I smell the rations ya earn off our misery. Meed must a given you ale or a thimble of his prize rum."

"Only gave us dried meat and a taste of ale."

"Perhaps I need to learn to write so I can get me sumpin' fer nothin'."

❖

At first light the crew opened the hatch cover, letting in blinding sunshine. The men wore their blue and white striped blouses and blue breeches with bandanas tied over their sunburned heads. Sweat ran down their faces as they maneuvered crate after crate to the dock.

That night, boots, heeled shoes, and women's voices along with bottles clinking kept me awake as we lay in the dark, waiting for bowls of porridge that never arrived. The next morning, sailors crossed the deck, singing rowdy songs from the tops of the sails while we remained chained below deck.

The following morning, the sailors opened the hatch to load cargo. The smell of ripe fruit and musky grass filled the air as dozens of barrels and small, padlocked crates were secured in our sleeping area.

The flurry of activity slowed; the anchor chain clanked up inside the ship. The sailors took up their now familiar ditty as they unfurled the sails.

Let's drink a fine toast to our schemes.
To villains, robbers, and knaves.
We'll sail 'em away for many a day
To become distant farmers' slaves.

When we were allowed on deck, Edward and I stood together, watching the last trace of land become part of the horizon. "Glad the crew and soldiers are happy, but it's no help to us stashed below deck."

"At least the new crates smell better," I said. "The ones they took off smelled nasty."

On wash day railings and walls held damp, rotting clothes drying in the wind. Our modesty disappeared long ago when we were forced to use the privy buckets and when we stripped to receive our now ragged exile clothing. It was difficult to decide whether we exiles or our clothes most resembled scarecrows.

Edward tightened his breeches with a hank of rope and stared across the unending sea. "Wish they'd quiet them cows and sheep with a quick slice of their throats. I dream of a taste of fresh meat instead of porridge and tasteless beans. I remember a time when an elderly priest came to the gaol. We promised our everlasting souls to him for two bites of meat and stale bread."

"We do what we have to do to survive, Edward," I said.

He sighed. "How long until we get to the new gaol?"

"Scotty says we're not yet half way. Still got a stop in Africa."

"Next time you see Scotty, ask what else he's heard."

Scotty shook his head. "Can't ask him anything. He's busy with Mister Meed. They won't let me in the cabin. Had to sleep on the deck."

Captain Woodwright appeared.

"Oh, oh!" Scotty hopped up and raced across the deck toward him.

At dusk we received three food buckets, two water buckets and two privy buckets. Our thirst was greater than our hunger. Fights broke out as exile hands grabbed for the buckets only to find they contained vinegar water. Cursing filled our space as laughter filtered down from the deck.

"Bloody thieves. They've taken our freedom and now our water."

From the dark corners of the exile deck, a voice called out, "Cheer up, lads. 'Tis meant to keep us from gettin' scurvy. Soon ya might wish ya were back here, swillin' the vile mix."

We resumed our routines, our jobs, and our grumblings. On each Sabbath we lined up on deck in the hot sun or the pelting rain while Woodwright read from The Scriptures about sin, forgiveness, and damnation. How could the crew and sailors who drank, swore, and much worse be better humans than those of us below deck?

The further we sailed, the more the weather cooled. For a fortnight the rain blew up severe storms. Winds rushed us forward. The sailors scurried like monkeys to adjust the sails to keep our speed true. Meanwhile, walls of water burst across the deck, washing through the open hatch to soak everything and everyone below.

Exiles took on the deck duty of catching rain off the sails, saving it in barrels for drinking water. They braced themselves to stay upright during storms while exchanging empty barrels for full and moving them to the gunwales, where sailors secured them.

When the wind and rain subsided, we enjoyed tropical air across the deck while Woodwright spoke to us. "We've re-crossed the Great Sea, and we'll round the Cape of Good Hope within a week's time. After Port Elizabeth, we'll begin the final leg of the voyage."

Charley turned toward me. "What a lie. Cap'n calls this a voyage. And good hope? We left that back in London Town."

I shrugged. "But rumor says we're half way."

"Half way? Is that all?" Charley sighed and returned to his job.

❖

Pulling into the harbor, I expected sounds similar to Rio: lots of busy feet and foreign languages; instead I heard Englishmen. Their voices spoke of cargo and weather, of slave and spice traders, of prevailing winds, and of Indian Ocean pirates.

Mister Meed called us scribes to update the logs and write crew and soldiers' messages to send to their families in England. They'd be carried aboard the first ship sailing that direction.

After the crew and soldiers finished dictating their letters and Mister Meed had not returned, I continued to write.

Edward grabbed my arm. "What are you doing?"

"Writing a letter before Meed returns. Now keep quiet so I can think."

Charley grabbed a paper as well. We tucked our letters into the bundle going ashore. My message read:

> *Dear Fiona,*
>
> *I am near the south end of Africa on my way to gaol. Please tell Master John I am innocent.*
> *Ask the clergy to send your message to Port Arthur, Tasmania.*
>
> *Lovingly, Ean*

Writing dozens of letters caused my shoulder to ache. Below deck, I rotated it, trying to extend it to full length, but, with the head space so low, I could only twist a few inches.

The dark-skinned man lay next to me. "I've been tol' the pirates roam the waters 'tween here and Australia."

"Will they capture this ship?" I asked.

"I doubt it. The cap'n will fly a slave trade or a plague flag to keep them away. They're after riches and spice cargoes, whatever they can sell."

I thought a minute. "They could sell us, couldn't they?"

"Yes, but they want quick riches rather than a hundred or more mouths to feed."

In port, the crates from Rio were removed. Over the next week, they replaced the crates with green fruit, dried fish, and cured meat. The deeper hold took on dozens of live pigs; cattle and sheep were hoisted on board to replace the earlier animals that fed the crew along the way to this port.

Black dust filtered into our exile space from deep within the ship. "Iron ore" one exile explained; "for the foundry."

Once the ship set sail, the captain unshackled us to resume our work and roam the narrow edges of the deck.

New rules were announced. Water became highly valued since the captain saved cargo space by no longer carrying ale for us exiles. He also limited our meat to once instead of twice a week. I prayed for rain to quench my thirst, not realizing before now what a dipper of water could mean in my life.

Scotty sat on the forecastle, whistling as he mended a line. I watched him work new hemp in with the old.

"Haven't seen you for a while, Scotty."

"Got meself in trouble back in port."

"How?"

"Got meself nabbed. Cap'n said ta leave the waterfront, but I didn't. Two buggers took my coins and almost took me. One of our sailors heared me yellin'. Came right up and stabbed the man, he did. I took off runnin' and jumped back on the ship."

"Where have you been since then?"

Scotty fingered the rope around his shoulder. "Got meself locked in Cap'n Woodwright's cabin."

I said nothing more as I watched his fingers finish the end of the rope with a tight braid.

He stopped working and looked up at me. "Didn't like bein' locked up."

"It's not fun, is it? See to it you mind the captain from now on." I prayed Scotty escaped being thrust below deck in our hell hole.

He nodded. "Cap'n says we'll find cooler weather before much longer. 'Twill be rain and snow to fill the barrels, plus we may see floating ice the size of the ship."

"Do you believe that?" I asked.

"Yes. The cap'n said. He also said we'll soon find weather opposite from England."

"What do you mean opposite?"

Scotty scrunched up his face. "Cap'n says it's not like spring anymore, not like home. It'll be May when we get there; 'twill be wintertime."

"How can that be?"

Scotty shrugged. "If the cap'n says it, must be so." Scotty coiled the rope he was working on over his shoulder and scampered away, leaving me to stare across the unending sea and run my fingers along the nearly unending knots in my rope calendar.

I thought back to my life before Newgate gaol and this terrible ship. As a printer's devil, an apprentice, I worked hard, but that life proved easier than this. There, I'd thought myself held down. Here, each day contains uncertainty, shackles, and grueling work. My long hours bent over a press had been free of torture and starvation. I missed that life more as each day passed.

Lately, the ruffians that ruled many convicts had taken on an interest in working on deck, especially whittling bones and jigging for fish. Below deck they'd forced those of us who slept near the hatch to trade places with them, so I now lay pressed into the darkest corner with no chance to find any light. Their whispered conversations day and night worried me, but I kept my concerns to myself lest they pull me into their scheming. Whatever they planned could only mean one thing. Trouble.

6

Over the next week as I holystoned the deck, the air turned damp; the coldness soaked into my bones. It took all my energy to push the holy-stone in small circles as I thought about May and sunshine in Langstone while we wallowed in wintry weather.

Maybe the cold chill also came from the ruffians' warnings spread cautiously from convict to convict: "Keep what ya hear to yerself, and we'll let ya live. If y'ur not part of our plan, stay deep in the hold and guard yer words."

Scotty sat watching me as he finished braiding the end of another frayed rope.

"What do you hear, Scotty?"

Before he could answer Woodwright yelled, "Scotty!"

The cabin boy wrapped the rope around his body like a soldier's bandolier, grabbed a line, and swung across the yardarm. He jumped down on the other side of the ship, where he handed the rope to a crewman before following the captain below deck. I continued to wonder what threat the man held over such a young lad.

The change in the weather and in our rations created angry moods within the groups of exiles. Tempers flared and the ruffians below deck took more and more control of our food and water.

Charley and I stood behind a group of men on the port side of the ship. Suddenly, he dipped his hand in the rain barrel and gulped down fresh water. "Ah-h. That was worth a lashing. How can the cap'n let us die of thirst when we're so close to the new gaol?"

"Easy," I said. "Must not matter what condition we're in when we arrive, so he can do as he pleases. I see he's eating enough food to keep his breeches taut."

"Serve him right to explode from gluttony."

I had to admit to myself that I'd begun to crave a decent meal and dreamt of food instead of Fiona and working for Master John. How could that happen? Things surely would improve once we arrived in Port Arthur. In the meantime, I hoped the captain would call us scribes to work and provide an extra portion of food in payment.

In two days' time my wish came true; captain called us to update his logs. It must mean we're approaching the new gaol, but none of us dared ask.

Mr. Meed burst into the cabin. "Captain! Trouble's brewing."

"Mr. Meed! Look around you!" Captain Woodwright shook his head and pointed toward where we sat working.

Meed stepped in front of us. I kept my head down and entered another line in my log, pretending I'd heard nothing. He slammed his hand on the log book in front of me. "What have you heard, scribe? Answer me!"

"Nothing, sir." I dared not look up lest he read the truth in my eyes.

Woodwright turned to Charley and Edward. They both shrugged and looked back to their log books.

Mr. Meed paced the cabin. "It's the four exiles we're using to crew since Rio. They ask too many questions of the regular crewmen. I hear that more scoundrels are volunteering for jobs, but nothing gets finished. We're too close to Port Arthur to allow troublemakers to interfere with our voyage."

"Double the guard," Woodwright said. "Provide every soldier and crew member with ample weapons. End all unnecessary details. Secure these men below deck as soon as they finish their work. Lock the cover at night."

Charley, Edward, and I stole glances at each other.

For the rest of the time working on the log book, my hand trembled so much I spilled ink on a cargo listing and needed to request a new page. Woodwright absent-mindedly handed me a new one.

When we completed our work, soldiers shackled us and took us down a back stairway, shoved us into a dark cell, then slammed and locked the barred door.

I convulsed from the darkness and the stench as I sat in silence beside Charley and Edward, praying Mr. Meed's notion of trouble was untrue. That's when I heard clinking chains and heavy breathing.

I leapt to my feet and whirled around, stumbled, and tangled my shackles. As my eyes adjusted to the dim light, I saw two dark lumps of men sitting in the back corner.

"What's happenin', lads?"

Bile rose into my throat. "Nothing," I said as I relived my panic from Newgate when thugs beat on me and denied me food. I vowed this time would be different.

I clenched my fists, ready for an attack

"Ain't ya a scribe?" one man asked.

"Yes," I gulped. "Mr. Meed decided I didn't write fast enough."

Both men clamored closer. "What of you other two scribes?"

Charley laughed. "The Cap'n caught me tryin' ta steal paper while I worked. Caught Ed here takin' a piece from my hand. Right, Ed?"

"Right."

"Huh," the other man said. "With our rations cut, I thought a prisoner's party was comin'. The soldier who left us here last night hinted he'd be busy cleanin' his weapons tonight. Said he'd pick off as many exiles as possible if there's trouble."

"There's to be a party on *this* ship?" Edward asked.

"These gents don't mean a party, Ed." Charley strode up to the two men, his body puffed up, his arms crossed. "They mean an uprisin'." He paused. "What if a bloke knew a secret or two? What's it worth?"

"Got nothin' to trade," the first man said.

"How about your head scarf? If you muster up three of them, I might have somethin' for ya." Charley backed up and sat down beside Edward.

I stared at Charlie's dim outline. Would he trade information for a head scarf? If so, I'd best not trust him with valuable information. I scooted away from him and sat with my back to a wall in case trouble began.

Time crept along. Suddenly, the sound of muffled footsteps and gunshots seeped into our cell. A war erupted above our heads. Shouts and cries approached us. Pounding and hacking broke open the lock. The door swung wide. The two prisoners we'd shared the cell with raced out.

"On deck! Hurry! We're taking the ship." Two burly men pointed their metal shafts at us. "Go on! Move!"

We ran from the cell, but Charley yanked us aside. "Follow me!" He pushed Edward ahead of him. "Hurry!"

We followed the noise and confusion. On the deck soldiers swung their bayonets at exiles. Convicts swung buckets, ropes, and their tunics at soldiers.

Shots rang out. The smell of gunpowder filled my nostrils. Exiles charged at soldiers, using their bare hands as claws and their bodies as battering rams.

Crew members hung off the masts, avoiding the mêlée. Some dropped ropes around convicts who stepped below them. The noise and confusion could never be mistaken for anything but a mutiny.

"Down here!" Charley pulled us behind him as he raced for the exile deck. We hurried after him, down the steps, crawling into a narrow space behind the steps, where we lay on top of each other listening, watching, waiting for the battle to end.

Minutes passed like hours and hours like days. As daylight dimmed, the deck above quieted to a low grumble of voices, thumps of bodies on the deck, and a clanking of chains.

"Search the ship for missing exiles," Captain Woodwright said. "I want every exile rounded up and on the deck as soon as possible."

Soldiers scoured the exile deck with torches and dragged out handfuls of exiles as well as the three of us. Lengths of rope, shattered rain barrels, debris, exiles, and dead bodies lay strewn across the blood-spattered deck. Soldiers forced us to join the men already face down with their hands bound behind their backs. Leg irons were affixed to any exile not already wearing them.

We remained face down on the deck while the crew put things in order and reset the sails. Meanwhile, the soldiers read tunic numbers aloud, marking our presence.

It started to rain. I craved the chance to capture a few drops of moisture, but any movement I made was met by a jab from a bayonet. I lay on the bloody deck, unable to drink in even one drop of the rain water I desired and needed.

We remained face down on the deck all night, shivering, hungry, and thirsty. Soldiers stood over us, holding torches, stabbing anyone who twitched. At first light they ordered us to stand as if for Sabbath Service. The Captain stood on the platform, his right arm rested in a sling. He glanced down at the eight canvas body bags that lay on the deck. "Proceed."

At his command, soldiers pitched the canvas bags into the sea, then stood at attention facing the captain.

A row of men draped in chains with gags in their mouths were dragged before us.

"Your mutiny failed," Woodwright said. "Each of ya had a duty ta report the uprising to me. Mutiny is punishable by death. I'd earn more gold coins carrying bricks than the likes of what's standin' in front of me. I should shoot the lot of ya, but that's a waste of ammunition. Drowning will be faster and cost nothing."

Is this where my life would end? Captain and his soldiers owned us. Did that entitle him to murder us as well? I braced myself as the soldiers stepped forward.

Captain Woodwright drew in a long swallow of rum and stared at the men bound, gagged, and chained on the deck. "You twelve instigators will receive fifty lashes each and be chained on deck for the rest of the voyage, which means yer fellow exiles will have limited space and time on deck until we arrive.

"Yer new sentence once we reach Port Arthur is life at hard labor. Ya may live, but I believe y'll wish for death before we finish with ya." He nodded to Marcus, who stepped forward and dipped his cat-o-nine tails into the one remaining rain barrel.

We stood on deck all day as Marcus released his whip fifty times across each mutineer's back. I winced at the first few swings of the 'nines, then slid into a trance, feeling no sympathy for the twelve who caused us to stand, watch, listen, and go without food or water.

After each mutineer received his lashings, he was given a salty back of seawater, cut down, and chained to the deck. These strong, brutal men who bullied the exiles two days ago now writhed on the deck like half-trampled snakes.

That night, uninvited thoughts crowded into me. I revisited my calmness at the endless floggings I'd witnessed. How could I change from being a printer's devil who's set aside a stray cat in the path of a wagon to a man who could watch men being beaten and not feel any sympathy for their plight. I shuddered at the coldhearted exile I'd so quickly become.

On deck the next morning, we received mouthfuls of food and thimbles of water. With so many buckets destroyed during the mutiny attempt, there'd be no more buckets of food or water below deck.

Each of us devoured our meager rations, wishing for a second helping that would never come. Port Arthur must be within a few days or else the captain planned on starving us. But then he'd lose his income. I doubted he'd want to transport us all this way and receive no bags of coins for his efforts.

The captain watched us eat, then shouted and pointed toward me. "You! Scribes! Follow me."

A soldier grabbed my arm and dragged me toward the captain. Charley and Edward were also grabbed, but disappeared with Mister Meed.

I trembled as I stood in the cabin, uncertain of my purpose. The captain handed me three death certificates. "Fill these out for the dead crew members. Cause of death: typhus."

When I finished, I handed the certificates to the captain. I avoided looking him in the eye. We both knew the true number of exiles on board began at one hundred fifty, but the revised log showed one hundred thirty-eight. The deaths during the illness were recorded, but those from the mutiny were erased as if they'd never stepped on board.

I sat waiting for an extra ration for my work, but none was given. At least I'd survived another day.

Soldiers replaced our hatch cover of crisscrossed wooden slats with a solid cover of wood, which allowed no fresh air and only dim light below deck. Any men sleeping in the back corners were forced to inhale stale air and live in near-darkness, much like Newgate gaol.

Leg irons scraped toward me. I pretended to be asleep, but soon a hand shook me. "You! 'twas you who tol' the cap'n about the prisoner's party, wasn't it? I'm talkin' to ya, scribe."

I sat up and closed my fists, ready to defend myself. "No! I was in the brig when the mutiny started."

The huge body with a mangled face knelt over me. "If I learn ya gave us up, y'll be over the edge to feed the sharks." He drew back his arm to strike me.

I cowered behind my hands and ducked. His fist hit a post, but he didn't as much as whimper. I feared another strike.

A voice boomed from my left. "Leave him be. He was locked up with me. He's not the one."

My attacker lowered his arm and backed away.

I closed my eyes and thought about all I'd heard about the mutiny. How *did* the captain learn of it? Most days he or Mister Meed ignored us, but the soldiers knew our habits. They must have noticed changes and tipped off the captain.

Chains dragged closer again. I tensed until I recognized Charley's face in the dim light.

Anger rose through me like a fever. "Go away, Charley. Leave me be."

"Why are ya mad at me? I took ya ta the hidin' space, didn't I?"

"True, but I heard you conniving with the man in the brig."

Charley inched closer and grabbed my arm. "I don't know what y'ur talking about, Ean."

I yanked free of his grasp. "Yes, you do. You offered to trade information for head scarves."

Charley snorted. "That? I have no idea what I'd tell that dumb bloke, but it was worth a try to get each of us a scarf."

"I'm not sure I believe you, Charley."

He edged closer and whispered. "Best decide, Ean. Y'ur my friend or my enemy, nothin' in between." He scooted away into the shadows.

Over the next week, as we resumed our jobs, the cold air soaked into my bones even though I worked hard and sweated profusely. I craved more than my small daily ration and prayed for the rains to resume so the captain might allow us more portions of water.

Daylight hours shortened. The clouds formed and broke apart into heavy mists. The ocean became fickle, swinging from wild and angry to a chop that barely wrinkled the surface. Rain failed to arrive.

The twelve convicts chained on deck depended on food and water from their former friends. That alliance weakened as each of us struggled to survive. From the looks of it, one or two of those once hearty men might not live to see dry land.

Scotty was right about one thing: within a few days, biting wind and snow swirled across the deck. Thoughts of Fiona and Langstone that usually crowded my mind were now replaced by visions of trays filled with food and more buckets of water than I could consume.

Below deck I lay near Edward, keeping my distance from Charley, still wary after the incident in the brig.

Charley tried to regain Ed's good graces while we stood on deck. He draped his arm over Edward's drooping shoulders. Edward pulled away and tossed Charley an irritated stare.

"I wonder what the new gaol will be like," Edward said.

"Relax, Ed." Charley patted Edward's arm. "We'll stick together and watch out for each other. I can teach ya how ta lift watches and money pouches."

Edward shoved Charley's hand away. "I don't want to learn to be a thief. I want to learn a trade and take care of myself. I want to be somebody."

"You are somebody, Edward," I said. "You're—"

"I know I'm a nice lad, but no one will trust me when they find out I've been in gaol."

"Don't tell them," Charley said. "For now be the great friend of Charley and Ean. Aren't we enough?"

Edward stared at us. "For now. But I'll want more after I'm freed."

The next morning as I ate my mouthful of food on deck, the watchman yelled, "Land ho!"

Edward and I raced to the gunwale. "Have we arrived?"

"I don't know." I pulled my arms inside my tunic to warm myself while I watched land appear and disappear as the *Sara Jane* pitched through the wintry sea.

Edward shivered. "I'm freezing. Hope we get warmer and better-fitting clothes. Mine hang so loose I fear they'll drop to the ground when I walk off the ship. I doubted I'd last the whole way. I mean, I thought I'd die or fall overboard. But I made it."

"Of course, you did," I said, "and you'll continue to be fine, Edward."

Exiles crushed against us as we moved closer to land. Soldiers and crew alike focused on the fast approaching shore.

Cliffs higher than the walls of the Tower of London fended off angry waves. Large, black sea birds circled overhead. As we rounded a promontory, the wind dropped to a whimper.

The small harbor we entered was a settlement of tan brick buildings that lined the shore. Homes marched up narrow cart paths, their smart rows ending beside a dark green forest. Horse-drawn carts and a handful of men approached the pier. No ship save ours appeared in the harbor.

Edward shivered and huddled behind me. "Do you think this is it?"

Charley slid in next to Edward and laughed. "Looks like a quiet little village—not as menacing as Scotty repeated from listening to the soldiers' conversations."

I stared at the buildings and the long wooden pier. "It's hard to tell. Maybe they'll march us through the settlement."

"If they do, we'll stagger like drunken sailors." Charley laughed at his little joke.

"Stand aside," yelled Mister Meed as the sails dropped onto the deck. Behind me two sailors talked as they wrapped the sails against the boom. "This is the hell hole I remember from my first voyage. Never thought I'd return here."

"You said we'd be going to the Indies," the other man grumbled. "How did ya make such a stupid mistake?"

"Too much rum. Wrong alehouse. Bet the proprietor received double coins for duping us. At least we'll get to the Indies on the trip home after pickin' up lumber here and tradin' it for spices."

The men swung down from their perches and disappeared forward as Captain Woodwright shouted for us to be sent below while the ship readied itself for its stay in port.

When we were allowed on deck, the now familiar sway and rocking of the ship had lessened. The ship had been securely tied against the pier with a gangplank added on the dockside.

Soldiers marched down the gangplank and assembled on the pier in their dress uniforms of blue wool coats with gold buttons in two straight rows down the front. Their tall shako hats, reminiscent of the guardsmen outside Westminster, looked out of place in this village; but each man stood at attention with a bayoneted musket against his right shoulder. Each presented himself well for his new commanding officer, modeling an attentive stance even in the icy wind.

The youngest soldiers remained on board to tighten our leg irons and attach heavy chain gang links to join every group of twenty exiles. After they left, we staggered across the gangplank onto the pier before wobbling and clanking along the shoreline.

Every step became a chore as we swayed from being on the ship for so long and from our limited rationing of food and drink. Walking in unison meant we took tiny steps or shuffled our feet to keep from falling and dragging everyone to the ground.

The skin around my ankles burned where the cuffs bit in. I shivered as the chilly June wind penetrated my ragged clothes. Our nasty odor sent the gawking children and adults backtracking to their tidy pathways. I'd have done the same.

We passed convicts in scruffy black and gray striped clothing. They mirrored our weary line, dragging their chain gang links and leg irons.

Straining under the weight of the enormous log they shouldered, they resembled a gigantic centipede walking in perfect unison on either side of their cumbersome load.

No man's eye met another's, nor did words pass from seasoned convicts to new. Our shared humiliation hung on each of us like a necklace of stone.

Onlookers ogled the exiled women, their hands shackled behind their backs, hidden in the folds of their threadbare gowns. The women were herded into carts like those used to transport British prisoners to Tyburn Fair. Within minutes they disappeared out of the settlement.

I turned back to the ship's gangplank in time to see the dark-skinned man and the mutineers. They wore shackles and a gang chain as they were herded up the slushy path toward a low, gray building. Only eight of the mutinous convicts had survived; yesterday four bodies were dumped into the sea.

Soldiers unhitched our drag chains but left our individual leg irons intact. My feet felt frozen as I stood shivering in our rag-tag assemblage, trying to keep from swaying after my months on the ship

Exiles whispered until an officer yelled, "Silence!"

A tall, spare man stood on a raised platform. His beard reached his chest; his bushy eyebrows twitched as he spoke. "I am Governor Carver, commander of Port Arthur, the southernmost British outpost in the world. Our task is to harbor incoming ships, make bricks, cut roads, ship out coal and timber, and produce what food we can in this climate. Do whatever task you receive, and your time here might be shortened. Disobey and you'll spend time in irons, be flogged, or sent to the silent prison.

"After your shackles are undone, give a recording clark your name and information; then remove your ship's clothing and toss it onto the burn pile. Officers will hand out new clothing with your numbers painted on the jumper. The yellow and black stripes remind everyone you're recent arrivals and not to be trusted. Once you're reshackled, take the pair of shoes handed to you and return to your line.

"Keep track of these clothes as well as your bowl and your spoon. If you lose any, do not expect replacements." The governor smoothed his beard and glared out over us. He signaled his clarks with a nod to begin our processing.

I stood shoulder to shoulder with Edward, tempted to link arms to insure our time together. Bound by our ship's adventure, we'd planned to stay together, share food, and protect each other. We'd relented and kept Charley as part of that plan.

For my turn, I stepped from my shackles and moved before the clark.

"Name?" he said.

"Ean McClaud."

"Crime?"

I blinked and said nothing.

"Crime?"

I hesitated until a soldier approached me with his musket raised. He prodded me. "Answer the clark!"

"Thief."

I shuddered. Declaring myself a thief stuck in my throat like a lump of rotten meat. For as long as I remained a prisoner here, I'd carry that crime attached to my name. Ean McClaud, thief.

I disrobed and shivered as I donned the coarse wool clothing, watched my ship's number painted on to my new jumper, and waited as a soldier reaffixed my shackles. Another soldier handed me a pair of worn shoes, which I carried to my line on the parade ground. The shoes, several sizes too small, crowded my toes together and left my heels hanging out in back. Barefoot would have been more comfortable.

The commander left. A second officer mounted the platform. He tapped a riding crop against his short legs as he strode back and forth, clearing his throat.

"I'm Captain Joffard. When we assemble, we expect you to stand with your hands at your sides and your eyes on the officer who is speaking. No talking, no singing, and no rattling chains. This is a prison. You'll work long hours to repay England for your crimes.

"Speak only when spoken to or during the hour after supper. No more than four men may assemble in any one place at any time. Offenders will be punished severely."

One prisoner a row in front of me laughed and jangled his leg irons, dancing a sloppy jig. Two soldiers pounced on him and dragged him up the hill.

Captain Joffard shouted after them, "Four days. Bread and water."

I watched the trio ascend the hill toward a low gray building.

Captain Joffard tapped the riding crop against his breeches. "As I said, no offense goes unpunished. That exile will spend four days in the silent prison. Any more fools ready to join him?"

No one moved.

Joffard continued. "You're thieves, burglars, and murderers. Don't bother us with stories of your innocence. It doesn't matter to us why you're here. Do as you are told. When your time is served, you'll be given a ticket of leave.

"Your leg irons remain affixed until your conduct is acceptable to me." He looked over the parade ground and grinned. "If you sing out complaints like a canary, expect lashes enough to silence your voice."

I glanced at Edward; his face paled. He shook like a tree in a fierce wind as he stared straight ahead. Charley's smirk had vanished; he stared ahead as well. I swallowed hard and suppressed a shudder. This prison promised to be as bad or worse than the ship.

Three soldiers stepped forward. One shouted directions: "When I call your name, step forward. You'll be going to Point Puer, a school for young exiles. We'll teach you a trade so you can make yourselves useful."

He called several young boys before he shouted, 'Edward Maddox'.

I almost spoke. My body tightened like a slip knot. On the ship we'd made plans to stay together and look out for each other. Now what would happen?

Charley looked my way; his face showed concern.

Tears glistened in Edward's eyes. He staggered toward the waiting soldiers and looked back as he marched away around the harbor.

Edward was gone.

7

Captain Joffard scanned the remaining group; then he turned toward a row of white houses on the promontory we'd sailed around and walked off without a backward look. Row by row, we hobbled to a long, tan brick building, holding our bowl and a spoon. I longed to stop and remove the ill-fitting shoes so I could walk faster, but I feared a raised fist or worse. I moved along as best I could.

Armed soldiers lined our way as we entered. Our leg irons clanked when we climbed worn wooden steps. More armed soldiers stood in each doorway. They stopped Charley on the second floor and sent his portion of the line inside the doorway while I continued up the steps.

Inside the third-floor doorway, a soldier handed each of us a small loaf of heavy, dark bread and dropped a slab of salted meat and rock-hard squash into our bowls. He yelled, "Johnny Raws! Take your food to your pallets 'n don't leave any crumbs for the vermin."

I was assigned to one of a hundred double tall, straw-covered wooden bunks. A bear of a man sat on my bunk. He kept his back to me as I sat down and ate. The food needed to be cut, but we had no knives; I gnawed bits loose, grateful for anything to fill my growling stomach.

I surveyed the huge room as I swallowed the last of my meat. All the men around me hovered over their bowls. Those on upper bunks dangled their feet into the faces of those seated below. The grimy floor did not appear to have been swept for weeks. Frost hung from the ceiling beams; wind whistled through the open spaces at the top of the wall. I hoped the snowy weather would warm quickly and the rains of England didn't extend this far. If they did, our clothes would weigh us down like sodden moss.

My bunk mate's smacking reminded of a cow chewing its cud. I lowered my gaze, forced down every crumb, and wished for more. After eating, I felt a strange sickness and rushed to the doorway, covering my mouth. "Quick! Where's the—?"

A guard led me outside. I only made it as far as the grass before I threw up all I'd eaten.

"Ya must be new." The guard snickered. "Ate too much too fast, didn't ya? Now, clean up that mess."

"Is there a broom or—"

I didn't see the blow coming, but I was soon face down in the grass, narrowly missing my vomit.

"Scrape up what ya can with your hands and toss it in the bushes. Leave the rest for the critters, 'n hurry!"

By the time I finished and returned to the barracks, I was shaking and smelled awful. My bunkmate turned toward me and sniffed. His glare frightened me, but I wanted and needed to speak. "My name is Ean McClaud."

He grunted and picked at the food stuck in his teeth. "Tom."

"Been here long?"

He gave one abrupt bob of his head. "Keep your shoes on if ya don't want 'em stolen."

"They're too small. I should leave them to be stolen."

He frowned. "Never give anything away. Keep 'em and make a trade."

Groups of exiles ambled among the bunks, joking and laughing once they'd eaten. Others sat in silence, their faces blank as an unprinted page. All of a sudden, a skinny lad clambered onto a top bunk, spread his arms, and started singing:

> *I love the sea, the wondrous sea,*
> *Where my love sings and taunts me.*
> *She slips her gown free for all to see.*
> *I think she wants me gold, not me.*

Others joined in the song or clanked their leg irons in rhythm. As the verses continued, men danced jigs and whirled each other around like Fiona and I once did.

A soldier banged the butt of his musket on the floor. "Time."

Every man stepped back to his bunk and sat on the edge or curled up under his half of a blanket. Soldiers extinguished the lanterns by the doorway. The noise in the barn-like room dropped to whispers and heavy breathing.

All night, I listened to skittering mice, snoring and moaning of men, and wind howling through the rafters. My body reeled from the ship's violent motion and from the food I'd gobbled down. I became sick when I closed my eyes.

Cold penetrated the thin blanket I shared with Tom. The icy shackles made my legs ache as though I stood in snow. If I slept closer to Tom, I'd use his body heat, assuming he'd allow it.

I tried to warm myself by remembering Fiona's sunburned face, as well as the printer's overheated pressroom, but I remained awake and shivered through the long night.

A bell clanged. Last night's bawdy noise and laughter failed to restart. Instead, I heard shuffling feet and whispering. We lined up at the door for food and returned to our bunks to sit and eat skilly. For as long as I can remember, I've hated flour paste in hot water. But it's better than going hungry.

While I spooned up small bites, I whispered to Tom, "Where do you work?"

"I cut stone," he mumbled as he licked his bowl, tucked it under his blanket, and walked away.

The scrawny lad above me leaned over the edge of his bunk, looking at me upside down. I recognized him from his bawdy singing last night. "Tom shapes stone into bricks for the road to Hobart."

"Has he been here long?"

"Longer th'n me. I arrived two years ago."

"Why are you here?"

The scrawny lad hopped down and hitched up his sagging trousers. "I was the best forger in all London Town, I was. Got meself caught by the constable himself."

"How'd that happen?"

His head bobbled as he spoke. "Took too long for the ink to dry. He got his fingers damp."

I shook my head. "Too bad."

He hiked up his trousers again. "This ain't so bad a place. I get food, 'n all I do ever'day is I pretend ta sweep the floor. They think I'm daft." He started singing and grabbing at the air as he fetched his broom in the corner. He winked as he began screaming and waving his arms.

A soldier yelled at him. "Crazy William, stop that noise or I'll have to jab your skinny ribs."

William slowly lowered his tone to a hum and swept the floor with zigzag swirls. The soldier turned away to watch a crew of men pass our doorway.

I chuckled while I sat on the bunk, wrapped in Tom's blanket. If Crazy William was an example, life here wouldn't be too difficult.

While I waited to be taken to the clark, I planned what I'd say: *I'm a printer's apprentice by trade. I've worked several presses and can repair many as well. I'm willing to start over as an unpaid apprentice.*

All morning, I waited on my bunk. In the afternoon, a soldier came to the doorway and shouted names including mine. "Ean McClaud?"

"Here." I walked toward him.

He tightened each man's shackles. "You men follow me to the clark's office. No talking."

We walked along the harbor and ascended a hill. On the path below us, centipede gangs carried lumber to our ship, the *Sara Jane*. Captain Woodwright waved his arms and yelled at his crew. Remembering his cruelty, I shuddered.

We approached an old country house that overlooked the harbor. Before we entered, the soldier gave us rags to wrap around our shackles and sodden shoes. Inside, the dark wooden floors gleamed. We moved down a long hall and stopped at a closed door. The soldier said, "Don't speak or sit on the floor."

My body ached to sit and remove my tight shoes. As I waited, the daylight faded. When I entered the office, the heat from the narrow fireplace warmed me like a summer's day.

A tall lamp lit the clark's desk and filled the room with buttery light. A rail-thin exile sat at a small desk in a corner. A tingle of excitement raced through me; working in this office would be grand. I'd be warm and dry, sitting near the fireplace or working the press in the back room. My fingers fidgeted, remembering the feel of the type as if I stood working at a press.

The clark, a shriveled man, wore his spectacles perched on the end of his nose. He bent over a ledger; the lamp light reflected off his bald pate. I snickered.

He looked up and scowled. "Silence! Give me your name and birth-place and last residence."

"Ean McClaud, born in County Cork, now of Langstone."

The exile helper leaned over a ledger and wrote.

The clark stared at me. "Age."

"Sixteen."

"Here you'll be seventeen so you can work. We need men, not boys. Point Puer is overcrowded."

"But I'm not seventeen."

The clark held up his hand to stop the exile's recording. He took off his glasses, leaned forward, and signaled the soldier to step forward. "Have it your way. If I send you to Puer, it will be after you've received fifty lashes."

The soldier reached for my arm. I jerked away.

"Stop! Say I'm seventeen."

The clark went back to his task. The exile resumed writing. "You're a thief? Stole a handkerchief and silver spoons?"

I shook my head. "I stole nothing."

The clark signaled the soldier forward again.

"Yes, say I stole those things, but—"

The clark raised his hand to silence me. "Turn slowly toward the window and stop."

I turned. The clark recited my distinguishing marks for the exile helper to record. "Medium height, brown hair, shoulder-length. Thin beard. Brown eyes with one small scar below his left brow."

I'd gotten that scar from falling out of Mistress River's apple tree. I still remember the switching I took for eating apples.

"McClaud?"

I jumped.

"Turn away from the window. I don't like to repeat instructions."
I turned as directed.

"Take off your tunic and turn slowly."

When I raised my tunic, my left arm refused to straighten.

"What's wrong with your left arm?" the clark asked.

I slid my arm free. "My shoulder was knocked out of place while on the ship."

He continued his scrutiny. "No scars on his arms, a tattoo above his left wrist, an 'F'. Back shows recent flogging cross-hatches. Put on your shirt."

The clark's helper blotted the paper and turned it to face me. He handed me his pen. The clark stared at me. "Make your 'X' on this line."

I wrote my full name and straightened with pride. "I'm a printer's apprentice. I read and write. I can help you here in the office or on your press. I was about to—"

"What makes you think I want your help?"

"But, sir, I'm a printers devil."

The clark took back the paper and shook his head. "We have no need for an insolent exile in this office, but you'll have a suitable job by tomorrow." He pursed his lips and narrowed his eyes. The soldier escorted our group back to the penitentiary.

I sat on my bunk, watching exiles return from work and waiting for my meal. For the first time in months, hope filled my thoughts. Tomorrow I'd have a fine and proper job. I'd probably need to start over and mix inks, but I would be inside.

After dinner I decided to find Charley on his floor to tell him of my good fortune. As I approached the hallway, the soldier standing guard raised his musket and pointed his bayonet at my heart. "Halt!"

I backed up. "I want to find my friend—"

"No one leaves their floor after dinner. Back away, Johnny Raw! Wait until Sunday."

"But—"

The soldier raised his bayonet to my throat. "Back away! Now!"

Taunts from men behind me began. "Poor Laddie. He's alone without his little friend. He must be a wee lad who needs his ma. Hey, John, let's help the poor lad."

I clenched my fists and started toward the men. Tom appeared beside me and shoved me toward our bunk. He slapped my head. "Can't you figger this out? Back away 'n keep your mouth shut."

I sat on the bunk, looking at Tom's back, my fists still clenched. I lay down, waiting for my anger to fade. After tomorrow Tom would know that I spoke up and got the job I deserved. He'd soon think differently of me.

In the frigid predawn light, my name was called before the morning meal. I bounded up, ready to begin my printing job. A soldier dressed in a heavy wool coat led ten of us to the parade ground. I reasoned their print shop must be huge to need ten men.

The soldier's words puffed out and hung on the air. "This detail works on the Island of the Dead. Since you men like children so much, it should be an activity you'll enjoy. However, these children can't cry or run away from you. They died of influenza. Both the ground and the bodies are frozen. If we have a thaw this morning, the bodies will reek. Bury them quickly."

I stepped forward. "This is a mistake. I'm to work as the printer's helper."

The soldier scanned his paper. "What's your name?"

"Ean McClaud."

The soldier shook his head. "No. You belong with these other child devilers. Says here you like to kiss and touch young children."

"No! It's been a mistake. Talk to—"

I didn't see the blow coming. A second soldier swung his musket and knocked me to the frozen ground.

"Get up! You're slowing our work."

I struggled to untangle my shackles. Digging graves? The clark said I'd have an appropriate job. Why did he lie?

Soldiers herded us into long row boats. On the planking in the bottom of each boat lay two small canvas bags like those used for sea burials. We walked around them and sat down to scull to the center of the harbor.

My heart ached as I stared at the bags. I imagined how I'd feel if my wee bairn died. Such sadness.

Fog shrouded the harbor. Icy water seeped through the bottom and soaked the canvas bags as well as my shoes. I heard only the oars dipping and lifting and the sound of myself bailing water off the bottom of the boat.

Once we'd tied our boats to rickety posts, we stepped ashore. Quiet blanketed the island as fog swept around ghostly, gnarled trees that grew in small pockets of soil.

Rows of narrow grave markers stood on top of the domed land. This truly was an island of the dead.

As we carried the bodies across the jagged rocks, soldiers pointed to small rock towers. "Watch for burial cairns. Stay three feet away from each as well as from grave markers as you dig new holes."

"Are these piles of rock waitin' for grave markers?" asked one man.

"No," said a soldier. "Only the soldiers and officers have markers. Convicts' and commoners' graves are marked by burial cairns. 'Nuf talk. Get busy."

We worked in pairs to scrape a hole large enough to hold each human bundle. My partner was a sturdy fellow who swung the pick with great force. But the frozen earth didn't yield more than a few crumbled bits with each swing. I removed loose soil and rocks with my bare hands. My fingers stiffened; I flexed them often so they'd not freeze.

After each body was laid in a grave, we filled the hole and made a cairn. Each pile of rocks reminded me of a hastily made children's castle.

No prayers, no headstones, no crosses marked the graves. Did their parents know or care about their children, buried without ceremony on this small island? I said a silent prayer over the tiny bodies and hoped God listened.

At dusk, as we returned to the penitentiary, several angry-faced prisoners approached. A tall, scruffy man shouted, "Here come the child devilers. Let's show 'em what we think of their crimes."

Each man picked up pebbles and small rocks and bombarded us while the soldiers stood nearby, watching and smiling. The cascade of rocks bruised and bloodied me. I covered my face as best I could.

After a few minutes the attackers tired of their sport and left. The soldiers yanked us to our feet and laughed. "Stoning is too good for the likes of you. Clean yerselves up before mealtime."

As I entered the building, I chided myself. How stupid I'd been to expect the clark cared about my talents as a printer's assistant. I should have listened to his words and read his face. Digging graves was his way to punish me for my arrogance.

I sat on the bunk, wiping blood from my face and telling Tom about the attack. "I've never hurt a child."

Tom nodded and dropped his hands between his legs. "No good to complain. No one cares about your life; just dig the bloody graves."

❖

He was right. Regardless of rain or wind or snow or the hardness of the ground, I'd be expected to dig graves. With more food, I'd have energy to work. With no shackles attached to my body, I could work with more energy. With time to heal my arm, I could to work faster. But what was the rush? I had three years' time away from the place I called home.

As I dozed off to sleep each night, an owl hooted, warning unsuspecting animals of its nightly hunt. I started to understand my new life: I was the prey of my captors. Innocence no longer had anything to do with freedom or guilt.

One evening I returned from digging graves to discover our blanket and spoons missing. Other grave diggers had no blankets as well.

Tom stood, waiting for me. "What have you to trade?"

"Trade?" I asked. "What do you mean?"

He shook his head and disappeared. In a few minutes, he returned with a holey blanket.

'Where did you find that?" I said.

"Crazy William," Tom said.

"Can he find me shoes that fit?"

Tom shrugged. "I'll owe him for the blanket. We'll need to repay that first. Next, we'll get back spoons. Find a way to make your shoes work"

We ate with our fingers. Tom stretched out and fell asleep amid the loud singing of exiles. I sat looking at my shoes, examining a way to make them fit. I picked the heel seam loose and folded down the back edges, making the shoes into slippers. Tomorrow, I'd look for a string or a hank of rope to keep them attached to my feet. Tonight, I tucked them under my feet, knowing that slippers would fall off or find their way onto another's feet if I wasn't alert.

Two evenings later as I drifted off to sleep, I felt a tug near my legs. I sat up, ready to defend myself. Tom held my shoes in his hand along with a pile of rags.

"What are you doing?"

"If I give him your shoes and these rags right now, he'll trade them for two spoons and bigger shoes for you. We'll also need to give him our next two days' rations of bread."

The shoes were too big, but I appreciated having space for my long toes. Thanks to Tom and Crazy William, I had backs on my shoes to keep my heels out of the snow when digging graves on the island. I'd find a way to hide and defend these shoes as long as possible.

By the Sabbath afternoon we'd buried every body, so I was free to walk around the parade ground. I watched a group of children playing hoops in the damp grass up the hill from the penitentiary. I laughed when one boy toppled down the hill, ending up in a huge puddle.

Just then, four men approached me. Their closed fists and grim faces made me back away until I stood pressed against the stump of a tree.

A surly-faced man stepped forward. "Fancy little boys, do ya?"

I shook my head.

He grabbed me and twisted my weak arm behind my back. I shouted in pain.

"Sh-h-h," he hissed. "Ya don't want others ta join us, do ya?"

I shook my head.

The man pushed me to my knees. A second man grabbed for my breeches, forcing me face down on the icy grass. I held my breath and prayed for rescue.

I heard a scuffle. The next moment I was pulled to my feet.

Tom stood over me. "This lad is mine. Leave 'im be!" He wiped my face and held me so close I could not breathe. He fondled my hair and kissed me.

What was happening? Tom and I never kissed or touched each other, yet he continued to hold me against him.

He whispered, "Kiss me, now. On the lips. Quickly!"

I kissed his wet mouth, feeling his scratchy beard on my face. I struggled to get free, but couldn't.

When he released his grasp, I tried to pull away. He held fast to my arm. His breath smelled of ale. He brushed back my hair. "Laddie, I've missed ya. Come now. Hold me."

His fingers dug into my arm. The group parted as he guided me away from the men. He leaned his mouth close to my ear. "Say nothin' more. Put yer arm around me and keep walkin'."

8

When we'd crossed the grounds, he released his grip. I shoved him away and wiped his slobber from my face. "Ugh! You're horrid."

Tom snorted. "I saved you."

"I can handle myself. I—"

"No, you can't. Many exiles spend their bedtime wrapped around each other. I've been here ten years 'n fought enough fights to be left alone. Act as if you love me, or you may find a sharp stick through your heart."

"But, Tom—" I tried to think of what to answer.

He put his arm around me. "Come on, Ean. I don't fancy men, but if they think we're together, they'll torment someone else."

Each night, Tom put his arm around me. I lay rigid in his embrace, listening to his loud snoring. When I rolled over, his arm slid away. I curled into a tight knot and wondered if I needed Tom or if he wanted to harm me as the others intended.

One convict song flooded the penitentiary and my mind. The men sang it like a badge of honor; the words repelled me.

> *All heed my cautionary tale*
> *Of innocence and crime;*
> *Beware of thieves 'n rich men's gifts—*
> *They're guilty of a lie.*

A hundred condemned, wretched souls,
We dodged the hangman's hand,
Transported halfway 'round the world
To ne'er return again.

With storms above and storms below,
We sailed the endless sea;
Our spirits withered like our flesh
With ne'er a chance to flee.

We convicts crowd the ancient ship
For months, no land in sight.
We holystoned, we hauled the sails,
We felt the cat's deep bite.

Arriving in the untamed land,
We'll struggle to survive
Near gallows steps, 'n pillory;
Our quest: to stay alive.

As thieves 'n innocents alike,
We're bound and chained each day
To work as slaves to clear the land,
No chance to slip away.

A hundred condemned, wretched souls,
We dodged the hangman's hand
To dream of loved ones far away,
Safe from Van Dieman's land.

During our free evening hour, Tom and I held hands and walked the penitentiary floor. One night, he released me and walked with his beefy hands behind his back. "I came here from Norfolk Island, a hellhole east of here."

"Did you live there?"

He shook his head. "No, it's where I began my sentence. This place is bad, but Norfolk was evil through and through."

"What did you steal?"

"Nothing. I murdered three men."

I stopped and stepped away from him. "Why?"

He moved on, so I hurried to catch up to him. A sadness crossed his face. "Sometimes you have no choice." He grabbed my arms and shook me; his face clouded. "I'm a lifer with no hope of leaving this place. Wake up, Ean. Stop being a Johnny Raw."

"What does that even mean?"

Tom shook his head. "The soldiers call all new convicts Johnny Raw because they act stupid, green, raw. Pay attention to where you walk, what you do, and what you say." He shook his head and shoved me hard, then hurried away without any glance my direction.

The month crawled by. One June evening as wintery light splashed shadows on the penitentiary floor, I complained to Tom. "Burying bodies with one strong arm was hard work, but digging for the local farmers is difficult as well. I'm about to sit down and refuse to dig."

Tom grabbed my arm and squeezed hard with his beefy fingers. "Ean, don't cause trouble or you'll be ripe for a lashing or the silent prison. I won't be able to protect you."

"I don't need you to protect me, old man."

"You couldn't stand up to the men that circled you after you arrived."
I paced the floor. "I was new and injured; I didn't know what to do."
Tom shook his head and returned to our bunk with no comment.

When I thought about it, he was right, but I tired of holding his hand
and having him cuddle me like a lover on our bunk. Not even thoughts
of Fiona erased my anger toward this place and this pretense. I had to
admit I was grateful Tom shared his blanket with me, but I remained uneasy, wondering if I should trust him.

"Does anyone escape?" I asked.

Tom shook his head; his voice dropped to a whisper. "'Tis not worth
the risk. If you succeed, the gov'ner loses face with the Crown. And if
he catches you, he'll put you in the silent prison or hang you. Most men
who survive that gray torture leave part of their minds behind."

"Have you been there?"

Tom scratched his bald pate and didn't answer.

"Was it bad?" I asked.

He wiped his hand over his face before he spoke. "The silence kills
your mind, and then your body withers."

On the next Sabbath, it snowed. The houses on the hill resembled
miniature Christmas cottages I'd seen in the wealthy folks' shops near
Langstone. Back home, Fiona probably watched leafy trees shade the
lane while here I lived in a frozen winter. Home. Would I ever return to
my print job and Fiona? Each day, a thin slice of my hope disappeared;
maybe it never existed.

After church, we assembled on the parade ground before the triangle.
Charley stood beside me in the icy afternoon as we watched seven men
herded up the platform. I seldom saw Charley except on the Sabbath
or during floggings; neither permitted speaking. Inside the building we
signaled each other with nods but seldom had a chance to speak before
moving back to our separate penitentiary floors.

Captain Joffard stood to one side with his arms crossed. Two soldiers held cat-o'-nines in a menacing manner, whipping the air above our heads. Joffard paced as the first man was strapped to the triangle, his arms stretched wide to bare his back as broadly as possible. "This man was insolent on his work duty. Twenty-five lashes."

This day's punishments began. One had lost a shovel: thirty lashes and three months in irons. Another tried to sell a blanket and two spoons: thirty-five lashes and irons for six months. I flinched at each swing of the cat, remembering each lash I received on the ship. Around me exiles watched the flogging with vacant eyes. Were they immune to the pain or blotting out the punishments with happier thoughts?

At the end of the three hours, the sun slid behind the western hills. My toes were cold as icicles, even with shoes on. Captain Joffard replaced tonight's meal with a cup of water, saying, "This is your reminder. If you want food, obey my rules."

Tom sat on his side of the bunk, alternately staring at his hands and rubbing his neck. I backed up to him and turned around several times like a dog trying to find a comfortable spot. "Tom, I have to get out of here," I whispered.

His head popped up. "Quiet!" He leaned and caressed my back as he whispered, "More than a handful of men in here sell secrets for a bit of bread or a thimble of rum. Never speak of escape unless we're alone."

"Have you ever made a plan or figured a way out?"

He shook his head. "There's no way out. When—"

An exile passed our bunk and slowed to adjust his shoe. Tom spoke with more energy. "The only way to get away from your job, Ean, is to do it. Now stop bothering me."

It took me a moment to understand his sudden rebuke. I stared at him while I considered a response. The exile stood watching me, waiting for my reply. "Leave me alone, old man."

He moved on and slowed beside another bunk, repeating his motions. Tom lay down and pulled the blanket to his chin. "Like I said, only when we're alone."

❖

My new job placed me on a road gang. Lieutenant Dorn, the soldier in charge, shouted, "Pick up a food pack and a blanket. We'll be out several weeks. Move in unison so you won't tangle your shackles. I don't tolerate stumblers and doddlers."

We marched across Eaglehawk Neck, a narrow stretch of land linking Port Arthur to the mainland, where snarling dogs pulled at their chains, ready to chase down escaping convicts. The guards smiled and unleashed several dogs, allowing them to nip at our legs us as we hurried past them, trying to stay on our feet.

One guard shouted after us, "'Member this when ya think y'll make a run from Port Arthur. We keep 'em hungry and teach 'em to attack the likes of you."

We followed the finished roadbed for hours on our way to build the next portion. In the nearby trees, strange pink and gray birds bobbed their white topknots and squawked like maids working in the gardens in Langstone. Birds seldom nested near the penitentiary. Here their chatter would have been comical and worth a long look had it not been that we were shackled together and being pressed forward as quickly as possible.

"Drop your packs!" Dorn's yell startled me after so many miles of walking with only the sound of chains clanking and our heavy breathing breaking the silence.

He waited until all stood silent. "You twelve will advance this section of road three miles each day. If you don't make the distance, I won't get my extra pay and your rations will suffer, especially your dram of rum. Don't anger me."

He pointed to a bush with red berries. "Never eat these berries. You'll cry for your ma and vomit your insides out if you do, and I'll still expect you to dig."

No one moved or spoke.

He cleared his throat before continuing. "Guards, keep a watchful eye on the exiles as well as our supplies. A tribe of aboriginals roam this area. Shoot anything that rustles in the bush or anyone who tries to escape."

Days passed into months. We dug furiously to keep meat and rum in our meal, but every day Dorn and the soldiers found fault with our work: too shallow, too deep, not straight enough. They always had an excuse to feed us skilly, a shovel bread, while they hoarded our portions of meat and rum as their own.

The frigid winter weather shifted to early spring, and we worked amid daily rain. My clothing stuck to my body like a second skin; my shackles dug into my ankles, never allowing the skin to heal. My back ached from the rivers of muck I pushed aside to make room for the hand-hewn stones that Tom and a dozen stone cutters laid along the track behind us.

I appreciated Tom's arrival last month. At his suggestion I kept my distance from the men that worked beside me on the road. "Don't trust a one of them. They'll do what they can to gain your trust; some might steal your food if they think you're easy prey."

Day after day, I watched the others to see if Tom was right. He was. Many of the men took advantage of new convicts, dragging them into trouble or standing back to watch them squirm under Lieutenant Dorn's stern rules.

After eating another meal of skilly, I finger-traced the numbers scratched onto a broken stone I found on the ground beside me. Tom watched me. "Scratching our exile numbers onto each brick slows our work. It's a devilment officers devised for us to prove we're working. Like we have a choice."

"No one has ever said why our clothes have the bird footprint?"

Tom brushed down his rim of hair and stretched his arms forward and back. "It's not a bird, it's a broad arrow. Let's everyone know we're exiles and owned by the government. Some say the three sticks stand for exile goals: work, survive, and leave. Everything belongs to the gov'ner. We're here to insure his profit."

"Profit?" I asked.

He stretched out on our sodden bed mat. "Port Arthur gets paid to build these roads so produce carts can travel to Hobart. Local crops fetch a fair price."

"But we never see fresh food."

Tom yawned. "They sell our portion. Send the profit to England or slip the coins into their pockets."

I tossed the broken brick into the bushes. The broad arrow looked like a bird print to me. "I envy the exiles back in the penitentiary. They have their Sabbath to rest. We're treated like slaves, working dawn to dark seven days a week."

Tom shook his head. "I never long to return to that brick cage. Here we have space around us with no bells and no floggings."

"But we're not free. I want my freedom so I can return to Fiona."

"Is she all you think about? Quit your complaining and go to sleep."

He turned away from me and pulled the damp blanket over his body. I moved close to him for warmth, but could not sleep until I conjured Fiona's smiling face near mine.

❖

Dawn to dusk, I watched for distractions to block the pain of bending over and shoveling dirt and muck all day. This morning, I found a raggedy shirt under a bush. When the soldier patrolling our digging turned away, I rolled up the rag and placed it inside my jumper, securing it with the rope holding up my breeches. Back in Port Arthur, the rag would bring a good trade for rations or other necessaries.

More and more, I disgusted myself. I'd begun thinking like Charley.

I wiped my face, lifted my shovel to dig, and stopped. In the brush, inches from my face, two dark eyes blinked. I turned away. When I looked back, the eyes were gone. I told no one what I'd seen; who'd believe me anyway?

The next evening, a young soldier named Thadeus, who patrolled our camp area, spoke of the aboriginal people. "They've lived here since before the Brits. My father visited years ago and told me these abs are Pallawah. Some nights, he heard their ceremony drums. First time I heard their horns, I nearly jumped out of my skin."

"How did they sound?" I asked.

"Can't describe 'em. But you'll know if ever you hear 'em."

"Tom," I asked, "have you heard them?"

"No." He stabbed his finger into my chest. "Ean, don't you ever stop asking questions? You're wearing out my ears."

❖

Our work inland progressed rapidly, but we never regained our full rations. We ate our shovel bread while Bartlett Anders, a fellow exile, entertained us with his prattle like a busy old woman. He smacked his lips as he chewed. "Lordy, this ain't no Manchester Puddin'."

"What's Manchester Pudding?" I asked.

Bartlett smiled, showing the space where four teeth should be. "Where ya from, lad? Manchester Puddin' is custard wearin' ap-pree-cot jam, lemon, and sugar on top."

Another exile piped up. "How'd you ever get Manchester Puddin'?"

Bartlett laughed. "I 'member seein' it in the scullery when I stole the fine folks' silver. I grabbed a piece jest 'fore the gov'ner chased me out."

"Silence!" a soldier shouted. "Finish your supper!" He aimed the butt of his weapon at Bartlett's head. Bartlett ducked and went back to eating his shovel bread. No one spoke until we bedded down like a row of skinny sausages.

I lay shackled between Tom and Bartlett. In the dim firelight, I saw the old man's toothless mouth gaping like a dark cave. His rancid mouth blew hot air against my ear. "Call me Barty; that's my best name."

"Sounds like a bitty bird if you ask me."

Barty laughed. "Did you learn 'bout those bitty birds what live here?"

"Can't say as I have."

Barty whispered, "One soldier tol' me he seen 'em along these beaches. Called 'em fairy penguins. Said they're smart dressers with grey coats and white fronts. Their legs are short 'n they wobble when they walk; look like they're floatin'.

"The ma leaves her babies in the rocks all day while she and the da fish for food. The young'uns stand quiet, waitin' for hours for their parents ta return. You c'n pass'em 'n not know it. The soldier claims that if ya see one at night, y'll be rich 'n free."

"Have you seen one, Barty?" I whispered.

"Am I lookin' free?"

"Did the exiles who saw them get free?" I asked.

Barty's foul breath tickled my ear. "Not certain, but I hope 'twas true."

9

Each night we built fires to keep away Tasmanian devils, wombats, tiger snakes, and aboriginal people. Soldiers collected our shovels and locked them away with our dwindling supply of grain and hard tack, then patrolled our encampment.

One morning, we woke to gunfire and a rustling in the brush. Lieutenant Dorn raced around the perimeter with his musket, shouting and cursing. "Blasted abs took half our shovels and a week's supply of food. Private Thadeus! You fool! You fell asleep on duty."

Thadeus stood rigid, "Must 've, sir."

Barty spoke up. "We headin' back to Port Arthur for supplies, gov'ner?"

Dorn laughed. "Why would we do that? It's four days' round trip. Find sticks, share shovels, or dig with your hands." His glare focused on Thadeus. "You'll lose one week's pay for your carelessness."

Dorn scanned the area. A smirk crowded onto his face. "Perhaps Barty's right. Thadeus, take him back to Port Arthur for supplies. You can carry three sacks of food and a dozen shovels, can't you, old man?"

Barty straightened. "Yes—sir." From his appearance, I doubted he could manage much more than one shovel.

I stepped forward. "Send me. I'm stronger than Barty."

Dorn brought his face up to mine. "Who asked you? Barty'd be a lot more fun to watch carryin' the bundles than the likes of you." He shoved me; I stumbled backward over a boulder and landed in a prickly plant. "We need twelve kilometers finished before they return with supplies."

Scrape, toss, scrape, toss. As I worked, something or someone watched me. When the soldiers drifted away that evening, I gathered a handful of twigs, stacking them in a haphazard manner like a fallen bird's nest. The next morning, they'd vanished.

Another day, I stacked rocks like the burial cairns I made working on the Island of the Dead. The next morning, the soft soil held no trace of a single rock or indentation.

As I dug my side of the road, I found a shard of broken pottery. I laid it under a scrub gum bush with a chunk of dry, leftover shovel bread. Later that day, a crude rope lay in its place.

The three-foot-long rope was made from braided grasses. Small, disc-shaped stones were woven in, creating bulges along the length of the rope. I returned the rope to the spot where I'd found it.

That evening, my curiosity was greater than my need to secret away the rope. I pretended to find the crude rope when a soldier passed nearby. "What's this?"

Dorn grabbed it from my hands. "Where did you find this?"

"Under the bush."

Dorn hefted the rope. "It's an aborigine weapon," he shouted. "If you see these, don't pick them up unless you want the cat-o'-nines across your back." He swung the rope in circles around and around above his head, faster and faster until it created a whoosh, whoosh as it spun.

"They swing these 'round and let 'em fly toward those pesky, pink gallah birds. Not as good as a boomerang, but it stuns 'em long enough for an 'ab' to rush in and finish 'em off."

Dorn released the whirling rope. It flew high and dropped into the brush at a considerable distance.

"Why didn't you keep it, sir?" asked one exile.

Dorn grinned. "Against a musket a rope loses every time."

Each day after that, I left rocks and twigs, hoping the unseen person would take them. I saw no one until the day we entered a thicket. A man crouched beyond the brush I was hacking with my stick. His eyes glistened like moist, black stones; his deep brown skin resembled damp peat. Long, black hair curled near his face. I kept my eye on him as I chopped.

As a wee one, when my brother and I found trouble, we'd signal each other with blinks for the story we'd tell ma. She never unearthed our scheming. Perhaps that would work here. I blinked four times and left a flat rock on a mound of soil as I worked on.

When I looked back, the rock had disappeared. The man followed soundlessly through the thicket. I blinked four times and left another rock. The rock disappeared.

Again and again, I blinked to the eyes in the brown face, left rocks, and received nothing more than the first braided strand until the fifth morning. When I woke, I found a braided rope by my head. The rocks I'd left over the past few days lay in a circle by the side of the road. I laughed, feeling a bubble of excitement slide through me. I hid the rope inside my shirt and used my shackled foot to erase the rock circle.

"What's so funny?" asked an approaching soldier.

"Clearing my throat, sir." This bit of grass with stones woven in would make a fine trade if I kept it hidden until we returned to Port Arthur and showed it to Crazy William.

❖

Evenings, we drank a licorice-flavored tea made from the creeper vine that climbed in the brush beside the road. We ate small portions of porridge, hoping Barty would return with new supplies before we ran out of food.

Sure enough, he arrived late one afternoon on the back of the cart, swinging his legs, singing a bawdy song, and acting like the king of the cart. His arrival made the fiercest member of the road gang laugh as the banty-sized man eased off the cart and helped unload the supplies.

After dark he told me the story of his trip.

"That Thadeus was ornery. Had me hoppin' 'stead of walkin' so I started singin'. By the time we got back to Port Arthur, I got me a scratchy throat 'n my feet had blisters big as flat cakes on a plate. When the cap'n saw me, he yelled at him. Said to let me ride back here and to quit wastin' time."

Only Barty would get even with the soldiers and not realize he'd done it.

We continued on, making our next camp in a clearing beside the ocean, where we ate cold porridge with vegetables. We slept on the ground in a shelter of trees. The ocean's roar shook the earth like thunder as waves rushed the nearby beaches, drowning out the growls of my hunger.

The next morning, a farmer approached along the rough-cut roadway. He carried a sack on his back and a musket.

"How's the spring season beginning?" asked Dorn.

The farmer shook his head. "Poor to middlin'. Tryin' to head for New South Wales. Heared tell they've found gold 'bout a hundred miles inland."

I listened to the details, ready to share them with Tom to encourage him to try an escape. With gold we'd be rich enough to buy our way back home.

"Where 'bout's is New South Wales?" Dorn asked.

"On Australia, the big island north of here. Found the gold jest this past winter."

"Can you make passage?" Dorn asked.

"Nope. I'll have ta work my way to Melbourne. Heared they need guards on the ships."

The lieutenant took the farmer by the shoulder and moved out of our listening distance. They talked long enough for us to catch our breath and then shook hands before the farmer walked on.

"What did the farmer want?" asked one exile. "To trade a bag of seeds for a slave?"

Dorn shook his head. "He has a ticket of leave, 'n now he's begging us to stop and plow his rooted field for free so he can lease it out, ready for farming."

"We gonna do it?"

"For free? Nah. It would take a heavy bag of coins to hold us here."

"You spent a lot of time talkin' to him," Barty said. "What's else has he got to trade?"

"His daughter is weddin' age," Dorn said. "Wants me to take her in trade for a milk cow for his family."

One exile hooted and slapped his leg. "Mus' be a toothless wench, fer sure. Best keep the cow!"

Laughter spread through our ranks like bees through a field of clover until Dorn drew his whip and stared us down.

That night I told Tom about the gold. "Think about it. Enough gold to live the rest of our lives as free men. I could marry Fiona, buy a cottage, even my own press. If I got caught, I could buy my freedom with gold. You could—"

Tom grunted and shook his head. "Don't have the will. I couldn't take another stay in the silent prison if we failed."

"We wouldn't get caught," I said as I turned away from Tom. "You worry too much, old man."

Tom stretched out on our mat. "Ean, you don't know what you're saying. The silent prison is worse than the ship. At least on the ship you're allowed to speak with others."

"It's you who don't know what you're saying. The quiet would be a relief from the snoring and grumbling in the penitentiary."

"That prison's different." Tom grabbed away the blanket. "These people think we're animals. They can do whatever they want as long as we never return to England."

"What do you mean, never return?" I said. "We get tickets of leave!"

"Most do. But think a moment; how will you pay for the trip home? Or, if you end up in the silent prison, can you survive?"

"The gold," I said. "That's why we need the gold."

Tom turned away. "You forget I have a life sentence."

"All the more reason to get as far away from here as possible." My anger brewed inside me at his obstinacy. I clenched my fists and tried to calm myself. "You know what? The silent prison wouldn't be difficult for a young man. Besides, we won't get caught."

"Barty's been there. Look at him," Tom said. "He's not himself any-more. You've not spent time in that prison, lad. It breaks your spirit."

"But you said Barty only stayed a week, and last week he was sitting on a cart, singing."

"You think you know everything after being in this bloody place for a few months. It would do you good to listen to those who've been here longer."

❖

Spring nights, we worked until dusk, adding final stones as we retraced the road to our encampment. I felt a presence along the side of the road. I slowed, pretending to adjust my shoe. Was an aboriginal following us?

I flipped up the leaves of a scraggly plant inches from my foot, looking for any small treasure left behind. Instead I saw a bird no taller than the head of a shovel. His coat glistened like a gentleman's gray silk hat. By Barty's description, it was a fairy penguin.

His dark eyes blinked, but his body didn't move so much as one velvety hair. I stared at his stillness, wondering how long the penguin could remain motionless. I let the leaf flop back, covering his hiding place. Barty told the truth; fairy penguins were real. I hoped the story's promise of freedom and wealth proved true as well.

❖

Along the coast I spied a low island a mile off in the sea. Grasses covered the slopes; trees stood on the rise like bushy hair.

"No one lives there," a soldier said. "The storms blow too fierce for rowing to and from the mainland. But further north, a string of islands trace the coast. Settlers farm a few, aboriginals call others their land, and one is Maria Island, where the prison closed last year."

On our bed rolls at night, I talked to Tom about the islands. "I think we could live on one of those islands if we escaped. With grasses and enough trees to live in and—"

"Ean! Stop this talk of escape."

But all day, every day, I thought of escape and freeing myself from digging and eating skilly. I knew I must find a way to return to Fiona before she forgot me.

Crossing Eaglehawk Neck was impossible. Soldiers with torches turned night into day; their hungry hounds stood ready to chew into any who tried to escape. The thick undergrowth beyond the settlement let no man through, except the 'abs'. The sea must be the best route of escape. But how?

10

At the end of August as we marched back into Port Arthur, I pictured myself sleeping in the penitentiary on my wooden bunk. Sounded like heaven: no more insects, bush creatures, or mud. During our walk around time after dinner, I spoke again with Tom about the aborigine.

"Be watchful, lad," he said. "The aboriginals would eat you before they'd befriend you. These roads destroy their hunting land 'n bring in more farmers and more sheep. They'll thieve the farmers' livestock if they can't find food and slaughter humans 'n steal their babies to stop their moving across their land."

"All I know is what I saw," I said. "The ab acted friendlier than the soldiers. I'm hiding the rope he left under the planks of our bunk. Could make a good trade through Crazy William. He'll find me shoes that fit."

Tom shook his head. "Your shoes are fine. Forget about trading for something you already have; save for something important you may need in the future."

The next week, while I turned a farmer's fields, time hung like the weight of the rain on my clothes. I distracted myself by thinking about working Master John's press back in Langstone. I worked beside the open window, moving the type into place, smelling the ink. Those long hours and my sore muscles were small discomforts compared to my current situation. I doubted I could keep working this hard on so little food for more than a few months, certainly not for three years.

A soldier arrived, calling out, "Attention!" He waited until we stopped work and leaned on our shovels. "If I call your name, put up your shovel and follow me."

He called out the names of several rough-looking men, followed by my name. Had a convict heard me speak of escaping? Was I to be punished? Since I had little in common with these men, I worried where we were headed.

The soldier dropped off the other men at the warehouse and led me to the offices where I'd been interviewed when I first arrived. The same snarly, bespectacled clark sat at his desk. As we entered, he eyed the mud and water dripping off my shoes and onto his plush rug. Without looking higher, he said, "I understand you can read and write."

"Yes, sir."

"Call me Master Glevins."

"Yes, sir, Master Glevins."

He handed me a paper and pen. "Write what I tell you."

Glevins cleared his throat and paced. "And I command you at that time, saying, The Lord your God hath given you this land to possess: ye shall pass over, armed before your brethren, the children of Israel, all that meet for the war."

I hurried through the words, attempting to add flourishes to impress him of my skill, but he spoke so fast it was truly a test. I finished and handed him the paper.

Before I had time to consider the words I'd written, Glevins glanced at my work and nodded. "Acceptable." He balled up the paper and tossed it into his wood bin. "Macquarie Harbor's penitentiary has closed. Their exiles arrive any day, probably tomorrow. You will report to me after breakfast, record their information, and stay until I dismiss you each afternoon. Since transport from England has ended, they will be our last arrivals."

Transport from England had ended? Surprise followed by anger raced through me. If only it had ended a year earlier, none of these horrible events in this strange world would have happened. I'd be home working, visiting Fiona, and planning our lives together.

"McClaud! Are you listening?" he shouted.

I pulled myself back to the conversation. "Yes sir, Master Glevins."

He stared at the puddle spreading through his rug. "In the future come with clean, dry shoes. I don't want water and mud smeared on my rug."

"Yes, Master Glevins."

The clark's job lifted my mood like viewing a brilliant sunrise. For at least a month, I'd be free of my shovel and out of the rain. I wanted to tell Tom, but he had returned to cutting stone at the quarry. Instead, I celebrated by talking with Barty after dinner.

"And no more convicts are being sent here from England. Barty? Are you listening?"

He ignored me and shuffled on toward the wall.

"Barty?"

He lowered his head and counted his steps. "Fifty-one, fifty-two—"

When we turned and retraced our steps, he kept his eyes toward the floor. I spoke louder. "I pray new exiles from Macquarie won't be added to our beds. I'm accustomed to Tom and want no other added to our cramped space."

Barty stopped counting. Tears filled his eyes. "Lad, I, I'm— I can't remember your name. My head gets soddy. The last visit up the hill and the whippin'—" He shook his head and ambled on.

"I'm Ean. Tom's friend."

"That's right, Tom."

I took his arm and steered him to a nearby window. "Continue doin' your job, Barty and—"

"I try, lad, but my body's too tired. An' if I don't work, they'll beat me or send me back up the hill." He grabbed my arm with force. "I can't do that place no more."

I patted his curved back and turned him toward his bunk. As he lay down, he smiled up at me. "Thank you—Tom. You're a true friend." He closed his eyes and drifted off to sleep amid the din of voices and the singing of bawdy songs.

Barty's terror surprised me. Would he get stronger and return to his storytelling and singing now that he was back at the penitentiary? With Tom away at the quarry, I'd need to keep track of him each evening.

The next morning, I entered barefoot into the clark's office after I wiped my feet dry on a rag at his door. As I entered, Charley, my friend from the ship, stood in a line. His eyes danced as he dipped a quick nod and a wink. I looked away from him and took up a paper, ready to begin my work. It would do no good to let Glevins know we knew each other.

Glevins looked up from his desk at the line of men. "I need additional helpers. You've been chosen because you *claim* you can read *and* write the King's English. Step forward now if that is untrue before I decide to have you flogged."

A shuffling of feet and bodies began. Six men stepped forward. Master Glevins' jaw tightened. "Guard! Remove these liars! Put them on bread and water and double chain them for the next week. I have no time for this! Now, the rest of you show me what you can write."

Over the next minutes Glevins tested the men and chose one to remain to work with me. It wasn't Charley. As quickly as he'd come back into my life, he left. We hadn't spoken a word, but I didn't worry. Like the thief he was, Charley always had a scheme brewing.

Glevins turned to me and the selected exile. "Record each new exile's criminal history and other details noted on the log sheets. Be quick, but record precise details or you'll be replaced."

"Yes, sir," we said in unison.

All day a continuous stream of exiles filed through the office. I wrote each man's criminal information and handed the forms to the other assistant, who recorded their physical characteristics as Glevins dictated. At the end of the day when Glevins left the room, I spoke to the man for the first time.

"My name's Ean. And you're—?"

"Lorcan."

I handed him a file. "Born of County Cork, lived in Langstone. You?"

Lorcan stood and stalked the empty room like a restless beast. "Are we allowed to talk?"

"If we keep working," I said. "When did you arrive?"

"Month ago." He lowered his voice to a whisper. "On the ship 'twas talk of a new commandant. Said to be planning to cancel all pardons and tickets of leave. He's bringing more troops."

Shock jolted through me. I grabbed his arm. "A new commandant? Why?"

Lorcan looked around the room and leaned closer. "There's talk of a rebellion among the convicts."

"What? We've heard nothing."

"'Tis true, I swear. Irish convicts sent word home about a planned rebellion and escapes. They've organized their kin who've migrated to Tasmania to slip weapons into the penitentiary. All true Irishmen must rise up."

"But we're not the only exiles here. Many come from England and—"

"Look at the records. More Irish here than Brits."

I stepped to the doorway and looked both ways along the hall, then returned to the desk. "How do you know this?"

Lorcan's eyes narrowed. "I have my ways," he said. "Join us or keep this to yourself. I'll know if you tell anyone."

I gulped to control a fear building inside me. "I ah-h, haven't seen you before."

"I've been up the hill since my arrival."

"In the silent prison?"

He nodded. "That mistake's been fixed. Enough coins fix anything. I'm back to England on the next ship. I need to stay in this office, so don't make trouble for me. If you do, I'll find you or send others to find you, understand?"

I watched his eyes narrow and his face twist with meanness. I clenched my fists, stepped back, and busied myself, putting away the ink and papers so I wouldn't say or do something I might regret. Lorcan went back to work as if we'd discussed nothing more interesting than the weather.

Over the next few days, Lorcan and I continued to interview a steady stream of exiles from Macquarie Harbor. Each professed his innocence, much as I had done when I arrived. I kept an eye on Lorcan, watching how he took extra time with certain rough-looking men. His manner made my skin prickle. The uprising might be a true threat. I avoided Lorcan once we left the small office, making certain I didn't look to conspire with him.

After a week and as August became September, Tom returned. I felt relieved to see him, but the thought of an uprising still bothered me. I mentioned it during our evening free time. "Lorcan frightens me. He knows troubling things. I have to work with him, but I don't want to be around him when he speaks of an uprising. I don't know what to do."

"Relax, Can. Talk of a rebellion circles all the time and nothing comes of it. He's another Irishman who wants to stir things up."

"But he's got money or influence enough to be sent back home. He talks with the groups of exiles most of us avoid. I feel them watching me. I fear they'll attack me."

Tom expelled a long puff of air and turned away. "In time you'll learn he's full of empty words."

I doubted Tom this time. I knew what I'd seen; Lorcan scared me as much as anyone I'd met in prison or on the ship.

Walking beside Barty one evening, I told him about Lorcan. "Tom thinks he's wrong about a rebellion."

Barty rubbed his chin and started swaying and singing before he whispered, "Best keep your distance from Lorcan." He walked away, counting his steps to the wall without looking back.

When he returned, he had a faraway look in his eyes. "I loved her, I did. Her smile made me heart dance a jig. But I lost her so long ago."

"Who, Barty?"

He wiped his eyes. "Me ma died, and me da, and the whole family." He shuffled toward his bunk. "Good night, Tom."

I stood over him as he pulled his blanket up to his ears. I brushed back his thinning hair and patted his shoulder more like a father than a friend. "Night, Barty."

My stomach churned with a sensation closer to fear than hunger. Day after day, Barty retreated further and further. He confused things and still didn't remember my name.

After lights out I tried to focus on Fiona and sailing back to England, but Lorcan's menacing face overshadowed my thoughts. I debated my next action. Perhaps I should tell Glevins or a soldier. No, soldiers never listened to exiles. More likely, they'd string me up, call me a squealer, and let exiles throw stones at me. Best that I travel across the sea to New South Wales and prospect for gold. Like Lorcan said, 'enough coins you fix anything'; they even buy freedom.

One week later, Lorcan didn't report for work. He wasn't in chains or flogged in front of us on Sunday. No one mentioned seeing him taken up the hill. Fear gripped me like a turn screw on the printer's press. What if he took my lack of excitement to join in the rebellion as a sign I'd blathered his secret? What if the officers learned of the Irishmen's plans and tried to stop Lorcan's influence. What if he told them I was involved?

Walking between the penitentiary and the clark's office each morning, an exile often followed me; other days, two or three trailed me, throwing pebbles at my back. I moved faster and faster to reach the safety of my destination; so did they.

On the Sabbath when Tom and I found a private spot along the parade ground, I couldn't hold back any longer. "I don't know what happened to Lorcan."

"People disappear all the time, Ean. Why do you care?"

"Because of the commandant's rant today about an uprising. I'm afraid Lorcan's friends think I spoke of the uprising to Glevins. I know I'm being followed."

Tom placed his hand on my arm. "Calm down, Ean. You're rattling on like Barty. You're imagining things. Rebellions take time to organize."

I stopped. My heart beat as rapid as a drum in a fife and flute corps. "You've heard something, haven't you?"

Tom closed his eyes and nodded. "You're right, Ean. I didn't want to frighten you, but plans are being whispered about enlisting all Irishmen, one way or the other. If they think you gave up Lorcan, they'll come after you. Best get yourself away from the office."

"But, Tom, the office is the safest place to be with so many soldiers around. Besides, when I'm working in the office, I write letters to Fiona."

"Does she write back?" he asked.

"It's too soon to know, but I'm certain she will."

He studied my face with a furrowed brow. "How many letters have you sent, Ean?"

"Three, no, four."

"Ean, she's not getting them, or she's found another to comfort her. Right now, you need a plan to focus and stay away from the men you think follow you."

I knew he was right, but I couldn't think of a way to ask Glevins to find me a job elsewhere. Plus, I enjoyed having the chance to work indoors during the spring rains.

With Lorcan missing, another exile arrived to assist me: Charley. When I saw his face, I gasped. He placed his index finger to his lips.

I patted his shoulder and whispered, "How'd you get sent back here?"

Charley smirked and picked up a wooden box of files. "I convinced the soldier ta put me first on the list. I can read wit' the best of ya. Plus, I gave him a silver coin I found on the ship we unloaded."

"Have you seen Edward?" I asked.

Charley shook his head. "Never get close to Point Puer. Never see those young lads. But Edward's smart enough; he'll do all right. His readin' and writin' will give him a better chance than many."

Little had changed with Charley. He looked scrawny like the rest of us, but he'd remained watchful and informed. While most exiles grew scraggly beards, he'd found a way to shave his face smooth as a baby's bottom. Perhaps he'd teach me his trick. I disliked my bristly chin.

He organized the files while he spoke. "Loadin' lumber onto the ships, I seen lots of crazy things happen. Would ya believe they don't guard the ships after loadin'? Instead, they fumigate the hold with smolderin' gases to kill rats and bugs. Last ship we loaded, three exiles crawled from the hold, coughin' their lungs out."

"What happened to them?"

"They were the ones flogged a while back and sent to the silent prison. Each got six months added to his sentence. Should've done their time. I never want to end up in that horrid place."

"But, Charley, being in the prison on the hill, away from the bedlam in the penitentiary, might be a relief."

"Ean, you're not thinkin' clearly. Have you seen anyone who's been in there?"

"Yes, but he's an old man."

We heard footsteps coming down the hall and resumed filing papers until the soldier passed. I checked the hallway; no one approached. "Charley, have you thought of escaping?"

He shook his head. "No. The chance of gettin' caught and sent up the hill's too great. I don't want ta stay a minute longer than I need."

"But New South Wales has mountains of gold."

Charley shook his head. "My brothers and urchins are keepin' my street for me, liftin' watches and such. I may be a thief and done things against the Crown, but I don't break a promise. I tol' 'em I'd be back. Now, let's get busy. I want ta stay in here for as long as possible."

In an instant my feeling about traveling with and trusting Charley cooled. I didn't miss him when he left one week later.

Glevins tossed a packet on my desk. "Take this to the ship before it sails at slack tide. I'll finish up and put the supplies away."

"Yes, Master Glevins."

After completing the Macquarie files, Glevins had given me a grey jumper, denoting me as a trustee. "I've watched you, McClaud," he'd said. "You've completed the records properly and not wasted my time. No pens, ink, paper, or any of my personal belongings have gone missing. Continue to prove worthy of this grey jumper. Do not embarrass me by abusing my trust in you."

"Yes, sir. Thank you, Master Glevins."

Now, wearing my grey jumper, I enjoyed the freedom to walk around the settlement without being stopped and questioned. My shackles were removed, so I carried messages and could even stop to dangle my feet in the harbor if I wished. I often slowed to watch the gulls circle and dip, rise, and then dive into the ocean, much as they had when I viewed them from the ship when we neared land.

This change in status created a thirst for more freedom; however, no further rewards would present themselves even if I followed every rule. Although Lorcan had disappeared, his threats and the men following me sent shivers through my body.

My letters to Fiona remained unanswered, but all kinds of reasons could explain why. Tom said I'd never return to England, but I knew differently. I pulled out a rumpled writing paper and old nib I'd stolen from the clark's waste basket and sat down under a tree to jot another letter.

Dearest Fiona,

You have not written. That makes me uneasy. Have you forgotten me? My love for you lives on. I must know if you await my return.

Ean

As I wrote, I pictured her asking the butler or the head cook in the Langstone manor to read my letters to her. I saw her face glow with a smile as she realized how much she missed me. I ached to hear from her.

After I inserted the letter into the mail pouch, I kicked a pebble, cursing myself; I should have taught her to read and write. She always laughed and said, "We've plenty of time. Teach me after we're wed." Now it was too late.

Gulls circled the harbor unfettered. No one threatened them or watched their movement. No one told them when to rise or eat or go to sleep. I wanted their freedom.

The next morning, Glevins instructed me to locate the record of Patrick Ordwell, a prisoner who died this past week. When I checked for his name, a blank letter of commendation fell out of the log book. I picked it up and slid it inside my jumper. When I returned to my bunk that evening, I folded the paper, tucked it between loose boards under the straw, and sat on it for good measure.

"Ean?" Tom watched and frowned. "Don't be a fool. Give that to me."

I handed him my treasure and watched him leave. When he returned, I asked, "Where did you put it?"

He stretched out on our bunk and closed his eyes. "Best you not know where I put things until you need them."

Day after day, I searched for blank forms, which I took to Tom to hide. I resisted taking the cracked ink pot and a handful of broken nibs. Glevins was a hawk about most things in his office. If he caught me, his punishment would be swift and merciless, but I wanted to gather as much as I could to build up any trade Crazy William could make.

The collected papers excited my dreaming, but I continued to worry about keeping myself away from the Irish rebels. Inside the penitentiary men followed me, stepped in my way, and whispered, "This may be your last day to join us." Near the privy they jumped me, pummeled me with their fists, and kicked me with their bare feet. Blow after blow, they slammed me onto the rocky ground, but I refused to say I'd join them.

One attacker shouted, "We know you turned him in. One day soon, we'll be back for you."

Tom appeared and interceded. He put his arm behind my neck and helped me sit up. "Leave my boy alone. Find your own."

They left before the soldiers arrived, but not before one final glare. I sat on the ground, trying to catch my breath. "Do you believe me now? Do you? Or do you think I'm imagining things?"

Tom pulled me to my feet. "Can't deny they're after you. Come on."

He helped me back to our bunk. My bruises convinced me that I needed to get away and soon.

The new Lieutenant Governor with his military reinforcements sailed closer each day. The talk among soldiers suggested they were scheduled to arrive within the next two weeks. With new rules and more soldiers, escape would become increasingly difficult. I watched the farmers and soldiers leave the penitentiary, free to sleep in their own cottages. I wanted a freedom like theirs before the new commandant arrived.

Tickets of leave remained as closely guarded as exiles. I'd need two: one for me and one for Tom. My chance came one afternoon when Glevins needed two tickets prepared. He laid them on the desk under a paperweight and left saying, "Guard these."

I paced and waited several minutes. When he didn't return, I touched them, checking the weight of the paper. They matched the commendation paper I'd found and hidden earlier. I slid one from under the paperweight and held it up to the light.

"You there! What are ya doin'?"

11

I whirled around to see a soldier watching me. "I, ah, the clark thought he saw a stain." I laid down the paper. "But it's fine."

The soldier paused a moment, then left the room as Glevins entered. "What did he want?"

"Checking on me, sir."

Glevins returned to the work on his desk. I sat down and waited for further direction. It shocked me how easily I could lie. If Ma was here, she'd box my ears.

The ticket of leave stayed fresh in my mind. The paper required a special imprint Glevins made, using the government stamp he carried in his coat pocket. Spiriting away two tickets of leave with his mark on them would be impossible. Liberty, a finger's length away, remained out of my reach.

Our month-long drought ended with a rainstorm that drove most settlers inside. At Port Arthur we initiated our new year standing in mud, as Governor Carver gave his usual speech before commencing with today's four floggings.

"It's my duty to prevent all exiles from returning to their wretched natures. These men continue to offend and show no remorse."

Carver recited each crime: singing during Sabbath prayers, talking back to an officer, wearing a different exile's tunic, changing a penitentiary file. Tom glanced my way as if to ask if I knew about the changed file. I shook my head, ignoring the feel of his eyes burrowing into mine. I'd not become brazen enough to forge papers, yet.

Much as I tried to distance myself from the floggings by thinking of the places and times when happiness filled my life, those images of my earlier life dimmed. Instead, I relived my turn beneath the whip when the whip struck my bare skin. I rubbed my shoulder, feeling the edge of one scar, and continued my vow to avoid any reason to be flogged again.

After the floggings ended, I walked toward the penitentiary with Tom. I could not erase the sights and horrible screams during the floggings. "Do the lashings and the screams still bother you after all these years?"

"Of course, they do. Not that we have any power to change them. The scars on my ankles and back never let me forget where we are." Tom kicked a pebble out of his way and leaned against a tree to rest. "Could you change files if someone asked you?"

"Not easily. Glevins guards his files like a hawk. Why?"

Tom shrugged.

I thought about his question. Could I? Would I risk it? No. Seeing the man receive twenty lashes, time in the silent prison, and half a year added to his sentence frightened me. But with the new commandant arriving any day, I needed a plan to escape.

After supper we paced the penitentiary floor with Barty, ignoring the bawdy singing in favor of conversation. In recent weeks Barty returned to his old self. He called both of us Tom, but he stood straighter. His new job may have been his salvation.

"How's the crate building, Barty?" I asked.

"Not bad, young Tom. I'm inside 'n out of the weather. I jest hammer nails 'n stay out of trouble as best I can."

Tom patted Barty's back. "For a banty-size man, you swing a hammer as easy as a summer faire sausage on a stick."

"Aye, but not so tasty." Barty leaned closer and whispered, "Lads, I saw me a blue sea critter last night."

Tom stopped and stared at Barty. "Where?"

"In the apple tree by the warehouse. He swung down 'n talked to me."

A sadness crept into me. Barty hadn't recovered and returned to real world after all. "What did it say, Barty?"

He looked around us then stepped behind a post before he spoke. "Tol' me to keep on seein' things. Then ever'one will believe I'm crazy and leave me alone." He bit his bottom lip and winked. He shuffled on, leaving Tom and me staring at his back and shaking our heads.

When I carried mail to the ships, I saw Barty repairing crates in the warehouse by the harbor. During January's warmest nights, he slept outside the building in a leftover crate.

As I approached him, two soldiers left, shaking their heads.

"What's happening, Barty? Why are those soldiers shaking their heads?"

Barty stretched and yawned. "I tol' those soldiers to keep away. I was guardin' the building from snakes and sea critters."

I had to laugh. Barty had figured out a way to distract the soldiers. "So, you like working here?"

He rubbed his bald head and his scruffy chin before he spoke. "I like the quiet, young Tom. 'Sides, when the gov'ner needs his crate loaded early in the morning—"

"Wait." I grabbed Barty's arm. "Tell me about the gov'ner's crate."

We sat on a pile of lumber in the shade outside the warehouse while Barty explained. "The gov'ner likes ta send presents to his sister. He always fills a crate and delivers it so late it can't be stowed below deck."

"That's after the ship's fumigated?"

"I guess. The sailors grumble and cuss when they have ta strap it on deck at the last minute."

I pulled Barty to his feet and took a deep breath to slow my racing thoughts. "How'd you like extra rations?"

He scratched his head, viewing me through squinty eyes. "How'd I do that?"

"I'll give you a portion of my meat and bread each night. Would you like that?"

Barty stared at me, twisting his head to one side. "Why would ya want to do that?"

I hesitated, looking around for soldiers or others standing nearby. "I need your help."

He pulled away from me with a quick lurch. "Oh no, lad. I can't help ya. I can't take the silent prison no more."

"I just need information."

"Leave me out of it, lad."

I held his arm, refusing to release him. "There's nothing to get you into any trouble. I swear."

Barty walked away, shaking his head. After a few steps he turned back. "How much food would I git?"

"Half my meat and bread. All I want you to do is watch the ships and listen to what the soldiers are saying."

"How long, young Tom?"

I made a quick tally. "Two weeks. I promise you won't get into trouble." My intentions were good, but could I keep Barty safe if I followed my plan?

"I'll think about it."

In an instant, he returned. "No trouble, promise?"

"I promise. No trouble."

During our next meal, I hinted my ideas to Tom. He frowned and thrust his jaw forward as he spoke. "What are you doing, Ean?"

"It's best my plans stay secret."

He pursed his lips. "Keep Barty out of trouble. He's got the soldiers convinced he's crazy."

"I promise. He'll be fine."

From that night on I couldn't sleep more than a few minutes at a time. While I listened to the exiles on my floor settle into sleep, snore, and call out, I worked through my plan. If Barty helped me, I could escape this place and the rebels, travel to the gold fields, then make my way back to England. I closed my eyes and pictured Fiona's smiles and the way she'd rush into my arms when she saw me. I smelled the ink of the printing press and the warm welcome home from the printer and his wife, greeting me as though nothing had happened.

Four nights later, Barty approached me as I lay on my bunk. "Meat *and* bread?"

"Done." I said and handed him half my scant meal. Hunger was worth my plan.

A wave of excitement washed over me like a refreshing waterfall. In no time I'd be away from here. No worrying about the dogs at Eaglehawk Neck giving me away. No flogging or being sent to the silent prison. I could escape and be far away before anyone missed me—assuming my plan worked.

12

Over the next week, whenever I worked alone, I glanced out the window of the clark's office to observe the loading and unloading of the current ship in the harbor. Exiles stored arriving cargo crates in the brick building next to the pier. Others loaded them onto long dray wagons for delivery.

Barty worked in a smaller building, where departing containers were stored. He repaired crates and sealed them closed for departing ships. The day before a ship left port, chain gangs loaded outgoing crates onto wagons, wheeled them to the ships, and shoved them up the gangplank. Heavy lines lowered each crate into the hold. Then the ship was fumigated and placed under heavy guard.

On one of our summer evenings, Barty and I discussed the special crates the gov'ner loaded on the deck after fumigation.

"How does the gov'ner get away with loading late crates?"

Barty shook his head. "He's the gov'ner, that's how. He c'n do as he pleases as long as he keeps this place workin' for The Crown."

"How heavy are the crates he sends?"

Barty cocked his head and frowned. "Why do you want to know that? Are you plannin' to send somethin' back to England?"

"Maybe," I said before I turned back to my bunk.

That night I couldn't sleep. The last piece of my escape plan fell into place. I'd send something alright. Me. I'd find a way to hide inside one of the gov'ner's crates.

Excitement churned through my body day and night as I worked out the details. What help would I need? What about food? Where would I get off and how? I vibrated with an energy I hoped none observed.

I'd need to get into the building, open a crate, hide inside, and reseal it the day before the ship sailed. I'd also need forged paperwork and food. At the harbor in Melbourne, I'd break out and swim to shore. How cold was the ocean in February? Tolerable if I coated my body with tallow. I'd steal tallow from the garbage bin outside the penitentiary kitchen door and find a way to save it for my trip.

I laid out my plan to Tom as we paced the floor. He kept his head down, then turned to face me and spoke in a whisper. "Are you sure you want to do this?"

"Another week is too long," I said. "The rebels continue to block my way and threaten me. I fear they intend to kill me. I know my plan will work. The only question is will you come with me?"

Tom shook his head. "I can't swim and I'm too big to fit into a crate." My excitement ebbed. I'd be making the trip alone.

Most ships sailed north, crossing Bass Strait and making port stops in Melbourne or up the coast in Sydney. Each day as I carried mail to the ships, I'd stop and watch Barty hammering. "How's today going, Barty?"

"Fine, young Tom, jest fine."

"Do many soldiers come through here while you make crates or nail them shut?"

"No, I'm usually alone. They hate the bangin'. Take my hammer 'n nails away every night, but they let me sleep here whenever I want."

"What if the gov'ner delivers his crate late to the ship, Barty?"

He squinted. "They give back me tools and leave 'til I call 'em to pick up the crate."

"Thanks, Barty." I left him scratching his head as he returned to his hammering.

The next time I took letters to a departing ship, I visited Barty again. "Can you make a crate with a hinge on the inside?"

His face scrunched up. "Course, but why?"

"You don't want to know. Just start sleeping here nights."

Barty looked me straight in the eye. "Means I'll not be gettin' any more extra portions, don't it?"

"Yes. It does."

Barty wiped his forehead. "You sure you want to do this, young Tom?"

"I'm sure," I said. Barty was my ticket of leave.

The *Maria Luna* arrived in port unexpectedly with more exiles and was scheduled to set sail for Melbourne in four days' time. Barty prepared one crate with a hinge on the inside. I wanted to protect him so I didn't share my plan to open the crate at sea to stretch my legs along the route to my escape.

Friday, I stood at the clark's window and watched the last of the crew exit the *Maria Luna*. A yellow haze of fumigating dust rose from the deck and out the portholes. The soldiers backed away, coughing and fanning the air, but kept their weapons drawn as they watched for prisoner castaways to disembark. None obliged.

I fidgeted as I thought through my plan. In a few days, I'd be on my way. My hand trembled as I returned to my desk and readied a forged bill of lading. I took deep breaths and exhaled slowly to steady my writing.

"McClaud!" shouted Master Glevins.

His voice startled me. Keeping my back to him, I slid the forged paperwork inside my jumper. "Sir?"

"Why are you still here?"

I turned to face him with my hands inside my breeches pockets to hide their trembling. "I, ah, you told me to wait for your letters home, sir."

Glevins frowned. "So I did." He placed his letters in a leather pouch and handed them to me. "Take these to the ship and be quick about it. They may sail on the morning tide."

"Yes, sir. So soon, sir?"

He studied at my face. "What concern is it for you?"

"None, sir."

As I stepped around him to leave the office, he grabbed my arm and said, "One more thing."

My heartbeat exploded in my ears, making it hard to listen to his words. "Yes, sir?"

"I won't need your help after today. I could send you back to digging, but you've proven yourself trustworthy. I'm assigning you as a clark to the Commissariat stores. Report back here to receive your paperwork in three days. Use the next two days to barter for more presentable clothes, trim your hair, and wash up, understand? Don't disappoint me."

"Yes, sir, I won't, sir. Thank you, Master Glevins." I hurried out of his office before my face betrayed my guilt. Should I forget about escaping? A clark's job with the commissariat meant continued freedom and a possible ticket of leave. Then I remembered: the new gov'ner was said to be a tyrant who planned to end giving out tickets of leave. I'd need to set my plan in motion right away.

As I carried the mail pouch to the dock, numbness settled in my mind and my stomach. I placed my letter to Fiona inside the pouch before I approached the watch command. I handed him the pouch and left.

Walking along the harbor to the penitentiary building, I watched for a sign to justify moving forward with my plan. A wizened exile passed me, hurried along by two young soldiers. His ankles were double chained, causing him to stagger as he dragged a heavy log.

The soldiers taunted him. "Faster, old man. If you can't do your job, we'll take you to the triangle, then toss you in the silent prison. The new gov'ner will have no patience with the likes of you."

They laughed and shoved him so hard he stumbled, falling onto the log attached to his ankle. His eyes pleaded with me for help I was not allowed to give.

His helplessness became my answer. I must leave before I went crazy and before the rebels decided to kill me.

I roamed the edge of the woods to complete my plan.

I could not eat my dinner, so I paced the floor to settle the jumpiness that coursed through me.

Tom grabbed my arm. "Ean, stop looking over your shoulder and sit down. You're drawing attention to yourself and me as well. Do you want me to bring you the papers I've hidden these past months?"

I shook my head. "Keep them. Barter when you need something."

Sweat dripped down inside my tunic. I wiped my hands on my breeches and sat down on our bunk. The minutes slowed. In a few hours I'd be away—on the sea or in it.

Tom and I walked the penitentiary floor together one last time, listening to a convict song:

As thieves 'n innocents alike,
We're bound and chained each day
To work as slaves to clear the land,
No chance to slip away.

A hundred condemned, wretched souls,
We dodged the hangman's hand
To dream of loved ones far away,
Safe from Van Dieman's land.

I'd dodged the hangman's noose, survived the voyage, and worked as a slave, burying bodies and building roads. I was about to set myself free.

❖

After the lanterns were extinguished and we lay awake on our bunk, I whispered my goodbyes. "Thank you for helping me every day since my arrival. I hope your new bedmate doesn't snore."

He laughed. "I'll always remember you, Ean. Use good sense. And take this. You'll need to blend in, if you make it. I found it along the quarry road." He handed me a torn, but wearable peasant shirt.

"Are you sure it wasn't hanging on a wash line?" I asked.

He laughed. "Could have been, but now it's yours."

I slipped it on under my jumper, feeling the crispness of the line-dried shirt against my skin. It resurrected my remembering when I too had clean clothes. In one week's time, I'd wash my own in Melbourne.

Tom reached for my arm. "Oh! It's happening fast." He groaned, stood, vomited on the floor, then staggered to the soldier guarding the penitentiary doorway.

I regretted that he'd needed to eat the berries I'd gathered. They were the ones Dorn warned us about when we worked on the road gang. They caused horrible cramping, vomiting, and uncontrolled diarrhea. But I wanted Tom out of the penitentiary to distance him from my escape.

Tom's moans caused a stir of cursing and loud complaints across the bunks.

"Silence!" the soldier yelled. He called a second soldier, and together they walked Tom out of the penitentiary. I spent my last night alone in the bunk I'd shared with a true friend.

Before sunrise, I stuffed my hoarded bread and salt pork into my breeches pockets and headed toward the warehouse. Sweat dripped down my sides. I took deep breaths to calm myself.

With each step closer to the dock, I imagined a soldier tracked my movements. At the slightest noise, I acted jumpy as a kangaroo, but when I turned to check for soldiers, no one followed my progress.

Morning sunlight backlit the Island of the Dead. A breeze fluttered across the harbor, cooling my face. The forests around Port Arthur remained black, waiting for sunlight to showcase their greenness. At this hour, most exiles remained inside the penitentiary, eating their first meal.

"You there! Halt!" shouted a voice.

I stopped. I turned toward the voice and slowly lifted my hands from my pockets, palms up to show my humbleness.

A soldier approached, his weapon pointed at my chest. "What's in your pockets?"

I slipped my left hand in and drew out a hunk of bread. "Breakfast." I said.

He stepped closer. "And your other pocket?"

My heart dipped like a sea bird diving into the water for a meal. I stammered and removed the papers. "I, um, I'm delivering papers to the warehouse for the clark."

"Be quick about it. Don't make me come to retrieve you." He turned away, moving back toward his barracks.

I exhaled slowly. My heartbeat drummed in my ears. Before continuing, I pretended to fasten my shoe while scanning for other soldiers. I straightened and took several more deep breaths before continuing along the path.

Barty dozed inside the warehouse doorway.

"Mornin', Barty."

He opened his eyes, stretched, and yawned. "Mornin'."

He lifted his withered body and twisted to loosen the kinks in his back. I handed him the forged papers. He fastened them to the special crate while I took off my trustee jumper revealing the peasant shirt Tom had given me. I handed it to Barty. "Be certain to paint over the numbers before you barter."

He nodded and tucked it inside his jumper. Tears glistened in his eyes as he handed me a mallet. "Might need this, young Ean."

He knew my name! I squeezed his bony shoulder as I took the gift and folded myself into the crate.

My knees touched my chest. My arms lay against my face. I closed my eyes and inhaled, preparing myself for the confinement and the darkness ahead.

Barty hammered two short nails to hold the side closed until I'd need to open it to exercise my body. He patted the crate twice and hollered out the doorway. "Lads, the gov'ner has a crate."

Boots scuffed across the warehouse floor. "Barty, you know we don't want no last-minute boxes."

"I do, sir, but he's the boss," Barty said.

"We'd better check it out with the commander." a voice said.

"Can't, lads. The clark said he's in Hobart. I was tol' ta git this on the ship, 'n then I could git me some breakfast."

I started to sweat. My chest tightened. I forced myself to focus on the slivers of light as the crate scraped across the floor, lifted, swayed, and dropped onto a flat cart. We crossed gravel and bounced over the uneven boards of the dock. The motion stopped. I held my breath. Had I been discovered? I listened for voices.

The motion began again, tipping the crate back as it traveled up a ramp.

Thump. The crate banged to a stop. "Careful with that, lads," an angry voice shouted. "Lash it down and get back to your tasks. We're short-handed on this voyage."

A second voice laughed, cursed, and kicked the crate. "What's the gov'ner sending off now? More wood for his carpenter in England. Let's open it and see what's so important."

I held my breath.

"Lash that crate down *now*," screeched a voice. "If we lose this one, we'll never hear the end of his complainin'."

My crate scraped across the deck. Tar-scented ropes slapped around it.

"Bloody last minute boxes crowd the deck. I didn't sign on for loading crates!"

"Quit grumblin'. We sail out at full tide. Got me a red-headed doxie waitin' in Melbourne."

❖

The voices and footsteps faded. Quiet filled the spaces around me as the *Maria Luna* swayed against the dock. In minutes the darkness clutched my body. I panted at the ship's rocking motion. My body cramped from being curled up like an unborn bird, but I thanked heaven we'd set sail soon.

I distracted myself from my pain by repeating my plan: escape the rebels, reach Melbourne, travel to the gold fields, dig buckets of gold, sail home, and clear my family name. I'd become a printer's devil and soon a paid assistant and wed my lovely Fiona.

Minutes passed like hours. My muscles creaked like small, loose bolts moving in a printing press. The decks remained unmanned. If we didn't get underway soon, I'd need to open the crate and stretch my legs before they became totally numb.

I concentrated on how I'd navigate Melbourne's busy harbor, where ships arrived from Great Britain and the Americas. Fortune hunters bought supplies for the gold fields, so dozens of shops and places could exist for me to get lost in the crowds. Digging gold couldn't be harder than digging graves or roadways.

The sun baked the space around me; the smell of tar-coated rope made me gag. Fear pressed in, twisting and knotting my insides while everything around me remained quiet. Should I chance opening the crate?

I picked up the mallet, twisted around, and started pushing the short nails loose. A sudden clatter of feet crossed the deck and hurried below. My breath escaped in a long, slow puff.

I listened for the ship's bells, remembering they recorded crew shifts. Eight bells: time for the crews to change shifts. Feet and voices moved about the deck. Cramps twitched in my legs and my back. Any minute now the cap'n would give the order to cast off. I ignored the swaying of the ship as I panted like a tired, thirsty dog.

One bell, two bells. Dull pain spread into my neck and arms. I distracted myself by reciting the names of my family, starting with my great-grand relatives who settled the family in County Cork: *Gavin and*

Martha O'Tavish, Mary and Berthram Carbol, Finn O'Tavish, Iris and David McDougal, Brendan McDougal, Mary O'Tavish and Shamus McClaud. When pain overpowered my recitations, I started over.

Three bells: my neck ached as though hands squeezed my throat. Brief twists side-to-side no longer relieved the pressure. I counted my breaths, mouthed chants from my childhood, and waited for the ship to pull away from the dock. We missed the high tide. Why weren't we setting sail?

The deck was quiet. I pushed the short nails free and inched the crate open to hang my legs out and regain feeling in them. The tingling brought a moan to my lips, but I shoved it deep inside myself as I kept a vigil for approaching crew members.

Four bells: I removed the rope holding up my breeches and slid it around one slat. After I folded myself inside the crate, I pulled the side closed and slid the rope inside with me, thanking Barty for adding the hinge to make the closing easy.

Five bells: I pictured Fiona's arms wrapped around me, her gentle hands soothing away my pain. I shivered from the closeness of the walls and because I could no longer feel my feet or my legs.

Bells continued. I lost count as daylight no longer entered my wooden prison. What delayed our departure? I began pushing the short nails loose, then stopped. Boots approached. Bodies bumped against my crate.

"This delay is costing us money. Where's the cartographer? He get lost in the woods?"

A hand pounded on the top my crate. "He's visiting the coal fields. Should be here before dawn."

Dawn? No! I couldn't stay in this cramped box overnight. I had to stretch my body. Maybe I should surrender now.

Sudden urges pressed through my lower body. I could not contain my bladder, so I relieved myself, hoping no puddle formed outside and gave away my location. The stench of my urine rose inside the box, suffocating me with its intensity. I thought, let them come soon if they are coming for me.

I dozed until a clatter of feet and conversations woke me, followed by the command, "Prepare to cast off the lines," followed by feet scurrying across the deck.

The ship swayed and lurched as sails were hoisted. Wind slapped them; we'd left the harbor and rounded Puer Point, where Edward was held. Next stop Melbourne.

The smoothness of the bay gave way to violent rocking as we entered the sea. I opened the crate and stretched my legs. Since no one approached, I slid from the crate, closed the side, and hid under a ship's row boat. I lay on the deck with my legs and arms stretched wide, waiting for the terrible pricking pain to subside. My stomach growled and grumbled, but I hesitated to eat the bread or salt pork; I'd need it for future days at sea.

Pre-dawn light woke me. No footsteps crossed the deck, so I replayed my days on the Island of the Dead and walking the penitentiary floor with Tom. It had been an uneasy alliance until I understood why he made me kiss him. He was right; the bully bosses left me alone after he intervened. Tom proved himself my friend over and over. I prayed he'd recover from eating the berries before I reached my destination.

More and more bells signaled the passage of time. I struggled to picture our road gang, remembering the way the ocean burst against the shore, the fairy penguin hiding under the low brush, sleeping out under the stars, seeing the eyes of an aborigine in the brush.

A sudden twisting wind whipped a drizzling rain across the deck. I crept back inside the crate even though my thirst made my tongue dry as an animal skin stretched taut in the hot sun. I prayed water might fall into the crate and into my mouth, but rain only dampened my clothes and made me shiver. Back inside the crate, I'd escape detection when the sailors swabbed away the water on deck.

I took small bites of my rations and whispered the penitentiary song until I fell asleep.

A buzz of commands and shouts roused me. A storm overtook us. The anchor banged from side to side inside the ship. *Maria Luna* shuddered in the long, slow rolls; we dipped and bucked like an untamed horse. My crate skittered across the deck, free of its ropes. Bile rushed into my mouth as I swayed back and forth, back and forth. I tapped the mallet to open the crate. I had to escape soon or sit in my own vomit.

Tap, tap, tap.

I gasped.

The open side of the crate faced the stern and flapped open and closed on its own. Far below, the waves collided and crested like angry fighters crowded into a small arena.

I unfolded my legs and hung them out the opening. Needles of pain bit into my toes, through my feet, and up my legs. I inhaled the salty air and kept a watchful eye on the churning sea below as nausea roiled my stomach.

My crate vibrated and came to rest against the stern rail. I stretched out, grabbing at anything to steady myself, but the container shuddered, moving away from the gunwale. As the ship rose from a dip in the sea, it broke free. I took flight off the stern of the ship like a wounded gull.

13

Down, down, down I plummeted, through the dark summer night into the black ocean. The sea swallowed me in its waves.

I fought my way to the surface, flailing through mountains of freezing water that crashed over me again and again, ripping at my clothes and forcing me down until my lungs ached. I struggled, thrashing waves as I gulped in sea water.

A rough object bumped my leg. When I reached for it, the ocean ripped it away and tossed me into a trough between two waves, where I floated like a twig on a stormy pond.

In the next instant, a massive log rode the calm beside me. I grabbed for it, trying to drape my body over its girth. But on each attempt to straddle it, waves pushed me away. Hope faded.

Another wave, another trough. Over and over, I smashed against the log. My stiff fingers clawed into small crevices in the bark. My arms shook from the cold and fatigue. I held my breath as more sea water cascaded over me.

When the waves calmed, I inched along the log until I found a narrow section. I tightened my grip and pressed my face into the rough bark. Endless waves lifted me and the log into trough after trough. I held tight and pulled myself onto the log, riding like a stable hand clinging to a wild stallion.

I rested and watched the moonlight skitter across the now-calm sea. When I turned my head, I saw the stern light of the ship sailing away, north to Melbourne, without me.

The log rode the waves and drifted on. I held tight, shivering but alive. I'd survived, but my quest for freedom ended far too soon. The place I floated ashore was within a day of Port Arthur, too close to ensure my safety. My dream for freedom might be short-lived.

I awoke barefoot and face down on a rocky beach beside the log. A thick fog surrounded me, blocking out everything beyond my out-stretched arms. Shivering and aching worse than the day in London Town when the soldiers shoved me into the hold of the ship that carried me to Port Arthur, I tried to turn over. Had I remembered to bring the tal-low I'd collected back at the penitentiary, I'd have had an extra layer of protection as well as less pain.

Slowly, I crawled up the coarse gravel beach and collapsed. The tide surged closer and closer. I shivered and clamored over nearby driftwood as the fog broke apart.

The land resembled a huge rock pile with trees in the distance. I crawled away from the water, seeking shelter. Beach grasses cut into my skin like tiny knives, but I kept moving until I could no longer lift my arms and legs. I rested.

The clearing sky turned dark with clouds. Rain began. I rubbed my arms and legs to draw heat to the surface of my skin while searching for cover.

As the rain became a downpour and a brisk wind circled around me, I staggered to my feet and scrambled up the crumbly shale cliff. I slid around roots of an evergreen and pulled fallen branches over me.

My stomach growled so loudly it woke me. The ground around me was littered with damp tree cones. I grabbed a handful and tried to eat them, but spit them out; their moisture had dried up long ago. I repositioned myself in the hollow and went back to sleep.

Sometime later, birds woke me with their cheerful songs. I stretched and peeked out from my gnarled root shelter. Sunlight hid behind puffy white clouds; the ocean waves riffled on the shore several yards below me. The beach held no footprints; no voices traveled across the windless day. For the time being, I was safe.

I worked myself to my knees but could find no energy to stand, so I lowered myself to sitting and watched gulls. Each dipped into the brilliant blue ocean and rose with a small fish in its beak. I needed food if I planned to survive, so I slid down the cliff in search of food along the shore.

Suddenly, I stopped. What if people lived nearby? They'd see me if I roamed the beach during the day. Best to search for food before dawn or after dusk. I sat down behind the wall of driftwood and wrapped my arms around my legs to wait.

At dusk I climbed over the driftwood to investigate the rocky shoreline. Between the rocks I dug around and found clams. I broke them open by hammering their shells together. Each swallow of pungent, salty nectar and chewy clam bodies reminded me of tasting them at the Langstone summer faire. I'd hated their texture as well as the idea of eating their brown, nasty-looking stomachs. Now I relished each bite, knowing I'd have ample food for the days ahead if need be.

After downing dozens of salty clams, I found rainwater puddles in rocks above the tide. I slurped them dry and made my way back to my shelter of boughs, grateful that my clothes had dried to a dampness I could ignore.

❖

Over the next few days, the wind whipped the land, carrying away my body heat. Thank goodness it was summer; any other time of year, the chill would be too much to survive. My concern turned to water. The saltiness of clam nectar increased my thirst. I'd need to find rainwater or a stream soon.

My pre-dawn and dusk trips to the shore for food and fresh water continued. On the fifth day, my energy returned; I began exploring the land. I scrambled up the cliff, searching for a place to enter the brush. The cockatoos, galahs, and kookaburras chirped and screeched around me as if to say, 'this is my land, go away'. I carried a driftwood club and a sharp-edged rock as protection from noises I couldn't identify.

The land curved away from the noisy sea. A small settlement lay directly across a fast-moving waterway at a distance of less than one of Lord Colridge's open pastures. Three ships swayed at the dock, but no people moved nearby. I kept to the edge of the brush with one eye on the settlement as I continued my search for a more permanent shelter and drinkable water.

At nightfall the winds dropped. I found no food or water, so I hid in the piles of driftwood and sat upright with my club at my side and the rock's exposed point poking out through my fingers.

The sunny dawn promised fair weather, but once again I'd slept too long to search for food. I stepped into the nearby grasses to wait for dusk. This beach, a collection of gigantic gray boulders, reminded me of a ramshackle stone fortress. I stayed behind their granite walls to shield myself from the settlement.

The area yielded few clams, so I broke open razor-sharp oyster shells and ate heartily of berries and wild greens I discovered before moving to sleep in the crotch of a eucalyptus tree. The pungent leaves reminded me of the herbal plaster Ma used on us when we had the croup. Did koalas find scaly eucalypt branches a satisfying sanctuary, or did the aroma and the leaves attract them?

When the tide changed, I watched the swift-running ocean race between me and the settlement. Perhaps I could swim or float across the narrows and join the settlement once I invented a story to explain my being here.

I found a rocky overhang. Moss and low branches created my sleeping pallet. I ate my fill of raw oysters and slept, glad the island held no interest for the people in the settlement. Or so I thought.

14

The first sign that the island had visits by humans came late one rainy afternoon. Muffled voices startled me awake. I shifted and rose to my knees, facing the direction of the voices.

Curiosity overpowered my need to stay hidden. I slipped through the brush toward the voices near the shoreline and stopped behind a tree. A dozen aboriginal men stepped from small, handmade boats and walked in my direction. Each wore short animal skin capes draped around their shoulders and carried long staffs.

My heart raced. I ducked down to hide. The ocean's loud surging hid my movements, but had they seen me? I rose cautiously and checked the breeze. It blew toward me, carrying my unwashed body odor away from them. I found a better vantage point.

The men were a variety of ages. Young men trailed after those with long hair and stooped backs. Each glowed with a white, chalky essence as if their bodies bore paint along their arms, legs, and chest. They resembled the aboriginal I'd seen in the brush back when I dug roads.

The old men chanted hollow-toned music and marked rhythm with slender sticks as a young man stepped forward, carrying two large shells like a treasure box. He opened them and removed smoldering coals, which he placed inside a ring of rocks he'd created from nearby stones. The others grunted approval as he blew on the embers and fed twigs to the tiny red coal until it burst into flame.

Once a fire burned brightly, the men settled around it on their haunches. One by one, each picked up a communal bowl and took a long draw, then approached an enormous gray-black boulder. With one hand resting on the rock, each man released an explosive puff of air, sending a white spray from his mouth. The splatter covered his hand and the space around it. When he lifted his hand away, his print overlaid earlier, faint shapes haphazardly covering the side of the boulder.

The ritual continued from man to man. Their repeating chants and rhythms lulled me into a dreamlike sleep.

Who-o-o-o-m—Om-o-o-om—Dyardoo.   Who-o-om—Wo-o-om—Dyardoo. Who-o-om.

A vibration shook the ground and sent the birds aloft in the rain as it startled me awake.

Who-o-o-o-m—Who-o-o-o-om—Dyardoo.

The deep, haunting sound throbbed in my body, pulling me into waves of sadness.

Was it a high wind? A violent storm approaching? The men around the fire pit hadn't cowered in fear.

I focused on movement in the nearby bushes. A native sat blowing into a long, curved branch that stretched across the ground in front of him.

Who-o-o-o-m—Om-o-o-om—Dyardoo.

This sound must be the one Thadeus couldn't describe to us during our road building along the shore.

He was right. Words could not explain it. I felt the sound as much or more than I heard it.

The aboriginal fire continued to glow with fingers of orange flames and lit the clearing as daylight faded. Young men rotated skewers of food angled toward those flames. My mouth watered as I watched them eat slabs of meat and dip out handfuls of food from communal bowls. Perhaps I'd find scraps once they left, if they didn't find me first.

When the young men dismantled their encampment, two elderly men scooped embers into large shells and carried them to a waiting boat. Others threw sand on the fire before they reentered their flat-bottomed canoes and poled out into the swift-flowing water.

I watched their course, noting the spot where they exited the ocean far north of the settlement and the setting sun. If I approached the land across the channel, I'd travel south to avoid these men as well as the community.

Waiting in my hiding place until darkness covered my movements, I then canvassed their meeting spot to search for leftover bits of food. Sandy berries, scraps of fatty meat, and a prickly plant became mine; I devoured them all without hesitation. With a stick I swept the fire pit and found one small ember. I blew on it, adding a tiny tuft of dry grass and twigs enough to bring it to life.

The flame brightened the clearing with a dusky light. I added more twigs and hurried to the beach, where I found two shells. I wiped them dry and smiled at my cleverness. I owned fire.

My small fire burned and crackled; I relaxed, imagining its warmth if I were to let it grow to a full blaze. Before the last remnant died, I gathered twigs and stuffed them inside my shirt to keep them dry should an unexpected rain begin. Overlapping the shells, I picked up and carried the coals to my newly-discovered rocky overhang.

At the entrance of my nighttime sleeping area, I built a ring of rocks as the aboriginal men had done. I nestled twigs with small, dry branches and added my ember, waiting for the fire to brighten and warm the night.

Before dawn I woke with a start. My fire had gone out. I grabbed a stick and scraped through the ashes until I found a smoldering cinder. I hurried into the brush to gather handfuls of twigs and dry branches. When the fire restarted, I scoured the beach for fresh shellfish but satisfied myself with the oysters I'd hidden earlier in a rocky saltwater pool.

I cracked them open and roasted them on pointed sticks, savoring each salty bite. The fire excited me more than any Guy Fawkes bonfire near Langstone.

Every evening before I allowed myself to sleep, I watched the flickering light create shadows on the rocky ceiling of my sleeping cave. When I grew tired, I banked the fire and slept, dreaming of my summers in the meadow with Fiona.

Fiona. She remained my reason for attempting an escape. But now a hollowness grew inside me; my remembrances of her were slipping further and further away. I prayed for her safety and that she awaited my return.

During the long hours of summer light, I continued to debate my next steps: stay on the island and hope to hide from the visiting tribesmen, or travel to the mainland and take my chances with the local people. If I stayed, I'd soon run out of food and still be no closer to returning to London Town. If I left the island, I'd need a plan to explain how I came to this place, wherever this place might be.

Back and forth I argued the possibilities, but my choice became clear. I craved more freedom than living on the island allowed. A plan formed. I'd pretend I'd lost my memory, find work, and, after suspicion about me waned, move north closer to the gold fields in New South Wales and to Fiona.

I began a new vigil, watching the flow of the ocean through the channel. The current rushed past regardless of the tide. The aboriginals paddled north, and the settlement lay straight across from my position. I focused on crossing to land south of both and climbing out of the water before I passed the last bit of land I sighted.

My new life required a series of believable lies. Perhaps I'd fallen from a passing ship and lived on the island for several weeks while I recovered from my injuries. What injuries made sense? My head. I hit my head. That explained my loss of memory and not knowing which ship I'd traveled on. Thank heavens the scraggy hair on my face appeared weeks old.

Hour after hour, I rehearsed my life story, examining the details, planning how and when I'd mention bits and pieces of my identity. My hands bore no blisters, so I'd not been a crew member. I read and write; perhaps I'm a penniless scribe working for my passage to the gold fields. Lies would be easier to remember if I stayed close to the truth.

I scoured the beach for a suitable log to cross the channel. After a day's search, I found one wedged in a pocket of soft sand. For a string of evenings, I dug around it, pushing and rolling it closer to the water.

One night when clouds dimmed the moon, I shoved the log into the swift current and climbed on, leaving my island home. I lay flat against the rough bark, shivering as I paddled toward an uncertain future. Within minutes the strong current whisked me south of the settlement and its dock.

I paddled with all my power toward shore. The current dragged me beyond the last point of land.

Suddenly, my makeshift raft slammed into a sand bar, tossing me into the water far from the beach. Strong currents tugged at me, pulling my legs out from under me, threatening to erase my tentative footing. I fought the current, paddling with my arms, churning my feet, and reaching for a footing amid swallows of sea water.

A boulder loomed ahead in the channel. I reached for it, clutching at small crevices as I flattened myself against it to avoid the fast-rushing channel water.

After a brief rest, I swam for shore and pulled myself out of the water. The distinct smell of eucalyptus made it easy to identify after my nights in a similar tree on the island. I hoisted myself onto a low branch, hoping I didn't share the tree with a koala or other odd beast.

At sunrise I scanned my surroundings: no buildings or cottages, a few old fences, no people or animals. I sat on the tree branch until dusk, then investigated the shore to scout out shellfish. It appeared the local inhabitants had harvested most of the seafood, so I dug in the beach, unearthing small snails and sucking up handfuls of their salty, spongy bodies.

I climbed down to search for a better, safer home and fresh water. I found neither along the shore. I listened for people working nearby, but only the cawing, swooping seagulls broke the silence.

Moving into the brush, I stepped around the prickly debris scattered along the ground. I missed the shoes the ocean had stolen. Even my too-short ones from the penitentiary would be a treasure here and save my feet when I stumbled among the trees and rocky outcroppings.

Deep among the trees, I ventured into a cave. A nauseating stench grew stronger. More of the smell rose to my nostrils when I stepped into a slippery mass. Shudders ran through me as fluttering and crying began. I stopped.

Suddenly, the air filled with the frenzy of thousands of bats, screeching and flapping to escape. I screamed. My heart raced as I scrambled from the cave, slipping and sliding through their wet droppings, brushing those same stinky droppings from my hair and my skin.

After my heartbeat slowed to normal, I walked along the beach and located a second cave with a low entrance. I crawled inside, hissing and swinging a stick ahead of me to scare off any inhabitants. Nothing flew or growled, so I continued. In the dim light, I felt my way along the damp walls and entered a second, more spacious chamber. I straightened and inhaled. No stench.

The cave floor was riddled with brittle, needle-sharp sticks that tore into the soles of my feet. I stifled a scream, stopped, and lifted the broken bits, fingering a surprisingly smooth piece of wood with rough edges and unusual holes. I carried the sticks outside to examine them in a brighter light.

I gasped and threw them down. A shiver of disgust coursed through me. I'd fingered pieces of a broken skull, most likely human.

Moving on, I climbed a low, rocky mound, where I found an open cave with no bats or skulls. Though shallow, with water dripping down one wall, it faced away from the sea and provided ample shelter. I pressed myself onto its small, rocky ledge and attempted to sleep.

Emerging the next morning to find pewter-toned clouds hanging in narrow layers above the horizon, I headed north along the tree line until I came to a decrepit split rail fence surrounding a maintained orchard of fruit trees. I sat waiting for any sign of people. When none appeared, I grabbed a handful of small apples and would have taken more, save for the barking dog moving toward me.

I leapt over the fence and raced into the woods. The dog stopped at the fence line. When no one appeared, I hurried to an outcropping and sat down to feast on apples.

The juice had a hint of both sour and sweetness. I savored several as I thought back on the ancient gnarled apple trees in the Langstone woods. Fiona and I met there many late summer evenings. I'd shinny up a tree and drop the best-looking apples into her outstretched apron. We ate heartily and threw the pitted or shriveled ones away, knowing small animals would finish them. We kissed away any sweet traces of juice that lingered on each other's chins.

Would Fiona visit that tree with another once her summer arrived in six months' time? Had I truly been gone from her for a year? I stretched out, straining to remember the details of her face.

Over the next few days, I avoided the orchard for fear I'd roust the dog. I continued my routine of hunting for food along the shore before dawn and after dusk, then sat beside a small stream I'd discovered. I washed myself and my ragged clothing and sat naked beneath a nearby sheltering rock pile, glad for sunshine.

To fill the endless hours, I collected and braided moist grass, twisting the fibers into long cords like the aboriginal weapon I found back when I built roads. I fumbled with the cords but added small, flat stones, creating bumps along their length to use as a weapon or to stun birds for a meal. Day after day, I practiced swinging the cords above my head. My efforts never gathered enough speed to hum like the aboriginal's cord, but it became my basic weapon. However, it was not powerful enough to take down a bird or to prevent my capture. I gathered more grasses and wove a simple belt and a small basket to store any future apples or other treasures I found.

Time traveled slower than a snail's pace. I counted back, estimating my days on the island and my time on this mainland. Gouging a small hole in the sand inside my cave each day, I dropped one pebble in it. When I reached seven, I replaced them with a larger stone marking a week. To date I estimated my time since escaping from Port Arthur as three large stones and six pebbles, nearly a month. My dream of freedom remained unfulfilled.

I realized living next to the settlement with scant food and ragged clothing was not much better than Port Arthur. Turning myself in at the settlement could be my only chance to survive. But returning to Port Arthur promised severe punishment and an extended sentence or worse.

I decided to stay with my plan a while longer and start north in the next few days.

❖

Each dawn, the wet grasses along the beach trail soaked through my tattered breeches and chilled my bare feet. I turned up the collar of my shirt to deflect the wind and began my early morning search for food along the shore. I stepped onto a huge, flat rock, where giant waves crashed around me before disappearing below.

A deep rumbling began, followed by a spray erupting through the fissure in the rock and sending water soaring into the air. I backed up, startled by this unusual occurrence, then sat down to wait and see if it blew skyward more than once.

Swoosh. Thoom.

The water exploded upward again and again. The spray blew over me and the surrounding area like a gigantic fountain.

That afternoon, as I selected a new hiding place in the tall grass, I composed another letter to Fiona; one I'd never be able to post. I chanted it like a priest:

> *I pray my letters reached you. I pine*
> *for you and dream of our lives together.*
> *Wait for me.*

Far below, the gray waves lifted in swells before they curled their frothy green-blue edges and splashed on the rocks. This ocean reached around the world to England, yet here I sat like a dullard. This wasn't helping me return home.

In a moment of recklessness, I descended to the shore during daylight and picked up a stone. I drew back my arm and threw the stone beyond the foamy surf. "Send me a sign! I need a sign!"

Nothing.

When I turned my back to the waves, I spotted her. Fiona? Could it be?

She stood on a nearby outcropping of stone. Her skirt blew back from the sea, outlining her trim figure; her hair flew in tangles about her face. I ducked down. My heart pounded louder than the surf.

I inched forward to see if the image was real or imagined. No one appeared in any direction.

I watched day after day, but no one returned. To be safe, I avoided the place where I'd seen the vision of the woman. Since no soldiers or settlers searched for me, she must be an apparition. But what if she was real? Maybe I should follow her path away from the beach and take my chances with people in the settlement.

Night after night, the woman filled my dreams; day after day, she filled my wakefulness. Always she resembled Fiona. I imagined her on the cliff, reading my letters and letting the breeze carry them into the sea. What did this mean?

One early evening as I searched for food along the shore, I spotted her. A fog dipping across the land gave her a ghostly appearance. Mustering my courage, I stepped closer, tapping a long stick on the rocky ground to announce my arrival.

As I approached, she turned to face me; her long, auburn hair was pulled back in a tight braid. She closed her shawl and crossed her arms over her chest.

I kept a distance between us. "Is this your beach?"

"No, but it's not yours either. This is owned property."

I tapped the stick on the ground to hide my frustration. This woman resembled Fiona but was a few years older. "I thought I saw you here a few days ago."

"That surprises me," she said. "You were so busy shouting like a mad man that I'd not think you noticed anything."

Her words stung like blowing sand against my face. I clenched my fists to hide my shaking and stared at her with a bravery I didn't own.

I leaned on the stick, attempting to look fierce. "You tell me how you'd act if *you* didn't know who you were or where you were from."

Her eyes widened. "What do you mean?"

I pointed my stick out to sea. "Somehow I ended up on that island before I floated here. What is this place?"

"You're near the Bicheno settlement on Van Dieman's Land. How did you arrive here?"

I dug the ground with the stick, dislodging a stone that I flicked over the edge. "Van Who? I've never heard of that place."

Her lips tightened. "Most call it Tasmania. I prefer the old name. The nearest settlement is Bicheno. Now, tell me how you arrived here."

I shrugged, realizing the time had come to begin weaving my life in lies. "I have little memory of my life before the island, except my childhood."

She tipped her head and scrunched her eyebrows together. "You don't know your name?"

I shook my head.

"How long have you been here?"

"By my count and the scruff of my beard, more than fifty days," I said, adding a few days to obscure which ship I may have been aboard.

"Where are you living? What do you eat besides our apples?"

"I live in the woods, in trees and caves. I eat oysters, berries, and your apples."

A flicker of a smile crossed her lips. "You must be the one our dog barks after."

"Could be. If you have work, I can repay my thievery and help your husband with chores."

The young woman pointed toward the woods. "If that is the truth, follow the path north to our farm. The harbor master lives nearby. He'll know what ships passed this way."

Panic swelled in my chest at the thought of meeting the harbor master, but I swallowed it down. "Thank you."

"Until then, see to it that you stop stealing our apples. You're eating one of our market crops."

I nodded and turned away, worried that I'd blather on about my true self if I stayed longer.

All night, I contemplated my choices: remain in the woods and live in near starvation, offer to work on the farm and take my chances with the harbor master, or start walking north toward the gold fields.

15

I made my decision: tomorrow I'd walk the path toward the farm but stay alert for settlers with weapons looking for me. The quiet suggested I remained alone, so I relaxed enough to continue napping until dusk, when I foraged along the beach for maybe the last time.

At dawn, I watched the young woman feed the work horses and hang the wash. Men's pants, a woman's petticoat, towels, and undergarments fluttered and snapped in the breeze. Mid-morning, she weeded a large vegetable garden with the help of an older man. Late afternoon, she worked in the outbuildings and took down the wash, then disappeared into the cottage.

A man roamed the farm, repairing fences. When another older man approached along their twisting road, the two exchanged waves. The arriving man walked inside without knocking. The first man put his fencing tools away and retreated to a small outbuilding with a chimney. The young woman carried a covered plate to that building. It appeared to be supper time.

A third man, perhaps the woman's husband, arrived and entered the house. Food smells wafted my direction. My mouth watered for a taste, even leftovers of their meal.

After dark, I heard a woman's voice singing, accompanied by a concertina. I stayed close until the lights in the buildings were extinguished.

Then I crawled into a dugout in a tree by their fence line where a dog sniffed around my hovel but didn't bark.

In the morning, the older man emerged with an overly stuffed canvas backpack, waved, and disappeared down the road.

I paced and kept watch until midday, inhaled a deep breath, walked to the cabin door, and knocked.

The young woman from the shore opened the door. "You came. Come in, Mister—ah—what should I call you?" She brushed strands of auburn hair away from her face and smiled.

I shrugged and dropped my gaze to my dirty bare feet before looking back to her.

She pursed her lips and tilted her head. Her green eyes danced with light. "We already have a Galen and a Robert. How 'bout Quinn? I fancy the name Quinn. Do you know it means strong?"

"No, Ma'am, but that's a fine name." Did she see my face flush? If truth be told, my eldest brother's name is Quinn.

She extended her hand. "Quinn, it is. My name is Maudie Claire O'Carroll." Her gaze drifted to a spot behind me. "And this be Galen."

I turned, looking up to face a brooding man far larger than Tom, my bunkmate in the penitentiary. He held my gaze.

"Galen, meet Quinn. He's new to town and wants work. I thought he could earn his keep helping Robert."

Galen crossed his arms over his wide body and scanned my clothing and bare feet. He frowned. Embarrassment flooded through me as he eyed my condition.

"Maudie, who gave you permission to hire another stray? I'm reminding you, again, we need no more help."

She crossed her arms and raised her chin. "This is my property too, Galen. Quinn needs a job."

"We'll talk later, Maudie." Galen turned on his heel and shouted over his shoulder as he headed toward one of the fenced fields. "He'll be your responsibility, not mine."

I fumbled the hem of my threadbare shirt, waiting for her to speak. "I should go. Your husband doesn't look pleased you took me in."

"He'll be fine." She laughed. "How 'bout I fix you breakfast before I send you out to work. That way you'll pick apples for market rather than eat our profits."

She brought out a plate of food and invited me to sit on a bench outside the cottage door. I savored the slab of ham and the cold biscuits and drank an offered cup of cool water. My stomach growled as the rich food slid down my throat.

Mistress O'Carroll bustled about, hanging laundry. When she spoke to me over her shoulder, I saw the sprinkling of freckles that dotted her cheeks. She had a pleasing and kind face.

"I know you can find the apple trees," she said. "Pick all you can reach. Store them in the barn with the others already picked. We'll take them to sell at Saturday market."

She handed me empty bushel baskets and busied herself feeding the animals in the corral. I decided that Galen O'Carroll was fortunate to find a lovely, energetic wife. I wondered if Fiona could be content working on a small farm, wearing plain clothes and sturdy shoes. I doubted her willingness to live thus.

In no time I filled the baskets with ripe apples. Their sweet aroma reminded me of Lord Colridge's orchard, where I'd spent time snuggling with Fiona. I rested, sitting on a low branch of one tree, allowing the sun to warm my aching body. Back home I'd soon have become a paid printer's apprentice. 'Twas surely lost to me now.

By late afternoon I'd picked all the apples and carried numerous bushels to the barn. Luckily, no strangers approached except for the mutt that followed me back and forth between the orchard and the barn. My first new friendship unexpectedly began with a dog.

At dinnertime I joined Robert, the field hand, in the worker's bunkhouse. The small four-bed building had two windows, a wooden table with four stools, and pegs for hanging up our clothes. A pot-bellied stove stood in one corner with a dusty coal scuttle nearby. If I lasted 'til winter, I'd be warmer here than in any cave in the woods.

Robert was a small man with grey hair, a white stubble, and muscular arms. He reminded me of Barty as he bent over his pork, beans, and cornbread, scraping every morsel as if his next meal might be days away. After he washed out his tin plate, he eased his shoulders back against the wall and crossed his ankles. "Mistress O'Carroll fixes a fine meal. She invites us into their cabin to eat with her family on the Sabbath. Right nice lady, she is."

I finished my tea and followed Robert's lead, rinsing out the bowl and cup and setting them on a shelf by the door. "How long have you worked here, Robert?"

"Three years. Tried whalin' 'til the huntin' took us farther and farther out to sea. Didn't like the rough water. How long you been 'round here?"

"Not long. Passing through. Plan to try my hand at gold mining and earn money for passage home."

"Home?"

I flinched. Now I'd done it! "I mean, to wherever I'm from."

Robert brushed back his thinning hair. "No talk of any gold 'round here."

"No. It's in New South Wales. It jumps out of the ground and right into your pan."

Robert sat a long minute, then chuckled. "You're a trickster, Quinn."

Sweat ran down my back as I hoped Robert wouldn't share my comments about New South Wales with anyone. How could I explain the gold fields if I'd lost my memory?

"I have an unusual story about coming here. I think I fell off a ship, but I only remember bits of information, like the gold fields. I don't know my name. Mistress O'Carroll gave me the name of Quinn."

"That so." He took out a pipe and lit it with a twig from a log in a bin beside the pot-bellied stove. "Must be strange."

"It is, but I'm grateful to be allowed to work here. I promise to do my full share."

I stretched out on my bunk of crisscrossed ropes covered with a straw-filled mat. I pulled the worn quilt on my bunk over me and closed my eyes.

The next moment Robert was shaking my shoulder. "Quinn, wake up!"

I sat up and shook my head, trying to remember where I was.

"Hurry up. It's time to get to work. Grab the boots sittin' by the doorway. I saved you a biscuit from breakfast."

As I started out of the bunkhouse, I met Galen face to chest. His body filled the frame side to side and top to bottom. "Can't have you work here if you're a laggard. See that you're up on time from now on."

"Yes, sir," I answered as I jammed the biscuit into my mouth and stepped into the spare boots. Galen watched until Robert and I had picked up our tools and entered the first gate. Then he disappeared.

Robert and I mended fences until midday meal, then sat on the grass and opened a dented miner's lunch tin. Inside were two large potato and bean pasties. While we ate, I scanned the surrounding fields, watching the cows munch grass and the flocks of birds fly from tree to tree. The underlying stillness brought a calm I hadn't remembered since before I left Langstone and Fiona. I closed my eyes until Robert shook my arm and we returned to work.

"You sure sleep a lot, Quinn. Last night a'fore you told me where you are from and again jest now."

"I don't mean to seem unfriendly. I'm just catching up on my rest. As for where I'm from—probably England like the rest of you." My mind raced for a truthful answer, knowing my hesitation raised suspicion. "I'm grateful that Master O'Carroll's wife invited me here."

"Wife?" said Robert. "She ain't no wife. Galen's her brother."

"Who was the older gent who stayed the other night?"

Robert eyed me intently but said nothing about my spying on the farm. "Her da. He's a government man."

"A what?" I wiped my sweaty brow and hoped Robert didn't notice my nervousness.

"A convict what's got his freedom from Port Arthur and stayed on."

"What was his crime?"

Robert shrugged and handed me a hammer. "He never said, but he's a God-fearin' man and true to his word."

I kept my head down, nailing the fence rail into place before I spoke. "You ever been held in Port Arthur, Robert?"

"Nope." He handed me another board. "I got my ticket of leave from Maria Island. In one year's time I'll have earned my pardon, so I'm free to leave. But I might stay. Kinda like this country, 'n there's nothin' to take me back to England."

"What was your crime?"

"Say I stole a purse. Wasn't me, but they'd sent me on the ship a'fore they caught the real thief, my neighbor. Too late 'n it didn't matter any-way."

"How'd you find out it was your neighbor?"

"Saw him on the prison ship with me. He figured we were still best friends. I knocked that idea out of him one day; he stayed clear after that."

"Don't you want to go back to England?" I straightened and twisted to loosen the muscles in my back.

"No reason anymore. Passage is costly, 'n my family's all gone. Sickness took the lot. Heard another sickness took thousands 'round London Town the year just past. How 'bout you?" He wiped his brow with a rag.

Time to return to my life story plan. "I don't know where I'm headed. Maybe those gold fields I mentioned earlier." I reached out to Robert. "Pass me a longer rail for this space, will you?"

That evening as I lay on my bunk, I wondered about Fiona. Had the sickness reached her in Langstone? How about the printer and his wife? I turned over and closed my eyes, waiting for sleep.

At first light Mistress O'Carroll called inside the bunkhouse, "Quinn, I've found clothes for you. They're patched, but good for work. I'll leave them out here on the bench beside your breakfasts."

Robert stepped out and brought in our food. He also grabbed the clothes and tossed them to me. "Can't remember Galen wearin' these. Doubt he'll shrink down to wear 'em. Loves his ale too much."

The pants and work shirt hung loose, but after my time in rough convict clothes, the worn fabric felt smooth against my skin. "I'm grateful he doesn't need these for whatever reason."

While we ate biscuits and drank our tea, I asked Robert, "Where did the O'Carroll's come from? I mean—where did Galen's father find a wife?"

"He met her after he finished his prison sentence." Robert said. "Issa had been sent to the Female Factory, the prison for women convicts where women weave and sew. Others provide comfort for prison officers, if ya know what I mean.

"Master O'Carroll became an overseer. They met at a holiday meal where she was servin'. They courted, got married, settled here, and Galen came along a year later. His wife died birthin' Maudie Claire. Her da raised the two of 'em with help from an elderly woman. Once they grew up, he took a job as a surveyor; that's why he's away for weeks on end. Lucky for us—means we have permanent jobs."

I finished my tea, wondering if these settlers acted more kindly toward convicts than those living closer to Port Arthur. Robert stood in the doorway, waiting for me. I put my cup on the shelf and slipped on the boots. "What's our work today, Robert?"

"Back to fencin'," he said. "Galen's due back with sheep, so we'll also need to fix the rotten boards in the barn. Winter's here are mostly mild, but he likes to pasture his sheep close in case it's stormy. Then it's Sabbath dinner."

We worked until dusk, returning to the hut to wash up before our Sabbath meal at the O'Carroll's cottage. Robert combed his scant ring of hair and brushed the dirt off his boots. I took the washtub behind the hut to hide my scars from view as I washed. If anyone saw the lash marks on my back, my story of being forgetful would be destroyed along with my freedom.

I shook the dust out of my clothes and combed my scraggly hair and beard. Since my first meetings with Galen hadn't gone well, I needed to make a better impression if I expected to stay. I also needed to avoid revealing too much about myself too soon.

Mistress O'Carroll met us at the cottage door. She carried an empty laundry basket. "Go on in and pour yourselves tea."

"Let me take in the laundry, Ma'am." I said. "I used to do it for my ma."

Her green eyes sprang open in surprise. "Quinn, you remembered something!"

"Yes, Ma'am, I mean no, I mean—" I fidgeted under her gaze. "I remember bits of my early life, like taking in the clothes."

"Thank goodness you remember fragments. I can't imagine how it feels to lose all rememberings of your family." She handed me the basket. "Now, since you're bringing in the clothes, I'll stir up a batch of my favorite muffins to go with dinner." She stepped back into the cottage, humming a melody that reminded me of home.

"Now you've done it," Robert said. "When she starts hummin' when she's workin', she'll think up more work for us."

"That's fine by me. I want to work."

Robert headed in for tea as I unpegged the clothes and folded them the way my ma showed me years ago. The smell of fresh clothes dried in the crisp air reminded me of my rambunctious family. My brother Quinn, the last of my family, lived so far from me. But soon as Fiona and I wed, we'll begin a family and invite Quinn to join us in Langstone.

Galen O'Carroll stood by the fireplace, lighting his pipe as I entered. He turned. His large body soaked up all the heat in the room. His eyes drilled into mine, giving me no time to look about the cottage. "So, Quinn," he said. "Tell us about yourself."

"Not too much to tell, sir. The past few years remain blank."

"Let me see your hands."

"Sir?"

"Hold out your hands," he said. "You can tell a lot about a man by his hands."

My palms were wet as he took them in his rough paws. He slid his fingers over my blisters. I flinched.

Galen stared at me as he continued to press his fingers into my palms. "Building fences is toughening up your hands." He stopped and looked up. "Why are your palms so wet?"

"I, uh, I sweat easily, sir. I'm not accustomed to warm rooms."

Mistress O'Carroll carried steaming bowls of food from the large cook stove to the table. "Please, everyone, sit down."

Galen released his grip but held my gaze as we took our places. I swallowed down my discomfort as I sat along one side, facing Robert, with Galen and Mistress O'Carroll seated on the ends.

After Galen said grace, Mistress O'Carroll passed him our plates. I watched him mound the plates with lamb, crispy potatoes, steaming beans, and a fresh buttermilk muffin. My mouth watered as I received my supper and sat waiting for the others to be served. Thank heaven Master John's wife had taught me manners.

It had been more than a year since I'd sat for a Sunday supper and felt the cool touch of silverware in my hands. I cut everything into small pieces and chewed slowly, savoring each bite, while watching the others do the same. Arriving at this farm truly proved to be a blessing.

When Galen cleared his throat, I looked up and waited for more questions.

"So, Robert, is Quinn a good worker? Does he do his full share?"

"Yes, sir, Master O'Carroll," Robert said. "Quinn is a fine worker."

"Good. Are you about done with the fences?"

I relaxed as Robert took over the conversation, sharing the condition of the various fences, the number of boards we'd used, and our progress in the barn. "And, sir, with Quinn's help, I think we'll get the work caught up before winter."

Galen nodded.

Winter. I'd appreciate staying here through the winter. I could make my way north in the spring and cross to the gold fields without the worry of facing harsh weather.

I kept my face down or stole glances at the room, hoping I didn't appear rude. Everything was tidy and polished.

When Galen placed his fork on the edge of his plate, Mistress O'Carroll took the kettle from the fireplace arm and filled a chipped teapot with hot water. She added a scoop of black tea and set the pot on the table to steep. Within seconds, I inhaled its smoky aroma.

"Maudie Claire tells me you don't remember much about your life."

"Yes, sir. It's hard being a stranger to myself."

Galen folded his hands around his cup. "I'll have the harbor master stop in one day. Maybe he can locate a man missing from a ship."

"That might help, sir." I blinked and looked away, hoping to hide my anxiety. When I looked back, Galen continued to watch me. The air around the table vibrated as though charged by a lightning strike.

Robert set down his fork. "Quinn knows a lot about farms and fences."

"Do you remember being a farmer?" Galen asked.

"No, sir, but I enjoy working with my hands."

Suddenly, Galen's chair scraped back.

I fought the impulse to cower as if expecting to receive a blow to my head and shoulders.

Mistress O'Carroll appeared startled. "Are you leaving?"

"Yes," he said. "I promised Widow Planchett I'd stop in tonight. If the rug you made for her is ready, I'll take it to her."

Mistress O'Carroll packed up a muted green and blue rug, and Galen left.

The warm gingerbread she then placed on the table melted on my tongue and slid down my throat like sweet tea. If I continued to eat this heartily, I'd soon fill my baggy clothes.

Mistress O'Carroll washed the dishes, refilled the kettle, and returned it to the metal arm at the side of the fireplace. She fingered the three books on the mantle and turned. "Do you think you know how to read?"

"Yes, Ma'am." I searched for a way to explain this sudden memory but had no lie ready.

"Will you teach me?"

I adjusted my shirt collar as a rush of heat surged through my body. "Of course, Ma'am."

She touched each book spine. "We have our family Bible, Galen's copy of *Pilgrim's Progress*, and a book of convict poetry Da gave Ma. He taught Galen to read but had no time to teach me. I've always wanted to learn."

She gathered up our empty gingerbread plates. "This winter when it's too cold to work outside, you can teach me. And—" She scanned the room, then turned with a smile as bright as the sun. "I'll make you a vest as payment."

"That's more than a fair trade, Ma'am."

"How 'bout you Robert? Do you want to learn to read?"

Robert shook his head. "No, Ma'am. I'm too old; besides, I got me no one to write to."

It appeared we were allowed to sit at the table after supper and enjoy the fire. I'd follow Robert's lead, but now I watched Mistress O'Carroll bustle around, straighten things, then move to sit at a floor loom.

I watched her shuttle dart from side to side and saw her draw a wooden bar toward her with each pass, tamping the fibers snugly together. Clack, clack, clack. Her feet danced across the treadles, moving bars up or down to create patterns. I swayed with the steady rhythm, watching the rug lengthen and spill onto the floor. Robert took his leave to smoke his pipe outside.

I started to nod off, so I stood to take my leave too.

"Do you need to go so soon?" Mistress O'Carroll stopped weaving. "I'd like to borrow your hands, if I might."

"Ma'am?"

She laughed and leaned toward a basket, lifting thin handfuls of spun wool onto her lap. "I'd like your help preparing the yarn for dyeing."

"I'd be glad to help," I said.

"Good. Step over here and sit beside me." She slid to one end of the bench and patted a place beside her.

I stepped toward her and settled onto the other end.

"Sit closer." She took my hands in hers.

I enjoyed the gentleness of her touch and fought the urge to pull away.

"Now, hold your hands in front of your waist, as wide as your body. I need to wind loose hanks for the dye pot."

For the next half hour, she looped the yarn around and around my hands. Sitting so close to her, I mirrored her breathing. To distract myself from her closeness, I surveyed the dusky rainbow of colored yarns that hung on pegs behind her loom. A nearby nail barrel held long sticks wrapped with yarn and tools used during weaving.

Each time she reached the end of the yarn and patted my hands, I jumped and pulled my hands back. Her eyes queried my face before she removed the yard from my hands and hung it on one of the pegs behind her loom.

"That should do it. Thank you—Quinn?"

I pulled my thoughts back to Maudie Claire. "Huh?"

"You're wearing a strange expression on your face. Do you remember another detail?"

"No, Ma'am." I stood and backed toward the door. "Thank you for the fine food. If you need help in the future, I'll be glad to lend you my hands. Night, Ma'am."

Maudie Claire laughed. "I'll keep that in mind. Good night."

I left, waving my hand without looking back. I wanted to hold onto the sparkle of her eyes and her hair glowing like a summer beach fire. Happiness flowed from her. For the first time since my arrest, so many things reminded me of home: the touch of a woman's hands, shared laughter, a full stomach, and feeling rested.

Evenings after Sabbath supper settled into a routine. I lingered in hope that Maudie Claire found tasks for me, allowing me to stay in the comfort of her company. So many things about her reminded me of home; a few reminded me of Fiona.

Often, I became an extra set of hands, preparing yarn for dyeing or for winding balls of yarn. Other nights, I created fuzz sticks as fire starters, enjoying the chance to stay near her.

As I brought in firewood one evening, she looked up from her weaving. "Has Robert spoken of the Saturday market to you?"

"Yes, Ma'am."

"It's a lovely market. We enjoy good profits from my weavings this time of year as people prepare for winter."

"Who taught you to weave?" I asked.

"The Widow James. She showed me the forest plants for the best dyes." Maudie Claire stopped the shuttle. "Did you know wild blackberries make a soft rose color and onion skins make pale yellow?"

"No, I didn't." I watched her eyes sparkle, seeing that she loved weaving as I loved printing. I dreamt I'd soon return to arranging black-inked letters into words and seeing words grow to thoughts on paper. For now, I'd remain content, watching her work with the wool.

"You should go to market with Robert. It would give you a chance to see Bicheno and meet the harbor master."

"Yes, Ma'am," I answered, but inside I knew that was one place I intended to avoid when I headed north. The constable had information about escaped convicts. Luckily for me, I had few distinctive scars to arouse any curiosity.

Saturday evening, Robert returned from market with a small berry
pie from Widow Morgan, which he shared with me. "She's a good cook,
Robert. You should court her."

"I don't want me no wife," he said. "Tried it once, before I ended up
here. Not happenin'. She's too fussy for me. I hafta back away if I want to
talk with the farmers about their crops. Otherwise, I'm trapped listenin'
to her prattle." His face turned red with embarrassment.

"Sounds like she's courting you, Robert."

"Could be, but she's outta luck."

He acted uneasy, so I changed the subject. "Any news from town?"

Robert took out his knife and picked up a small block of wood. "No
cattle thieves this week. No drunken whalers in town much anymore,
now that the whales stay farther out to sea. You know, these bays once
boiled with their slick-backs. You could step from the island to shore and
never get your feet wet."

I laughed. "Now who's telling tales, Robert?"

He shrugged and opened his whittling knife.

"Have you been to the island off shore?" I asked, trying to sound
curious.

"Only the abs go there. Most folks think the land is haunted and spirits
live in the trees." Robert shook the blade of his knife around, pointing to
the island where I'd lived. "One fella saw chalky marks on the rocks like
white ghost hands. Made his hair bristle like an echidna's."

"E—what?"

"Echidna. It's a little critter that lives in the brush. Has quills all over
its body and a snout longer than a pig's. Don't hurt people, but they look
scary. Ain't you never seen one?"

I shook my head. "You're making it up, I believe."

The evening light faded. I lit the lantern as Robert continued to shape the wood into a gentle curve with four thin sticks, building a mound of shavings around his feet. His hands moved quickly and with skill.

A pig-like snout emerged from the wood. Next, he cut rows and crosshatched them into short spines. He stopped working and handed me his carving. "This is an echidna. Folks like these little statues. Why don't you drive the wagon to market next Saturday? You could see the settlement and sell things too. Put a little extra money in your pocket."

"Nah. I'm not good with a knife or whittling. Be wasting my time."

"Suit yourself."

My hands trembled; I slipped them in my breeches pockets. "I'm fine right here for now. Besides, if you didn't go to market, Widow Morgan would want to come out here and see about you."

Robert chuckled. "Lordy! She might do that."

That night I thought about going to town. What if I forgot my story or the constable got suspicious? I planned never to visit there.

After the next Sabbath supper, Maudie Claire sat at her loom. I handed her long pieces of fine yarn she threaded through small holes in a wooden bar that fit across the front of her loom. Next, she inserted each through a looped string before carrying it to the back of the loom. Warping a new project appeared to be a tedious process.

She looked up. "Season's changing. I hope you remember your promise to teach me to read this winter."

"Yes, Ma'am," I answered.

"Quinn, please call me Maudie Claire. Ma'am sounds old." She straightened the rows of yarn with her fingers and tied them in small bundles, which she attached to the loom frame.

"Yes, Ma'am, I mean, Maudie Claire." Watching her straighten and twist side to side to loosen her back muscles distracted me. I turned toward the fireplace to clear away thoughts of her and remain true to Fiona.

"Have you remembered anything about where you lived? What you did on days you didn't work?"

With each question she asked, my deception grew more difficult to continue. She trusted me; I wanted to speak the truth before I became too comfortable with lying. But fear of being sent back to prison stopped me. I fidgeted with the buttons on my shirt to keep my hands busy. "Maybe I lived out in the country. I don't remember my work or my friends."

She laughed. "Surely, you'd remember a sweetheart!"

I blushed. "True. Must not have had one." I prayed Fiona would never learn of my lie.

16

Over the weeks, Maudie Claire and I talked, and I read aloud from the family Bible or Galen's book, *Pilgrim's Progress*. We'd not read the book of poetry yet. Back in Langstone, Fiona and I eavesdropped behind the stone gate when a groomsman recited to the upstairs maid. They spoke of stars, of sweetness, and of love. I knew I couldn't read them aloud to Maudie Claire without feeling a flush of heat rise through me. But my heart still belonged to Fiona, didn't it?

In the workers' hut one night, Robert spoke of Maudie Claire's brother. "Galen is a hard man to know. Keeps to hisself 'cept he visits Widow Planchett, his lady friend that lives four miles down the road. He helps with heavy chores since her husband died two years ago. She's a pretty thing and lonely. Says it's the neighborly thing to do, but his face gets that funny smile of a man who's in love. Like the one sneakin' onto your face."

I stopped brushing dust from my pants. A shock slammed through my body. "*My* face? Who'd I be in love with?"

Robert pursed his lips and narrowed his eyes as he watched the heat rise in my cheeks. I inhaled and released my breath slowly. "No, Robert, you're wrong. I don't know Maudie Claire that well."

"I know what I see. You're 'memberin' your life before you came here, 'n seein' Maudie Claire brings back feelin's for another."

Finding no words to reply, I stretched out on my bunk and turned to face the wall. "Night, Robert."

The father, Patrick O'Carroll, returned home between surveying jobs during most weeks. After Sabbath dinner he spoke of working on a road along the wild northern shore. Like Robert, he kept his hands busy whittling.

He stared at me while he worked. "Have you ever been up north or other parts of the island?"

"Like the small one in the bay?" I said and gulped down a swallow that crowded my throat.

Patrick scrunched his eyebrows together. "No, this island, Tasmania."

He twisted his latest work, a dipping spoon, as he continued making smooth passes with his knife. "The west is wild, full of deep forests, lakes, and steep cliffs. More 'roos than people. Closer to here, the northern port town of Launceston is growing. The government men build roads to connect it to Hobart."

"Laun—what and Hobart, sir?"

Patrick stopped whittling. "Sorry, Quinn. I forget you're not from here. Launceston is our closest port to Australia and a full, two-day sail to Melbourne. Hobart is a busy harbor down south by Port Arthur. You've heard of Port Arthur?"

"Yes, sir. Robert spoke of it."

Patrick O'Carroll ran his hand through his hair. "Spent my time there, I did. Not a pleasant place."

I picked up the hearth broom, swept up the shavings around his feet, and placed them in the tinder box beside the fireplace. "Are we close to Port Arthur, sir?"

He surveyed my face as I sat across from him. "'Bout a two-day ride. But you'll not want to go near there. With no identification, they'll hold you 'til they find a body who knew you. Exiles do escape, but them that do steer clear. Not good to be close without your papers."

"Yes, sir." I kept my eyes toward the floor to avoid his piercing stare. My heart jittered and thumped; my palms became slick with sweat as the silence continued. I picked up one of the spoons he'd made and turned it over in my hands, feeling its smoothness. "Where's your next survey job, sir?"

He didn't answer until I met his gaze. His eyes asked questions I knew lay on the tip of his tongue. "I'm heading north, then west along Bass Strait. Be out a few weeks."

I slowed my breathing, laid down the spoon, and moved toward the cottage door. "I'd like to find me a job like yours. Perhaps you'd teach me how to use the tools I see you toting."

He spoke as my hand touched the door handle to leave. "When I return, if time allows, I'd be glad to teach you. Maybe by then you'll remember your background."

I hesitated, then turned to face him. "Yes, sir. Good night, sir."

My future at the O'Carroll farm depended on my growing pile of lies. Each day, truth slipped further away. I dreamt of pouring out my story to Maudie Claire, Robert, Galen, and Patrick; but my safety and theirs held me back. I longed to find a way to confess yet stay free.

Daydreams and tender thoughts of Maudie Claire blossomed within me, though I worked to push them down. I watched her cross the fields, work the late crops, cook meals, and weave rugs and shawls. The longer

I remained here, the more the gold fields and returning to England and to Fiona faded; meanwhile, my freedom remained distant.

One Sabbath after dinner, Maudie Claire handed me a piece of her weaving.

"What's this?" I asked.

"The vest I promised. Autumn will soon change to winter, plus, I decided today's your birthday."

A warmth crept up my neck and face. Then her fingers grazed mine, creating a brief spark. "Thank you, but I've not earned it. We've had no time to teach you to read."

She finger-combed the auburn tendrils of her hair that covered her cheek as she let her gaze wander over my face and shoulders. "I know, but we'd never have finished the fencing if you hadn't shown up. I've enjoyed listening to you read while I work. Besides, time's coming during the long string of frosty nights ahead."

"Yes, Ma'am." I unfolded the vest and slipped it on. The moss green fabric bore a raised chevron design in darker green. I fastened the small, oyster shell buttons down the front panel and straightened. "'Tis a wonderful gift. Thank you."

Her hand reached forward as if to brush down the front of the vest. Then she stopped and stepped back. "You can wear it when you go to market on Saturday."

"Market?" Though the vest warmed my chest, a cold trickle of sweat ran down my back.

"Don't you want to go to market?" she said. "You've been here a long while and haven't seen the settlement."

"I, I ah—"

She looked at me as if waiting for me to continue. When I said nothing more, she closed her eyes and shook her head as if tossing the thought away. "Never mind. Robert enjoys the trip. He'd be disappointed if I sent you."

I picked up the broom and busied myself sweeping up every tiny twig and clod of dirt. She watched me, but I refused to meet her glance.

Suddenly, she stood and walked to the fireplace. She fingered the books before taking down the volume of convict poems and handing it to me. Her eyes narrowed, suggesting a challenge. "Let's read this tonight."

I turned my head away, pretending a cough tickled my throat. Reading poetry promised to be as harrowing as any trip to town. I opened the book and began.

The writings spoke of love, loss, and betrayal. I kept my face down so Maudie Claire couldn't see my stress at reading them aloud. I stood to take my leave as soon as I finished a third poem, fearing the words would reveal my truth.

When I handed the book to her, she returned to weaving. It appeared those convict truths had scant effect on her, making me feel all the more foolish.

Why did reading poems to Maudie Claire cause my heart to race? I figured my only worry would be about going to market. I knew I could put off the trip easier than reading aloud to her. But my trip to market arrived long before I could have anticipated or prepared for it.

At dawn the following Saturday, I stood in the workers' hut, willing Robert to feel strong enough to drive to market. His fever and delirium had resisted four days of care from Maudie Claire, and now she'd contracted a fever and cough. Galen remained in Launceston; with her father not due back for days, I knew I needed to drive the wagon to market. How could I refuse when the farm produce and her weavings created income to sustain the family over winter?

I paced the worker hut, biting my lip, trying to calm my jumpiness. Robert pushed himself to a sitting position and coughed as he spoke. "Can you remember the man who'll buy the corn?"

"Yes. Baxter. He sells harnesses."

"And remember, don't sell Maudie Claire's weavings for anything less than her asking price. I bargained once and she sulked for weeks. Also—"

"Robert, you've told me all this many times. I'd not dare make a mistake. Lie back and rest."

"Remember to buy me two—"

"Tins of tobacco from the general store. I'll remember."

Robert coughed. "Good. Watch what you say to the widow."

"Widow Morgan. I know. She'll want to come here and nurse you back to health. I'm to tell her you were too busy for market this week."

Robert doubled over coughing before lying back and closing his eyes. I watched him settle down, then left to hitch the horses to the wagon.

With everything loaded and lunch wrapped inside a kerchief, I put on my vest, pulled myself up onto the seat, and headed down the road to town. Looking back, I tamped down a pang of sadness that Maudie Claire hadn't come to see me off. Why should she? I remained here as a hired hand, nothing more.

I tried to relax and familiarize myself with the land, but my focus on myself prevented me from scouting back roads to follow when I traveled north to cross to the gold fields. In a few hours, this venture into Bicheno would end, and I'd return from market with every task completed. Then I'd never go there again.

The crisp May breeze signaled an early winter. I anticipated spending rainy Sabbath evenings with Maudie Claire, teaching her to read and write, giving myself the perfect opportunity to mention bits of truth about myself. While reading, I'd pretend to recall being a printer's devil. That would explain the lack of deep calluses on my hands. I disliked each lie that came between us. But what else could I do? If I thought my reveals through carefully, my deceptions could be filled with truth more than falsehoods. That pleased me.

The village bubbled with activity. Shoppers scurried about with baskets and bags ready for buying vegetables, fruits, and fresh baked goods that spilled from stalls and the backs of wagons. I drove to the spot Robert described, turned the horse away from the street, and gave him his feedbag before I opened the back of the wagon. I took special time to display Maudie Claire's weavings, arranging scarves, quilts, rugs, and mats on the planks of the wagon and hanging vests and jackets on the sides. I laid out Robert's carvings and bushels of the O'Carroll's apples, then waited for customers.

Settlers tipped their hats to each other and to me as they passed. An elderly farmer approached. I tensed, waiting for him to speak first.

"Mornin'. Where's Robert today?"

"He's sick," I said as I reached my hand forward to shake his hand. "I'm Quinn. I work on the O'Carroll farm."

"Why didn't Miss Maudie drive in?"

I coughed, creating time to calm myself. "She's sick as well."

The farmer frowned. "Hope it's not serious. Give them my best. I'll take a half bushel of them apples you've got."

As he paid for his purchase, a woman from a nearby stall approached. "I've not seen you here before." She tilted her head and stared at me.

"I'm new. I arrived a few months back." I slid my hands in my pockets to hide their trembling as I explained why I'd come to market.

"Tell the O'Carroll's I asked after them. And tell Maudie Claire I need a baby sweater for my grandson. She'll know the size and color I like."

I nodded and hopped down to remove the feed bag from the horse.

A bustling woman in widow's weeds swished up to the wagon. "Mornin'. Where's Robert?"

"He's too busy to come today," I said. "Are you Widow Morgan?"

"Yes-s. Why?"

"Robert said to tell you hello and that he'd see you next week."

She straightened her bonnet. "He's comin' to my house? He promised he'd stop in one day."

"Yes, Ma'am, but I think he meant he'd see you here at the market."

Her shoulders dropped. "Oh." She leaned close and whispered, "Tell him I asked after him."

"I'll do that, Ma'am."

Widow Morgan bustled down the street and into the general store.

Sunlight broke through the clouds as clutches of shoppers strolled along the street. Market folk were friendly. It appeared I'd been wrong to worry about visiting the settlement.

With the sun and the friendliness warming me, I took off my vest and rolled up my shirt sleeves. The nearby fiddler's music set my feet to bouncing. If I closed my eyes, I'd easily imagine myself back in Langstone.

A short, muscular man stood nearby, talking with a group of settlers. Why did his stare send a shiver down my spine? When he left, I released a long, slow breath, chastising myself for my wariness.

By early afternoon, I'd sold all the apples, two of the sweaters, and all the rugs with orders for five more. Robert's carvings sold out, plus he had orders for six toy sheep and dozens of clothesline pegs.

As the sun dipped in the west, the street emptied. Settlers headed into the general store to finish their shopping. I packed up the wagon and prepared for my return to the farm. Robert and Maudie Claire would be pleased with my handling of the market.

A breeze arose and I slipped on my vest. That's when I noticed the short man approaching the wagon, accompanied by the constable and three townsmen. Their gait showed intent. I slid off the back of the wagon as they moved closer.

"I know you," the short man said.

I swallowed hard and shook my head. "No. This is my first day in town, sir."

"Where did you say you were from?" the constable asked.

"The O'Carroll farm."

"Before that?"

I shoved my hands into my pockets and shrugged. "I, ah, I'm not certain. I was on a ship."

The constable crossed his arms. "What ship?"

"I'm not sure, sir. I hit my head as I fell into the sea. I can't remember any details."

The short man asked, "What's yer name?"

"Quinn."

"Quinn what?" the constable asked.

An empty feeling invaded my stomach. I pressed down the desire to race away. What could I say to encourage them to leave me alone? "I told you I can't remember." I crossed my arms.

The men circled me as the constable continued his questioning. "Got a strange tattoo on yer arm, lad. Where'd ya get it?"

I lowered my arms and rubbed my hand across my wrist, hiding the jagged 'F' tattoo. "I don't remember."

The short man pushed through the group. "Wait!" he said. "Let me see that tat."

The constable held my arm and pushed my hand away from my tattoo.

The short man leaned forward. "Thought so. I remember that 'tat'. I helped give it to ya on the convict ship. You was a scribe for the cap'n, a favorite boy as I 'member."

The constable crossed his arms. "Is that so, mate? How do you know?"
The short man laughed. "Was me only time doin' a 'tat', constable."
"Travis, you've earned a reward for catchin' this runner."

I stumbled backward, stunned by their discovery. The constable wrenched my arms behind my back; his meaty hooks dug into my skin as he wrapped a rope around my wrists.

17

Escape was not possible.

The constable invited the others to step forward to escort me to the gaol. As we passed the woman in the next wagon, she cowered as if I planned to attack her at any moment.

"Please, take the wagon back to Mistress O'Carroll," I shouted to her.

She glared at me and turned to the constable. "I'll take her money and wagon back to my farm. I can't believe the O'Carroll's would put us in danger like this."

As the men shoved me down the road, I called back to the woman, "Mistress O'Carroll didn't know. She didn't know."

Three days later, Maudie Claire stood inside the settlement gaol. A somber bonnet shaded her face from view. Her pale skin and damp forehead revealed that she remained ill.

"Quinn?" Her eyes conveyed a mixture of questions and sadness.

I stepped forward, uncertain of what words she'd speak to me. When I clutched the bars that separated us, she stepped closer. I looked toward the floor. "I'm sorry, Maudie Claire; I didn't want to deceive you."

"I guessed as much."

"You knew? What gave me away?"

"No one thing. It's strange to find a new person in the settlement, especially one who appears from the island in the bay." Tears slipped from her eyes.

I ached to see her so troubled.

"I don't understand. How did you become a convict?"

"Does it matter?"

"Yes, it does."

Over the next minutes, I explained my true name and where I'd come from before my transport to Port Arthur. I talked of my jobs in the prison, my escape, and my pretending to have lost my memory. I left out the violence I'd witnessed and experienced.

When I finished, new tears trailed down her face. She wiped her nose and her eyes on a small white cloth.

I wished I could remove the sadness I'd caused. But now it was too late; I'd lost any chance to preserve the O'Carroll's trust.

Maudie Claire faced me and watched my eyes. "Was your escape worth the risk you took?"

"Yes. Can you imagine being considered a criminal and carted away to London Town like a goat headed to market? After I found my way to escape, I didn't expect I'd fall off the ship. I thought I'd sail to Melbourne, head to the gold fields, and then create a new identity before I sailed back to England. Now I can't claim a shred of innocence. I've broken so many rules."

"What will happen now?"

"I'll be transported back to Port Arthur. They'll lengthen my sentence and punish me, or hang me. They don't like to admit any runners gain even limited freedom."

Maudie Claire bit her lip. "Will you be free to return to England?"

I shrugged and swallowed hard before I faced her. "Since I've gotten to know you and your family, many things have changed. I'm thinking.

I'd enjoy a better chance of being accepted in Tasmania among other exiles than in England. Besides, it would take years to earn enough for passage, and then I doubt I'd be welcomed."

She took hold of the cell bars. I covered her hands with mine. Heat radiated from her gloved fingertips. I pressed down the urge to touch the cuffs of her sleeves or pull her forward, closer to where I stood.

She searched my face; her eyes wandered to my mouth and chin. "Where will you go once you are freed?"

I shrugged.

"You could return to our farm."

A lightness washed over me at her words. "Your family would allow me to return?"

"Once I share your story, I'm certain they will."

The constable entered the cell area. I pressed her fingers against the bars, then backed away to the bunk. "It's a long time before I'd be able to return. Your family will probably change their mind."

She shook her head. A smile gathered at the corners of her mouth. "We'll need to hire a new farm hand until you return, one that doesn't yell at the sea or steal apples. You promised to teach me to read and write. I'm holding you to that promise."

She opened her reticule and handed me a folded paper. "The constable gave me permission to give this to you."

I recognized it as a page from Galen's book of convict poetry.

"Maudie, I can't take it. The book belongs to Galen."

"He knows I took it. He approved, reluctantly."

The constable arrived. "Time to leave, Ma'am."

I handed her the vest she'd made for me. "Keep this. They won't—I can't take it with me."

She laid the vest over her arm and turned toward the door. I watched her auburn hair sway across her shoulders. At the last moment she turned, giving me a sidelong glance from under the edge of her bonnet. Then she was gone.

A restless joy rattled through me. I'd be welcomed by the O'Carroll's and by Maudie Claire, if I survived. I'd hold that thought and the vision of Maudie Claire's face through whatever lay ahead.

I unfolded the page, remembering my nervousness when she took the small purple book of poems from the shelf. She only chose to hear them when Galen and Robert were not present. Reading them aloud, I often stammered and my face heated up.

I stared at the page she'd selected, recognizing this poem as one that made both of us blush when I read it aloud. Realizing that my possessions would be confiscated within the next few days, I memorized each line, savoring its language.

> When my whole life dims to its final days,
> I'll trace each moment that I've spent with you.
> Though clouds and rain obscure remembered views
> And life is crowded with regret and pain,
> My faults shall glare across my aging eyes,
> Excusing not my sins nor absent faith.
> I'd thought my life would be a bright'ning ray
> Filled with your love, your face, your gentle grace,
> But ne'er did I foresee our looming fate
> That men would block our love at every chance.
> As fear and pain become my daily life,
> I rant against the coming of my death.
> Remember me, hold fast onto my love,
> For all's not lost until I cease to live.

I read it over and over until night darkened my cell. Its words assured me that I wanted to survive, to become a free man and return to the O'Carroll's farm and to Maudie Claire.

Two days later, the prison cart rattled into Port Arthur. Now I stood bound and shackled in Glevins' office. He held my papers in his crossed arms. "You've been free for more than three months' time. I need to know how you escaped."

"Yes, sir." I wove my tale, staying close to the truth. "I stole a crate and attached false papers I made from my time in this office. I told the old guy and the soldiers that the crate was a last minute one being sent home by the Commandant well after the ship was fumigated. That night, I climbed into the crate and waited for it to be loaded onto the ship."

"You must have had help."

"No, sir. I acted alone."

Glevins set aside the papers and stepped to his window. "I thought you were trustworthy."

"Sir, I—"

He turned and lifted his hand to silence me. "Guard!"

When the soldier arrived, Glevins grabbed up the papers and read the order aloud: "Ean McClaud, by order of Lieutenant Governor Forrester, you're to receive a severe lashing and time in the silent prison. Your sentence will be extended one year, forward from this date. Take him to the triangle."

18

The dark history of the triangle returned to my mind as I approached the assembly yard, hurried along between two soldiers. Four steps above the gathering place, along a wooden platform, the wide wooden top of the triangle dominated the space.

Sweat ran down my sides. I remembered the hours I'd been forced to stand near this spot, watching men whipped for petty thefts and broken rules. The closer we moved, the more my stomach roiled from viewing the brown stain of dried blood that trailed off the platform. Soon mine would be splattered atop others.

Bile rose in my throat.

The soldiers stretched my arms and legs to their extremes, attaching me to the wooden structure with wet leather straps. In the heat of summer, these straps would shrink and tighten to dig deeper into my limbs. Today, I received a small amount of good fortune as May's crisp autumn breeze crossed the platform.

One soldier ripped away my shirt and tossed it to the ground. I watched the poem flutter in the wind, carrying away my connection to Maudie Claire. I shivered from the approaching punishment and the loss of the poem, hoping it didn't signal a greater loss: not being welcome at the O'Carroll farm.

The soldiers retreated to a nearby tree, where they eased into smoking, laughing, and joking about the new lasses living in Port Arthur. Another soldier joined them.

"What's this? We've no flogging scheduled for noon."

"Naw. Forrester wants this one on display 'til tonight. He's a runner."

They laughed, then appeared to forget I existed.

Hour after hour, exiles passed, but none paid me any mind. What would my escape cost me in skin, thirty lashes? I shuddered, remembering my ten lashes on the ship. Could I muster more bravery this time? Surely time and living through the harshness of Port Arthur toughened me for the punishment to come.

As dusk approached, the penitentiary bell clanged, calling the exiles to assemble. When Lieutenant Governor Forrester climbed the platform steps, the bell stopped. I gulped in air, bracing myself for the approaching punishment.

Forrester grabbed my hair, pulling my head back. My body strained from the leather straps. I viewed the assembled men upside down. He yanked my hair and shook my head about.

"Witness this and heed my warning. No one escapes from Port Arthur! This evening, you'll all forego your meal to watch this man receive his punishment." He released my hair and shoved my head against the triangle. He paced the raised platform, then stopped. "Ean McClaud, your punishment shall be: fifty lashes, a week in the pillory, followed by eight months in the silent prison. Your sentence is extended by one—" He stopped. "No, make that *two* years of hard labor. I doubt your short-lived freedom was worth the trouble. Commence with the lashing."

The string of punishments sent a shock wave through my body. Fifty lashes? Two years added on to my sentence? I'd hurt no one. Why such a severe number? I trembled, feeling my resolve fade. Only hanging would be worse.

A burly soldier flicked the cat-o-nine-tails whip over my head as he mounted the steps. I closed my eyes and held my breath as I'd planned. At the first flick of the leather whip, I flinched but made no sound. Between each lash of the whip I inhaled and held my breath. Four switches, five.

"Ah-h-h!" My resolve broke. I heard my scream. My bladder released, dampening my trousers. I closed my eyes, knowing my blood splattered onto the platform and mingled with the blood of a thousand other men before me.

Six, seven. My screams continued as the tails dug deep into my back. Eight, nine— Pain flooded my body. The world of Port Arthur dimmed, then disappeared.

The splash of salt water woke me. I screamed and began shaking as the water trickled down my shredded back, burning like a hundred hot pokers twisted under my skin. I gasped, taking in shallow breaths, unable to open my eyes.

Again and again, I felt the lashing. Again and again, I fainted. Again and again, I awoke when the saltwater splashed into my wounds. Finally, I lost my hold on wakefulness.

When I awoke the last time, it was dark. The convicts forced to watch my punishment headed toward the penitentiary as unsympathetic to my pain as I had been for theirs. I wept.

Footsteps mounted the platform. Someone stood near me with a torch. A man fingered the edges of my wounds. I screamed at his touch.

"Hold still," a man's voice said as he continued to press my back. "We need another bucket of sea water here."

The new splash of water took away my breath. In short order soldiers dragged me, face down, toward the harbor. With each step they took, I cried out as my wounds opened and closed. Hades could not burn hotter.

They dropped me like a bag of grain beside a wooden pillory, opened the partitions, and fastened me upright. I shrieked in agony, wishing for unconsciousness.

"How high'll we crank this one up?" asked the soldier holding the torch near my face.

"Forrester said keep his toes touching the ground. What's his crime?"

"Not sure. Didn't murder anyone or he'd be hangin' from the gallows."

I drifted in a fog as they chained the wooden cover around my neck. When I tried to loosen the muscles in my arms, I realized each arm was chained into another set of cutouts, preventing me from even the smallest wiggle.

I awoke at dawn, screaming. The doctor had returned. He rubbed my shredded back.

"Hold still," he said, "your wounds will putrefy before your week's end without this ointment."

I floated between nightmarish sleep and days where fires and blistering suns, canons and bullets paled in comparison. In wakefulness, I struggled to stand on tiptoe. Constant pain shot up my legs into my back and radiated out to my fingers. If I relaxed my legs to relieve that pain, the board below my neck choked me. I discovered I could turn my head an inch and get relief by clenching my jaw.

My left arm, re-injured during the lashing, ached worse than when the soldier pushed me into the ship's hold back in London Town. I prayed the doctor would shove my shoulder back into place when they took me from the pillory.

I couldn't remember what punishments were promised after my time in the pillory, but it didn't matter; I'd need to endure every one of them if I wanted to become a free man some time in my future.

Daily, a handful of exiles threw pebbles at me, but most kept their distance as if to say, *Stand back or you'll catch his runner's disease*. Twice a day, soldiers fed me bread and water. The rest of the time, I hung like a dead capon in the butcher's shop.

The doctor's visits daily were my only solace. He applied salve each evening but didn't speak with me, Gov'nor's orders. After six days my wounds crusted over, but the wintry air chilled me and made my back throb.

Bits of dreams punctuated my thoughts. Fiona's hands soothed my back, or were they the hands of Maudie Claire? Both apparitions sustained me through each long day and night.

On the fourth morning, before the sun rose above the Island of the Dead, a man rushed toward me, waving his arms. I closed my eyes. He stopped so close his shouting hurt my ears. His rancid breath blew over my face. "You scourge, you vile beast sent by the Devil."

I started to drift off to sleep. He slapped my face and forced a chunk of meat into my mouth. "Chew fast! Tom sent me. I'll bring food when I can. Chew faster!" He looked around. "Hurry, before men stop to watch!"

I chewed faster.

"Now, close your eyes. I'm going to splash water into your mouth. Swallow what you can."

A blast of water flew across my face. I gulped it down and coughed, wishing my hands were free to capture more. Passing exiles laughed but kept walking.

True to his word, the man reappeared daily, shoving bread, bits of meat, and vegetables into my mouth. When no one stood nearby, I asked, "What did Tom pay you to do this?"

"A shirt and papers from the clark's office."

I nodded my thanks. The crazy man's bravery and kindness nourished my heart as well as my body.

Through the agony of the pillory, I watched for Tom, Barty, or Charley's face. I'd hoped to see them, to take strength from their presence. But none entered my narrow vantage point. Perhaps they'd been punished for knowing me. I might never know.

At the end of the week, soldiers opened the pillory. I dropped into their grasp with no feeling in my arms and legs. They dragged me to a waiting cart that rumbled up the hill. I groaned and cried out as they wheeled my battered body inside a dark building and dumped me on the floor like a sack of grain.

19

The stone floor cooled my fevered face but didn't ease the pain from my lashing. Precise footsteps approached. Scuffed black boots circled me. A whip slapped against trousers. Bits of cloves splattered close to my face.

"Ah yes, the runner."

I strained to look up to see his face but saw no higher than his knees. I closed my eyes.

The boots circled me again. "I'm certain you'll be with us more than your scheduled eight months, depending on how you follow *my-y* rules."

The man's menacing tone floated in and out of my thinking. I closed my eyes.

"Exiles live in sol...morning bells...hammock...Divine Service...ill...not respond—"

The man kicked me and spat out clove fragments, then used the heel of his boot to grind them into the stone floor. He nudged me as a farmer might nudge a lazy beast and spit more pieces near my face.

"Answer me. Do you understand?"

"No," I cried out, using the last of my strength.

A boot crashed into my ribs. "Didn't you listen? No speaking! ...keep your wicked ways."

The lashings still burned like fire as I was gagged, placed face down onto a rough wool blanket, and carried off, swaying side to side. I whimpered in pain as each step opened and closed my wounds.

A bolt slid. They lowered me onto a cold floor. Someone touched my forehead as I drifted off.

Light and darkness entered and exited the space where I lay. Thirst woke me; my growling stomach kept me awake. I twisted toward the light entering through a high, narrow window. Dirty gray walls dripped with rivulets of dark green slime that traced a wandering path to the floor. A battered wooden door with no visible hinges or handles covered most of one wall.

I heard faint clicks and slipping, like a person skating on dry grass. A slot in the door at eye level opened and closed. A second slot at the base of the door scraped open. Three small, misshapen buckets slid inside. I made no move to inspect them.

Wakefulness and sleep circled as containers arrived and departed. Sometime later, dawn, dusk, or a cloudy day, I awoke and moaned as a fierce burning sensation knotted every muscle. In a flash, a soldier entered, kicked me, and left. I stifled further cries of pain by shoving my hand into my mouth so deeply I gagged. Someone watched me through the viewing slot, but no one entered.

Thirst roused me. I crawled toward the buckets and peered inside: food, water, and an empty privy bucket. I lapped the water like a dog, then shoveled in food. Within minutes all I'd eaten flew from my mouth and splattered onto the floor. Shivers shuddered through me until I gathered enough energy to crawl to retrieve a thin blanket crumpled in a corner. I covered myself and slept.

Rustling grass and clicks approached along the hallway. I shoved my containers forward as the lower door slot opened. Buckets were exchanged, and the opening slid closed. I used a tin cup I found and drank the water bucket dry. Then I crawled toward a dusky corner and dozed, ignoring the stench of my earlier vomit.

At first light I surveyed the space around me: gray floor, gray-green walls, and gray ceiling. My cell appeared two crawls wide and three crawls from a bench by the back wall to the door. Today's food bucket contained equal amounts of flies and porridge but I brushed the top clear and slurped down the cold, lumpy mixture. I guzzled gritty water from my bucket, then retched up all I'd swallowed. A bell clanged once. Nothing happened, so I curled up and slept.

As the day brightened, I woke to the sound of snoring and rustling grass. Two soldiers entered, threw a burlap bag over my head, and put cuffs on my wrists. They dragged me upright. When my legs buckled, I screamed, "Stop!"

I was slapped; the bag and cuffs were removed. The guards left. Their intentions bewildered me.

When daylight returned the next day, two soldiers entered and threw a bag over my head. I kicked and flailed, but they held my arms firmly until I relaxed. They dragged me out of the cell and carried me along the straw-strewn hallway.

A breeze sliced through the space where they dumped me. I inhaled the scent of dry soil. Was I outside? I must be. I shivered as I sat bound, unable to rub my arms to warm myself. I waited for whatever came next.

In the distance I heard chirping, muffled voices, and marching feet. I waited, inhaling deep breaths through the rancid bag.

After a short while, a door opened. Hands lifted me. I clenched my teeth to silence my pain as we moved along a walkway before another door opened and the bag and wrist cuffs were removed. I lay on the damp floor of what appeared to be my cell. My dried pile of vomit remained nearby.

On the high window sill lay a pile of tangled ropes I hadn't noticed earlier. I inched to standing and pulled them down. A hammock. I attached the ends to hooks in the walls, steadied it, and lay down. The ropes cut into my shredded back, but the motion of the hammock soothed me. I rocked and dozed, watching the sliver of sky through the window.

The cell door opened. A soldier entered, poked me in the chest, and untied the hammock. I landed in a heap on the floor. He pointed to a rumpled paper tacked to the wall and gestured toward the window sill. I rolled up the hammock and put it on the sill, he backed out of my cell.

I crawled toward the paper on the wall and pulled it down. A long list of rules ran the length of the page:

No exile may view another.

No exile will enter another's cell.

The way we were guarded, how would that ever happen?

No speaking or singing except during Divine Service.

No hammock after first bell. Hammocks remain on the window ledge until dark.

That's why the soldier untied my hammock!

No markings on walls, door, hammock, bench, floor, or buckets.

No shaving.

No buckets will be filled unless left by the door.

No pets.

Pets? In a prison cell? Where would I get a pet?

No medical assistance except for severe illness.

No more than 30 minutes outside in the exercise pen daily.

So. I was outside. How can anyone exercise in wrist cuffs?

No exile may miss Divine Service unless in absolute isolation.

No exile may be present in his cell during weekly inspections.

No clothing or blanket exchanges more than once a month.

Willful disregard or fighting lengthens an exile's sentence.

So many rules. No wonder I'd been kicked and slapped. How did the prisoners who couldn't read fare? What was absolute isolation? Wasn't each cell already isolation?

Time and silence lay heavier than a worn millstone. I focused on my heartbeat to still the nightmarish images that flooded my mind. One moment I was drowning in a well, flailing to keep my head above water. The next, blankets smothered me. I hummed my mother's breakfast song over and over while I swayed and tapped my head against the wall.

> *Today is my life, today is my dream;*
> *Today I taste biscuits and porridge with cream.*

Saliva filled my mouth as I pictured myself beside the hearth, watching her stir the porridge, then stopping to ladle it into my bowl. Oh, Ma, forgive me for disgracing our family name. I promise to make things right before I die.

Over a handful of days, I gained strength enough to exercise. Each morning, I sat on the bench, exercising my legs and arms until sweat ran down my body. I unrolled the hammock and climbed in. My back lashings still made me wince but I stretched out. Today, blue sky, no clouds, but icy air flowed in through the window, reminding me of my last winter back home in Langstone.

I remembered the seasons between here and home were opposite. Here, it was early winter, but a calendar would read June; in Langstone it was summer. I closed my eyes, trying to see flowers blooming and crops breaking through the ground.

Suddenly, I remembered. The hammock! I eased myself out of the ropes and rolled it up before a patrolling soldier passed. How could I forget the rule so quickly? Perhaps the luxury of moving off the damp floor to rock and doze addled my brain.

Outside the window only the wind and an occasional bird call broke the silence. I willed a gull to fly past. None obliged. If I were free, I'd not come within miles of this forsaken place.

As I stilled myself, I tuned in to sounds outside my cell: creaky door hinges, tapping on metal, and a man's hacking cough. I moved near the door to listen. People traveled back and forth along the hall, dragging their feet, scuffing the straw about.

Without warning, two soldiers arrived with the bag and cuffs. They lifted me. This time I staggered down the hall on my own. Through another door they lowered me to the ground and removed the cuffs. I waited several minutes; then I found the courage to pull the bag off my head.

I sat in a small yard with high gray walls and a wire cover like a bird cage above me. The air held a tinge of salt, reminding me of my rocky lookout on the coast where I first saw Maudie Claire. Images of her freckled face, her wide smile, and her hair tied back with a piece of braided wool flooded my mind. I swayed back and forth, remembering the rhythmic clack, clack, clack of her loom's shuttle and the feel of the soft wool wrapped around my hands. Did she ever think of me while she worked?

For the rest of the day, I crawled around my cell, crisscrossing the middle in wandering patterns. As the daylight faded, I sat on the floor and pretended the bench was a printer's tray. I flexed my stiff fingers, arranged fanciful pages of flyers and newspapers. I avoided the food buckets in favor of resting in my hammock, where I swayed myself to sleep.

❖

One morning, earlier than usual, two soldiers came in and covered my head but left my wrists unbound. They grabbed my arms and took me from my cell, turning me a different direction than the exercise cage. The air around me bristled with human energy. I moved amid a disconnected chain of sweaty exiles, sliding their feet. Crushed straw bits poked like needles into my bare soles. Our breathing unified as though one person inhaled and exhaled.

I stumbled up cold stone steps and along a smooth wooden floor before entering a space that smelled of freshly polished wood. Where were we going? To be punished for breaking rules? I convulsed like I did in Newgate Gaol and on the ship. Were we being sent for a beating? Off to another prison? To be pardoned and put on a ship back to England?

Hands pushed me up a series of narrow wooden steps. My long toes bumped the short treads, but unseen hands kept me upright as I climbed to an unknown fate.

Click, slam, click, slam.

Doors opened and closed. I hesitated after every slam, but hands shifted me right, then left like type in the printer's tray.

Click. Slam.

I flinched as a door closed within inches of my hooded head.

Waiting in the narrow space, absorbing the restlessness and ragged breathing around me, I hoped the fetid bag would be removed before I suffocated.

Click, slam. Click, slam.

I cautiously extended my hands and bumped my fingers against wooden walls. Was I being placed in a crate? I touched side to side. More wood. My heart raced faster and faster. Could I survive another crate, another voyage?

I reached above my head. The space was open. When a pole slapped my head I pulled my hands down and sighed; I wasn't in a crate. I turned, fingering the space at knee level. A wooden seat spread across one side.

Click, slam. Click, slam.

"PRAISE GOD!"

The booming voice startled me.

"All exiles, confess your sins. Uncover your heads to praise the Lord. Open your eyes to the Lord's greatness. Show your sinning hearts to the Lord!"

I removed the bag. Walls surrounded me on all sides. In front, the wall was only as high as my chest. Far below stood a white-haired clergy wearing vestments, stretching his arms toward heaven. A large wooden cross hung behind him. Was I in a church? Then I remembered the rules; this must be the Divine Service.

"Repent your sins!"

"Save us, oh God!" Shouts came from all around me.

"Praise the God of our fathers," called out the gruff voice of the clergy.

"Help us, oh God!" erupted in shouts, screams, and cries around me. Were the prisoners in pain?

The clergy pointed toward me. He shouted and thumped the lectern. "Your sins are too vile for the Lord God to forgive. Your sins send you straight to Hades."

A pipe organ wheezed wildly before a hymn's melody came alive. From all sides, off-key singing broke out: "Oh, worship the King of Peace."

Prisoners around me shouted or sang like true believers—or did they use this chance to hear their own voices? I stood and sat, spoke and sang, sensing a connection with others though they remained unseen. I listened and mumbled anything to hear my own voice, but the shouting around me covered any sound I made.

When the organ stopped, the silence reverberated as loud as the singing. The clergy read verse after verse, thumping the lectern as he spoke. "You're all sinners in God's eyes. Repent and ask for his peace and understanding. Drop to your knees. Praise the Lord!"

A shuffling of feet began. Many convicts must have knelt. I stood and scanned the chapel. No statues or banners adorned the gray stone walls. High windows let in light and a treetop view. I touched the wooden walls around me. Each bore scrapes and scratches but no gouges. Perhaps the soldiers checked these spaces to prevent any evidence of messages left behind by exiles.

Another song, another verse with a chance to respond. I joined in and pressed my hand along the pulsing walls. My connection to those around me grew stronger.

The clergy continued. "Abide with me, Lord, as I standeth before you in darkness."

I lived that darkness every day and night. How could God abide the existence of this prison?

Divine Service droned on and on. I sat back and covered my ears to lessen the screamed responses while the clergy reminded us of our vile nature. More music sprang from the organ before more prayers and more verses about repentance.

Suddenly, the clergy thrust his hands high over his head. "Oh, Lord, hear these sinners, these men beyond redemption. Help them accept their fate. We ask in Jesus' name, Amen. Cover your heads, wicked scourge of the world. Cover your heads."

The clergy disappeared out a side door. Restlessness erupted around me. The door of my space opened. A soldier motioned for me to put the bag on my head before we retraced our route: down narrow steps, across a wooden floor, down more steps, and along the straw-strewn corridor.

My cell floor felt damp; it had been washed. Clean clothes and a clean blanket lay on my bench. Must be the first of the month but which month, July? How would I find out without being allowed any questions or answers?

I rinsed my hair and body with my last cup of water and dried off with my dirty clothes. The touch of clean clothes on my skin provided a moment of clarity. If we received fresh clothes once a month, I could track time.

I was sitting in thought on my bench when a swoosh sounded along the hall. Time for exercising in the caged place outside? The food slot opened. My soiled clothing that I'd piled near the door and my buckets were exchanged. The silence returned.

The food for the Sabbath contained bits of meat, vegetables, and a chunk of bread. I took the meal to my bench to savor every morsel. Was this our reward for attending Divine Service? No. That was not an option. But I understood a bit more about this place. Next Divine Service, I'd gladly sing.

Lately, I'd decided that loneliness existed as a living, breathing condition. I craved companionship, the chance to see and touch others, to speak and listen to their voices. I decided I'd whisper a conversation, pretending I sat eating a Sunday supper at the O'Carroll farm while talking with and listening to Maude Claire.

Why did this happen, Ean?

I acted outside the rules. On the ship I showed off, being a scribe. Then I used Tom in the penitentiary as protection when men came after me. It was stupid to say I'd enjoy the silence.

Is the silence difficult?

Yes. Silence may be worse than death, but it's too late; I can't go back and change things. From the time I accepted the handkerchief from Lady Colridge, I was a fool.

But I thought she gave the handkerchief to you?
She did, but nothing good came from it, except meeting you.
Do you still wish to return to England?
I still couldn't answer that question. After I finished eating and set my food bucket by the door, I paced my cell and gave myself a dressing down. My arrogance had ruined my life. Why did I act so stupid? Look where I ended up. If I'd fought the rebels off or told the clark what I knew, I might be a free man by now.

I paced endlessly, trying to grasp any explanation. I pounded my fists against the walls, willing them to crumble to let more light inside. A new resolve grew inside me. *If they think they can make me crazy like Barty, they're wrong, Maudie Claire. They have to be wrong!*

The minutes, hours, and days dragged across my life slower than the small brown snail crawling up the damp wall. He swayed his feelers, testing the air and the green slime before moving toward the small window. "And where do you think you're going, my slippery friend?" I picked him up and put him on the floor. "You can't leave just yet."

The snail restarted his climb. "You're determined," I whispered; "I'll give you that, but you're my companion for a while longer."

Day after day, I repositioned him from the wall back to the floor. Day after day, he restarted his climb. Was my forcing him to restart his journey a torture? Was I becoming as uncaring and mean as my captors? After four more days, I let him escape. "Don't come back, little snail. If you're stupid enough to return, I vow I'll eat you."

❖

Wintry frost covered my thin blanket most mornings. I watched the morning light cross my window and ached to experience an ordinary day in the free world. My skin tingled as I imagined loving fingers traveling over my face. Did they belong to Ma or Fiona or Maudie Claire? Whose warming touch and faint pulse claimed my heart? When I touched my own face, the images faded away.

The food slot opened. I inched closer and shifted the buckets scant inches further inside my cell. The hand reached in and touched the water bucket. When it pulled the bucket closer, I grabbed the exposed skin between gloves and the sleeve of a uniform.

Crash!

"Ah ha!" I screamed as the slot closed, crushing my hand. "Almost got you!"

The food slot reopened to release my bruised hand. As I pulled away, my cell door opened and two soldiers entered. In turn each man slapped me across the face until I dropped to the floor. On their way out, they kicked me.

I stayed curled up on the cold floor. My face burned from their slaps, yet a laugh crowded out of me. I clamped my sleeve over my lips to stifle my laughter. I'd almost won.

For days following the incident, when my food slot opened, if my buckets weren't line up exactly in front of the door, the soldier moved past without exchanging empty for full. Each day I watched the soldier's gloved hands, remembering the downy feel of his arm hairs, knowing a beating was worth the added contact each slap placed on my skin. I hadn't enjoyed the warmth of skin to skin since the doctor checked on me when I stood in the pillory.

Mornings, the only required task was rolling up my hammock. Neither the cold floor nor the bench was inviting, so I worked out a plan to use my hammock during daytime hours. I listened for crunching straw, a sign of soldiers approaching. In the absence of swooshing or crunching, I'd hang the ropes and swing back and forth. When a swoosh approached, I'd leap up, toss the hammock on the window, and pace.

One time, I fell asleep and slipped into dreaming of Langstone. That was unusual; Fiona had disappeared from my dreams weeks ago. Just then the straw rustled near my door. I rolled out of the hammock but had no time to place it on the window ledge, so I undid one end and sat in front of its heap on the floor. The soldier passed. I returned to swinging and sleeping.

During my time in the exercise cage, I sat and stared at the gray walls, not bothering to exercise or toss pebbles out through the screened top. As a child I liked to build dirt piles and blow them away; now I had no desire to move around since I kept myself moving all day, every day, in my cell. I sat, listened for outside sounds, and awaited the soldiers return.

Daylight hours, I paced or crawled around my cell. I fingered my lengthening scruffy beard, pulling out hairs by their roots to amuse myself. Same with the hairs on my head; I created a bald spot above each ear. The brief twinge of pain from yanking out each hair reminded me I was alive.

Days bumped together. I needed a way to record my time yet obey the rules. Monthly clothes exchanges allowed me to gauge the changing of months, but I explored the smallest crannies of my cell, searching for a place to mark each day. That turned into pleasant whispered conversations with myself. "In the cave I'd used rocks in a small depression in the earth to mark time. If I brought back pebbles from the caged yard, where would I keep them? I can't write or draw on the illness slate; they clean it every Sabbath. I could pull a thread from my tunic every day, but where would I hide the threads?

Could the stone floor be marked so they wouldn't notice? I made tiny scratches on the spaces between the stones on the floor and walls, but the marks showed. At my next meal, I mashed a glob of porridge over each one to erase the evidence of my breaking the rule.

Next, I fingered the top and sides of my bench: smooth, worn wood, no scratches or dents. That wouldn't work either. That's when I realized they never checked my body for markings.

20

The handle of my tin cup bore a tiny sharp edge that I used to scrape narrow lines beside my tattoo. Blood trickled down my arm. I tasted its saltiness.

I added more slashes for the past six Sabbaths, lapping the blood after each tiny incision. I appreciated my own craftiness until I realized I'd need twenty or more cuts before my stay in the silent prison ended.

My daylight routine consisted of pacing, napping, and watching for food, followed by more pacing. Days inched into nights as I awaited permission to attach my hammock to the bolts in the wall. But sleep provided no solace.

One night Ma's ghost slid in through the watcher's window. She hovered near my head and whispered, *Remember your promise to me—to our family—you must not bring shame to our ancestors.*

"I won't, Ma," I pledged, then paused to let the image drift higher. "I promise I'll find a way to redeem myself and our name."

Her image swept close again, breathing warm whispers against my ear but not allowing me to grab hold of her misty presence. I wept as a hollowness inside me expanded. Clutching my throat, I swallowed down my loneliness.

Night after night, Ma's image returned, shattering my sleep. Then one evening a host of ghosts arrived to encircle my cell. I squeezed myself into a tight ball to ward off their presence.

Charley stood in a corner and jangled the coins in his pocket. *Ean, join me and my kin. We'll lift enough pocket watches and live in an old cabin I found near the wharf. Glevins will never be the wiser.*

That's not true, Ean. Edward's shadow slithered under the door and pushed Charley aside. *I'll report you and earn me a pouch of coins and a ticket of leave on the next ship.*

"No!" I sat up and covered my ears and screamed as I did during Divine Service. "Don't report me!"

Within seconds two soldiers rushed in. They tipped me out of my hammock and pummeled my head and shoulder. Before they left, they gagged and bound me like goose for a Christmas feast.

I lay on the cold stone floor in a daze. I ached from their fists ramming into my body. After gathering my strength, I raged against my bindings. The soldiers' actions suggested nightmares weren't allowed to enter this place. Another rule.

Tears ran down my cheeks as I twisted to find a position beneath my hammock, but sleep refused to arrive.

When I closed my eyes, Maudie Claire's ghostly upside-down image appeared on my ceiling. Yards of woven brambles grew from her fingertips. They reached through my hammock, wrapping their barbed tendrils around my neck, tightening, tightening, tightening.

Ean, you betrayed me. I gave you work, food, and clothing. Your misdeeds embarrassed me and my family. Never return to our farm.

I shouted through my gag, "No! Please, Maudie. You must believe in me. Please!" My muffled speech resembled an injured animal squabbling with another over the last piece of a fresh kill.

Once again soldiers entered. This time they grabbed me, dragged me down a corridor, opened a door, and tossed me in like a bale of straw.

The stagnant air reeked of human waste. I shivered. Could life become any worse? I sat in a corner and waited for dawn.

I listened for the telltale swoosh of straw in the corridor, disturbed by the soldiers' feet, but I heard no sounds. I dozed and awoke, anticipating morning light. None arrived. I stood and ran my face along the wall, searching for a trace of fresh air. Nothing.

No food or water or privy bucket was shoved through a slot. My ranting must have landed me in absolute solitary, where only darkness gained entry. This must be how it feels to be blind and deaf, except I heard my breathing and the endless thump, thump, thump of my heartbeat drumming in my head.

Day and night lost meaning.

Moments when I remembered who I was and where I'd been taken, I mumbled the lines from the poem Maudie Claire left with me:

When my whole life dims to its final days,
I'll trace each moment I have spent with you.
Though clouds and rain obscure remembered views
And life is crowded with regret and pain;

I whispered the comforting words ending the sonnet, words I'd never dared consider before now:

Remember me, hold fast onto our love,
For all's not lost until I cease to live.

Hour after hour, the rhythm and truth in the words circled in my mind, the only place Port Arthur and the prison couldn't control.

New sadness soaked into me, leaving me restless. I rolled about the floor with no fear of bumping into a bench, a hammock, or a blanket. None existed in this blackness.

I hummed and recited verses of songs my ma sang to me when I was a wee child. They filled the hours but brought no comfort.

When the door to my windowless cell finally opened, the soldiers covered my head before they dragged me to my feet. They hauled me down a corridor, opened a cell door, shoved me to the floor, and removed my handcuffs, my head covering, and my gag. I lay motionless, too weak to crawl or pull myself onto the bench I saw in the corner; too exhausted to hang my hammock.

I awoke from a troubled sleep and focused on the light streaming in through the high window. This cell had a viewing slot and a food slot in the door. I listened. Chirping and human work sounds filtered in through a high window. I'd returned to a cell where daylight was allowed to enter.

I lay still, waiting for food and privy buckets. Judging from the wretched stench of my clothing, I missed at least one Divine Service as well as my chance for clean clothes. I dozed, hoping for the return of my old routine.

Days crawled slower than the snails slithering on my cell walls. My time in the exercise cage failed to arrive. At the sound of shuffling and dragging feet, I stood beside my door, ready to attend Divine Service. My door remained closed. My cell remained unswept. I received no fresh clothes. What crime allowed me to be treated thus? My relief from the silence came from listening to the straw rustling in the corridor and hearing the once-a-day opening of my door slot to exchange buckets.

❖

Confinement to my cell continued. Mornings, I amused myself by licking frost from my blanket, then I curled into a ball to conserve my body heat until food arrived. I gave up my pacing and reciting to lie in my hammock during the forbidden times and wait for soldiers to enter my cell and dump me to the floor. At least I'd see other human beings and feel their punishing blows for breaking the rules. It would prove I still existed.

But no soldiers, no slaps or kicks arrived. I'd become invisible, even to the guards.

Weeks passed. Surely Spring would arrive any day. That meant we'd reached September or October, and spring rains could come at any time. I longed for the summer I was missing in Langstone.

When I was allowed to return to the exercise cage, I sat and let the chilly rains soak my skin. I shivered and cried before gathering my anger like a blanket and reaching for the narrow wires overhead. I hung, letting them dig into my fingers, using the pain as proof that I lived, breathed, and I survived, despite this suffocating silence.

In my cell I distracted myself by continuing to watch snails and bugs crawl along the walls. I crushed and ate each one, spitting out their shells. Foolish, worthless creatures!

Once I returned to Divine Service, I retched from the disgusting stench of myself and fellow inmates. I prayed I'd soon receive clean clothes. As we sang, I placed one hand on my throat to feel the vibrations of my screaming like a wild animal struggling to free myself from a deadly trap.

Divine Services and the daily sounds along the corridors were no longer enough to satisfy me. Tears slid down my face. I longed to speak with a living, breathing person, even my worst enemy.

Back in my cell, I struggled to determine how long since I'd made my tally marks of my time in the silent prison. Ten? Thirty? Ninety days? Longer if the clergy's mention of spring and rebirth were to be believed.

I dug a jagged fingernail into my arm and let my blood drip into my open hand. I smeared it along the wall. The dampness absorbed the brilliant redness, leaving a rusty streak behind. I slid my tongue across the wall, relishing the saltiness and the tang of my blood mixed with damp moss.

My hair hung in long, dirty clumps to my shoulders. I used my fingers to comb it back, touching the patches of scaly, dry skin above my ears. I pretended the fingers that caressed my face belonged to Maudie Claire, or was it the ghost of my mother?

Is this what happened to Barty? Was I becoming a lost, lonely wanderer?

Each day in the exercise cage, I focused on sounds I knew well, the steady clacking of Maudie Claire's shuttle moving back and forth as she sat weaving. I swayed, mimicking the motion of her shuttles—right, left, right, left. Her fabric lengthened, but the memory of her smile and the brilliant rainbow of yarn skeins hanging on the wall behind her loom dimmed.

As the days lost their cool edge, more bugs entered my cell and skittered across the floor. I watched them, not bothering to trap and eat them. New nightmares arrived. I stood tied to the ship's mast with a host of friends sentencing me to endless lashings. I woke drenched in sweat, yet shivering.

By day I resumed pacing and watching for eyes in the viewing slot. When it opened, I rushed to the door, but not before the window slid closed. When would this torture end?

I rocked from foot to foot, waiting for a soldier to approach. My heart beat as fast as if I'd raced a long distance. I strained, imagining the swoosh of straw in the corridor. With my face pressed against the viewing slot, I waited.

When the slot finally slid open, I saw blue eyes. I screamed. "Ah-h-h!"

The soldier pulled back, slamming the slot closed. I laughed aloud, replaying the startled look in his blue eyes.

He entered and slapped me until I collapsed on the floor and curled up like a sow bug. He kicked me for good measure as he left.

I kept my vigil, knowing my outbursts invited punishing slaps. After several encounters with the same blue-eyed soldier, I named him Conroy and invented his life. He was taller than I. The edges of his eyes held small creases, making him as much as two score years of age. His left eye bore a brown fleck near the pupil; perhaps he'd been struck by a stick or a sharp object.

Conroy had a mole over his right eye, and the edge of a scar cut through his eyebrow; he'd been in a serious fight or a battle. I chose a battle against Napoleon, where he'd disgraced himself by his recklessness and been sent here as punishment for his folly. That explained his brutal fists on me. Had he known I barely felt his attacks, he'd have found ways to cause me greater pain.

I waited for Conroy to appear. I had a plan.

Each day, I listened for the crunch of straw in the hall. Each day, I stood pressed beside the door. Each day, I waited for the viewing slot to open. One day it did.

I held my breath as the slot slid open. There was a pause; then it closed. I inhaled a quiet breath.

The cell door opened. I jumped out and grabbed the guard's face, holding it so close to mine I inhaled his breath. "I got you, Conroy!"

He pushed me away, knocking me across my cell. I shrieked with laughter and clapped my hands as he slammed my cell door closed. I knew he'd return soon.

Moments later, he stepped into my cell with a wall of a man. Together they bound my arms behind my back, gagged me, and put a bag over my head. As I stumbled along the damp, straw-covered floor, I knew my destination: a windowless cell.

The giant-sized man shoved me to the floor. The lock clicked. I shook the bag off my head. I'd guessed right. I lay in a room blacker than a moonless night. Once again, the heavy odor of urine penetrated the space. Another convict had been held here recently. I scooted to a corner away from the stench and pulled my knees to my chest. Was my chance to scare Conroy worth the punishment of spending more time in this darkness? Maybe.

My nightmares changed to dreams of sunshine, the smell of the printer's shop, and scenes near the small lake by Langstone. Sparks of light flashed across my eyes like fireflies, but nothing penetrated the darkness or the silence for long. When the door opened later, I squeezed my eyes closed against the sudden burst of light.

Back in a regular cell, I curled up on the floor and focused on the light coming in the window, knowing no food or exercise or a chance to shout during the Divine Service would soon include me.

With my hands now untied, I rubbed my arms, brushing across every slash I'd made and found them healed. I reached for the tin cup lying on the floor, searching for a rough edge, but this cup had none. Biting one fingernail to a point, I reopened each old slash and drank my blood like communion wine.

❖

One morning, my body ached; I could not rise from my hammock. I rolled onto my side and retched, then fell to the floor. One moment I shivered with cold, the next I burned with a fiery heat. When my food bucket arrived, I remained on the floor, unable to retrieve it.

When my cell door opened, I could not tell if I'd slept for hours or days. The tall, thin doctor who'd tended me in the pillory entered. He checked my hot forehead as two soldiers entered and raked my vomit into dry straw. Then they lifted me into my hammock.

The doctor felt my forehead. I grabbed his wrist, feeling the steady k-thump, k-thump, k-thump of his life beneath my fingertips. He loosened my grasp and patted my shoulder before he helped me sit up to swallow bitter medicine. Next, he washed my face and arms with cold water and patted my shoulder. I drifted into a dreamless sleep.

For days the doctor returned to check on my health and to help me eat. Each time, I held his hand. He neither spoke nor pulled away. Feeling a human connection sparked my interest in recovering. I summoned my strength, remembering my resolve to survive and prove my innocence.

As when I arrived at the silent prison, I needed to crawl before I could stand and walk before I could exercise or pace. The weather softened; sunshine lasted longer and longer each day. My spirit rose with each new sunrise. The slashes on my arm healed. My time in this dim, silent place must soon reach its end.

Expectation of my release grew stronger each day. Like a butterfly trapped in gentle hands, I'd soon be set free. I needed to be ready. I needed to return to my regimen of pacing and exercising to strengthen myself. I planned to walk to freedom with confidence and my head held high at my release.

Day after day, week after week, in the outside caged area, I forced myself to trot in circles. I pushed through pain to exercise my arms and legs until sweat ran down my sides.

A warm breeze swirled through my cell. Two soldiers entered too early for my turn to exercise or for Divine Service. They shackled, hooded, and guided me along the straw-strewn corridor and across a wooden floor, where the heels of their boots echoed off the walls.

When they removed the bag from my head, I squinted, trying to adapt to the bright sky after living in the dimness for so long.

"Move along," one soldier said, shoving me out the door.

I staggered as I walked on, blinking at the brightness while listening to the myriad of sounds around me: voices, marching boots, hammering. The town of Port Arthur spread below me like a colorful faire. Pale green grasses and dark green forests framed the town's dirt roads. I inhaled a cleansing breath, then sneezed again and again, clearing the stench of the prison from my nostrils. Soon I'd see Tom and Barty. We'd share our recent experiences, and this time I'd not brag or complain. I'd apologize wholeheartedly for my arrogance about enjoying the silence. From this day forward, I'd relish every voice that spoke, every sound I heard, never taking one minute of the noisy world for granted.

After I was allowed to wash in a trough by the penitentiary, I put on the clean set of exiles' clothes handed to me and saw my number, 57457, painted on the tunic. The yellow and black stripes of my clothes signified my untrustworthiness. That no longer mattered.

I'd lost weight and needed to cinch the breeches snug with a length of frayed rope the soldiers provided. I'd survived the silent prison and walked as free as any shackled convict held at Port Arthur could expect.

The harbor glimmered like a brilliant blue gem, and mid-summer flowers swayed in the breeze. The soldiers escorted me to the clark's office. A fresh beginning lay ahead. The thought of speaking with another person lightened my spirits. I'd now be able to shake a man's hand or pat his back without being punished. I straightened as we walked on.

In the clark's office, I encountered Glevins. He looked up from his desk and set down his pen. "Hm. You survived."

"Yes, sir." My throat constricted. The voice escaping my lips fractured like a young boy stepping into manhood. I swallowed hard to clear my throat.

"Two visits to the pit, huh? I see your attitude hasn't changed. We'll see if you can survive hard labor from now until your sentence ends."

Hard labor. I knew he hoped to shock me, but I planned to give him no satisfaction.

Glevins narrowed his eyes; a sly smile crowded onto his lips. "You're heading to the coal mine this afternoon. For the next six months, you'll be shackled day and night or until you prove yourself willing and able to perform your tasks."

I met his glance without blinking. Inside, I remained weak and frightened, but I determined to hide my disappointment that I'd not be with my friends any time soon.

"Guard!" he shouted. I jumped. He turned back to his work.

A soldier checked my shackles, then directed me to a waiting cart, where I was again chained to an iron ring. The cart driver whipped the horses as we clattered down the road and out of Port Arthur.

The scene around me could have been an English countryside if I ignored the exiles in ragged clothing, dragging leg irons as they carried heavy loads. New cottages dotted the hills. Kitchen gardens shared their abundance of summer crops.

I scanned the docks and the warehouse where Barty worked and the penitentiary building where I'd stayed with Tom. If the rumors about the coal mine proved true, I'd wish myself back in the silent prison before the end of my first day.

While the cart rattled along, I made a determination. If I kept my mouth shut, my eyes watchful, and my head down, I'd survive the coal

mine. I remembered my time in Newgate Gaol, the ship, and the prison.
Today I'd begin one more test in one more dark place.

21

Coal. The sooty taste and smell increased the closer we drove to the mining settlement. Soldiers led me into a squat orange building near the shore at Plunkett Point, a brief cart ride from Port Arthur. Once inside, I walked along a short hall to a door with the words 'Mining Commandant' printed on a small sign. One soldier knocked.

"Enter," a deep voice boomed from inside the room.

The man stood no taller than a half-grown child, with his girth matching his height. He reminded me of the drawing I'd seen of Napoleon. He wore a snug, ornate military coat during this muggy February day. I watched him pace beside his desk with his hands clasped behind his back. The soldiers that delivered me stood at attention on either side of the door.

The man stopped pacing and scanned me from head to foot. "My name is Commandant Robbins. You're here because you're beyond redemption and are sentenced to hard labor for the rest of your imprisonment. We do not tolerate your kind of exploiter. Here you'll sleep in a separate cell to prevent your partaking in unnatural crimes with other convicts."

I blinked. The false claim that I deviled children had followed me. How would I clear that from my record? I clenched my jaw to prevent making a response that could change this moment into a bad beginning.

Robbins shuffled papers, then looked up at me again. "You'll work with a partner twelve hours a day, six days a week. If you do not dig enough to fill thirty coal trolleys a day, your rations will be cut to half until you reach that goal. Watch where you stand; this coal ignites easily. We don't want fires started below ground because of your carelessness."

More rules. Endless, ever-changing rules. I gazed out the window, distracted by the chance to watch a bird light on a branch and chirp a short melody. I almost smiled until Commandant Robbins paused. I returned my attention to him.

"You! 57457! Look at me when I speak to you."

I straightened. "Yes, sir."

Robbins harrumphed and continued. "At my discretion or the mine foreman's, you'll remain shackled up to six months. You may not receive or send any posts. No exceptions." He paced in a circle as if considering what he wanted to say next. "Take him to the convict barracks."

They locked me in a small cell with an observation window in the door, a wooden bench attached to the wall, and a small window along one wall. I sat down on a battered three-legged stool and waited.

For the rest of the day, I remained locked in my cell. Men speaking a variety of accents passed by. Their words broke through my months of enforced solitude; their unending, fevered conversations disturbed me. I wanted to scream 'stop your squabbling. Appreciate what small freedoms you own.'

Clank, clank, clank. Men in shackles passed close enough to smell their sweat. I worried about myself, working underground where, like in absolute isolation, daylight made no entry.

After the evening meal, I was allowed to join the others in the open area between barracks. Men stood in small groups in the shadows of the courtyard lanterns, talking and laughing. All men, regardless of how tall or broad or thin each appeared, had rock-hard arm and shoulder muscles beneath their layers of coal dust. In time I imagined I'd gain similar strength.

As I listened, I looked around. Nearby stood a small chapel. The builders turned bricks helter-skelter to create rows of decoration and patterns on the entry arch. Why bother, I wondered. It's near a grimy coal mine in a prison.

An older man sidled up next to me and pointed toward the chapel. "Fancy place, huh?"

I shrugged. "Are we allowed inside?"

"Every Sabbath. The preacher c'n talk more 'n any woman I know."

I laughed and turned to study the man's thick mane of gray hair. The sleeve of his right arm was turned inside his shirt leaving an empty place where he should have an arm. The fingernails on his left hand and his ragged shirt were clean. He didn't work in the mine.

He sneered. "Do I pass?"

"What?"

He squinted, his agitation evident. "Do I pass yer inspection?"

Heat crept up my face. "I'm sorry. I've been isolated and—"

"Silent prison?"

I nodded. "Several months. It's hard to remember my manners."

"So I'm told. Name's Theo."

I extended my right hand, stopped, and exchanged it for my left. "Ean."

"Proud to meet ya. Can't offer ya a fine cup of tea or a cigar, just my friendship."

"Thanks, Theo. It's been a while since I had the freedom to speak. You don't work in the mine, do you?"

"Nope. Lost my arm during a cave in. Put me above ground. Now I'm weighing trolleys and running the steam engine. One hand is enough for them jobs." He spoke as if losing an arm was commonplace.

"How long are you here?" I asked.

"Lifer. You?"

"Two years or more."

"Plan on doing the work, Ean, and don't complain. Y'll be fine." Theo turned away and joined a group of men tossing rocks into a rain barrel. He didn't look my way. I waited, wondering if I'd be welcome to join them.

Theo signaled me forward. As I approached, I listened to their conversation about their work, coal, and mining. A sense of self-satisfaction wove through their comments:

"I hefted that trolley back onto its rails and went back ta work, diggin' twelve more loads."

"But have ya ever done more trolleys than Montross?"

"That devil. His last mate felt his anger and earned a broken jaw for his trouble. Glad he's not bossin' me 'round."

Heads bobbed in agreement.

"He's kept the record at fifty a day for some time 'n probably will for years ta come."

Men chattered and screamed into the night. The loudness of their voices caused me to cover my ears until an officer threatened them with isolation. But if I wanted to be friends with Theo and the others, I'd need to adjust to the noise and join in.

Back home, Fiona called me her magpie. I wonder if she uses that endearment for another. Would Maudie Claire have called me a magpie if I'd met her before I reached Tasmania? Not likely. I'd lived another lifetime since Langstone: gaol, the ship, the penitentiary, silent prison. Would I recognize myself if I went back?

In the morning after a breakfast of porridge, tea, and a dry biscuit, I marched up the hill with other shackled men. The closer we walked to the mine, the more my stomach lurched; I feared I'd heave my breakfast as I focused on the coming darkness. Could I survive below ground?

The shift foreman stood on a platform by the entrance to the mine and spoke. "I'm Colin Worth. We've important safety rules with severe consequences if you break them. First, shift yer own metal tag onto the mining duty board before ya step into the shaft. At the end of yer shift, move yer tag back to the main board. Failure ta do so will send ya to isolation with no food for at least one night. I'll pair ya with an experienced miner who'll teach ya how ta dig and remain safe in the mine. Listen to yer partner. Work hard. Obey the rules. Don't cause problems."

Mr. Worth rattled off our names and our partner's. "Ean McClaud, Devon Montross" I shuddered. My partner was the man the group discussed yesterday. That couldn't be good.

Montross stood a head taller than most men with a frown as broad as his shoulders. Like many, he wore no shirt in the chilly air. As we stepped closer to the mine entrance, he spoke. "I'm accused of murdering my brother. Found him in bed with a young girl. Spent twelve years in Macquarie; been here six. No chance of a ticket of leave. I own the record for the most coal in a day, fifty buckets. That's all you need to know. Don't ask questions, don't cause no trouble, and don't slow me down."

I stared at the cat scars on his broad back. Were my scars as hideous?

Montross stopped, turned his tag, and waited as I turned mine. "Hurry! Follow me."

We entered a narrow shaft alongside a heavy sailcloth curtain. Devon pointed. "Stay on this side. They build a fire below to draw air into the shaft where we work. Otherwise, we'd only work a few minutes before running out of air and collapsing. Stand clear of all lanterns along the walls. If you bump them and they fall and light a lump of coal, they'll throw out tiny flames that can set you on fire."

Devon's explanations distracted me as we descended through the chilly, stagnant air. When I realized where we were, my panic grew. Pressure created a rapid thumping inside me. My lungs constricted as if about to burst. "Please, can we stop?" I said.

"Can't. Got too much coal to dig. If we stop, we'll lose valuable minutes." He kept moving.

"I can't breathe!"

Devon turned and grabbed my shoulder, shoving me against a dark wall of coal. "Keep moving. I'll not have a weepy, whiney partner. If you can't keep up or stop chattering, I'll leave you here permanently, if you get my meanin'." He rushed ahead before I could reply.

Fear of Devon took hold. I caught up to him and didn't lag, but my insides continued to quiver the further and deeper we moved into the ever-darkening mine.

I distracted myself with useless conversation in my head: keep up the pace, dig the coal, and survive. Keep up the pace, dig the coal, and survive. I can do this. What choice do I have?

We followed long trails of rails where trolleys the size of a small printing press waited to be filled, pushed to the entrance, and dumped. The air chilled and breathing became more difficult, but I watched Devon's back as I dragged my shackles over the uneven ground. He slowed occasionally but never stopped to let me rest.

"Stretch out your steps. You're slowing me down!"

I inhaled deeply and took longer steps, stumbling as I went.

The timbers, secured by cross beams, made tiny adjustments, reminding me of the creaking ship I'd arrived on from England. Instead of a salty crust on my skin from my days at sea, I'd now wear a coating of coal dust until I completed my time.

The timbers we passed around and beneath held up the roof and created shallow passageways where pairs of men worked, pulling down coal. Thunk, thunk, thunk, thunk. None turned to watch us when we passed.

In the distance a vibration rattled through the shaft. "Sir, what's that rumble?"

He kept moving as he spoke. "The steam engine. It pumps water out."

"Water?"

"The mine lies close to the sea. This vein heads below water level. Seepage creeps in around the coal seams. Stop asking questions and hurry up."

The trail of coal car rails ended. We passed dozens of sputtering lanterns. The darkness gobbled up the light before we reached the next one. The pressure inside my chest grew.

Devon slowed his pace as we turned into a small, low-ceiling area. He lit a lantern and handed me a short-handled shovel and a metal bucket large enough to carry several bushels of coal.

"Stand back. Watch how I swing my pick. When I build a pile of coal, shovel the lumps into a bucket, it's called a hod. Rush the hod to the first empty trolley on the rail. Within the week I'll expect you to pick coal and act as a runner. I've a record to protect, 'n I'll not allow you to ruin my numbers like my last mate did."

I stared at him, waiting to hear what happened to his last mate, but Devon had turned to work. He swung the pick with brute force. Thunk—thunk. The tip of the blade stuck in the coal. He stepped back a half pace and pulled. A bushel of coal tumbled from the wall. He repeated the motion again and again, then turned toward me. "What are you waiting for? Load up hods and run them to the trolleys. Hurry!"

I scrambled to the pile and scooped up chunks and lumps of coal as fast as possible. After I filled one hod, I turned toward the trolley.

"Stop!"

What did he want now?

Devon leaned on his pick. "Where are you going?"

"To the trolley."

He shook his head. "Not with a single, half full hod you're not! Load 'em to the top, then go."

I scrambled to fill a second hod and hurried to follow the lanterns down the tunnel toward the trolleys. My arms ached from the weight I carried; my body stooped forward as I rushed through the dim tunnel. When I reached the trolleys, I struggled to lift each hod high enough to dump it into a waiting trolley.

An arm grabbed my shoulder. "What are you doing?" asked a young boy no taller than a trolley and no more than twelve years of age.

"Dumping coal." What did he think I was doing?

He held a lump of chalk in his hand. "Your prison numbers?"

"I'm 57457."

In the dim light I read impatience on his face. "Your partner's number?"

"I don't know."

The young boy punched my shoulder. "What's his name?"

"Devon Montross."

He took a piece of chalk and scribbled 7139 and 57457 on the outside of the trolley container. "Next time, tell me your numbers before you dump the coal. Make certain you put your coal into your trolley. And bring full hods, not puny amounts. You're slowing Devon down, and he won't take kindly to a low count."

I leaned forward over my feet, trying to inhale a chest full of air.

The young boy nudged me. "Now, what do you think you're doing?"

"Resting."

"Devon will strangle you if you don't speed up. Run back before he comes looking for you."

I raced back to Devon. He'd pulled down a huge mound of coal in my absence. He ignored me while I filled pairs of containers and ran back to the trolleys.

By the end of our shift, I hunched over like an old man. My arms ached. The shoulder I damaged when I was tossed into the ship's hold felt strained. I feared it might dislocate again. That would surely ignite Devon's anger.

My ankles were chafed from dragging my shackles all day. I'd only tripped once and considered myself fortunate when I saw other shackled men fall, dumping their loads of coal. At least I had shoes. I couldn't imagine navigating the mine barefoot like some men did.

At the surface of the mine, I investigated my hands. Broken blisters covered my palms. They oozed with coal-colored liquid. Before lock-up I'd wash my hands and search for rags to protect the exposed fire that burned from each open blister in hopes they'd heal before I started work tomorrow.

Day had turned to night as I straightened and inhaled fresh air to ease my parched throat. As I started toward the barracks, a hand on my shoulder stopped me. It was Devon. What was it *this* time?

"Where do you think you're going?"

I pulled away. "To the barracks."

"Not so fast. You need to shift your tag to show you're out of the mine. Next, go to the counter to check our total for today." He pointed toward a man standing by the mine entrance. "Then find me and tell me our count."

After I shifted my tag, I joined a long line of men waiting to learn their totals. The line snaked forward. Each miner wore a ghostly layer of black dust except for where his scarf had covered his hair. Most wore no shirts, so their chests were sooty. I glanced down. My shirt was filthy. No wonder men worked shirtless. They could wash away their coat dust, but I'd be sleeping in mine. It appeared my choices were to freeze in the mine or sleep in coal dust. I shook my head; I'd gladly trade printer's ink for coal dust any day.

Fear filled my steps as I approached Devon. He leaned against the barracks wall with his arms crossed over his black, coal-dusted chest. "Total?"

"Forty-three."

Devon shook his head, and walked away.

One day tumbled into the next. I lived in darkness, above and below ground. By the end of the week, I sped up my carrying; Devon and I counted forty-five trolleys a day. Next week, I'd be expected to pick coal *and* fill hods before running them to the trolleys. What would Devon do if I failed?

Coal seeped into my pores like sea water seeped into the mine. My light brown hair turned black, my hands dusky gray, and my clothes resembled widow's weeds. Saturday afternoon, I received a ragged towel for my turn to bathe. The tub water had already turned black with coal dust from the earlier bathers. Attempts to remove my grime in the overused tepid water proved impossible, though its color lightened to gray.

Many men preferred to bathe in the icy stream near the barracks while washing their clothes. The rust-colored rocks on the bank wore a black sheen. No one noticed their coal-dusted nude bodies until the

Commandant appeared with visitors and yelled for everyone to return to their cells.

Sabbath meant no work in the mines and sitting in full view of each other. Some sang with gusto; others dozed. Most talked with one another during the sermon without punishment handed out for their inattention.

As always, we were reminded of our dark sins, our unworthiness to enter God's world, and our immediate descent into Hades. Nothing could be as dark as working in the mine. My chest tightened every time I entered; a hundred lanterns couldn't stave off that darkness. Could our descent, away from God in heaven, be any darker than our descent into the mine?

This first Sabbath afternoon I exercised, stretching out my arms and legs, using my cell wall to test their strength. Tomorrow, I'd begin picking and filling and carrying the coal like a pack animal to the trolleys. I hoped to avoid Devon's closed fists by starting out strong.

I arrived at the mine before Devon and paced to settle my nerves. Devon led me into the mine and pointed to a spot several feet from where he worked. "Start there."

The pick was so heavy I stumbled as I made my first swing. Twang. It bounced off the wall and flew back, sticking in the nearest beam. I wiggled it free, took a deep breath, and swung again. This time a trickle of coal dropped from the wall.

Taking another deep breath, I swung as hard as I could. This time chunks dropped to the floor of the mine, almost too scant to locate in the dimness.

Devon stopped working and stepped toward me. I waited for his fist to strike me. Instead, he grabbed the pick from my hands and pushed me aside. "Put your back into it. Watch."

He started the pick moving near the ground, raised it backward over his head and dropped the tip into the wall. A huge chunk dropped. "You must create speed and force if you're to break the coal loose."

With practice, my picking improved. Before our shift was half complete, my back muscles and my hands cramped. I wanted to stop and rest, but I worked through the pain and considered my trips dumping coal into the trolleys as rest breaks.

When we stopped to eat a potato pasty, my muscles pulsed with pain. Lifting my hand to my mouth took all my strength.

Devon ignored me until I gave him our day's tally. "Forty-seven."

He didn't strike out at me then or over the next week when our tally continued to fall short of his record. I wondered how long he'd tolerate my lagging.

At the end of the first three months, I imagined I could handle anything. But a month later, on a frigid June day, a giant gust of air swirled into the tunnels and extinguished every lantern. I stopped working and reached for the side of the tunnel to steady myself in the dark. Tools hit the ground and feet scurried. I froze in place. I gasped for breath and clutched my chest, feeling my heart pumping double fast.

Devon cursed under his breath.

I said nothing, not wanting him to hear the fear in my voice.

"McClaud? Answer me."

"I, ah, ah—"

"Damn. I'll go." Devon brushed past me, following the other rushing feet. Were they leaving? Should I follow? Surely, if I stayed behind, this shaft might become my tomb.

I stood waiting, trying to reason what had happened. Soon light reappeared in the shaft, bouncing off the walls as footsteps and voices moved closer.

I heard Devon's voice. "He's too green to know his backside from his face."

Miners around him laughed, probably at my expense.

He approached with a flaming lantern, stopped to light candles that had usable wax, replaced exhausted candles, and went back to work without comment or criticism. My breathing slowed to normal. I hoisted my pick and resumed working.

The rest of the afternoon, I hurried to repay Devon for fetching a new flame. I realized I'd need to learn to navigate the tunnel in the dark and be able to secure new candles and lanterns if I wanted to survive as his partner.

As we ended out shift, I tried to find my way with my eyes closed to understand how to move in the darkness, but all I did was slam into Devon and receive a shove for my efforts.

After dinner I approached Devon. I waited for him to turn my direction, but he didn't, so I stood in front of him, forcing him to acknowledge me. "Devon, I, ah, I—"

"Keep up the pace, Ean. We need to reach days of fifty-one." He pushed himself off the wall to join other miner groups scattered around the open area in front of our cells.

"Wait! I could work faster if I didn't wear these shackles. Can't you ask the foreman to remove them?"

"I've no power to change that," he said and turned back to his group.

I grabbed his arm. He stared down at me. The men nearby stopped talking to watch and listen to us.

"I have an idea."

He laughed. "I suppose you want me to run the coal to the trolley." He started walking away again.

I grabbed his arm again. He turned with his fists clenched.

I ducked as he swiped the air.

Conversations around us stopped.

"Wait! Listen. If we could get shoulder straps to lift the hods instead of using handles, I could carry more weight."

Devon looked around. Miners stood watching and waiting. "I'll think on that." He walked away without a backward glance.

Nearby miners looked at me and shook their heads. I imagined they were thinking tomorrow might be my last day alive—that Devon might exit the mine alone.

Dark days underground spun into weeks; weeks became a month. By July, the middle of winter, Devon had found sturdy ropes to use as shoulder straps. This allowed me to tote more weight on each trip to the trolleys. When the foreman saw our improving numbers, he warily removed my shackles. That freedom sent our totals to fifty-six trolleys the following week.

Now I was free to walk, but instead I focused on Devon and his bluster. He strutted around the grounds, accepting pats on the back and hand wrestling challenges as if he had thought up our system and made the record by himself.

Theo stood beside me. "Looks like you've gotten on Devon's good side."

"Lot of good it did me."

Theo grabbed my shoulder with vise-grip strength. "Best be grateful. His approval will stand you well in the future if the need arises."

After Theo left, I picked up handfuls of stones and threw them into the stream, pretending each one hit Devon square in the face. I didn't see how anything he said or did would help me in any way. All I noticed was how it bolstered his standings with the other miners.

22

Eight months of days and nights in darkness, through the rest of winter, spring, summer, and into fall, we pulled down coal. We hacked deeper into the walls of the mine, pushing farther and farther into small passages off shaft number seven.

I no longer experienced tightness in my chest in the dim light, but knowing an extinguished lantern could throw us into total darkness still sent shivers through me. With better food than the main penitentiary, I'd gained muscle enough to swing the pick with ease. I focused on my job, avoiding any incidents that would delay my release.

Rumors circulated that recent inspection of the mine showed the drop in the quality of the vein of coal. Closure of the mine rattled our nerves. When Colin Worth, the shift foreman, called us to the cave entrance before our shift, I noticed that many men fidgeted with restless energy.

Worth stood on the platform and waited for us to settle down. "The rumors are true. The vein is depleted; the mine will close soon. I've worked with Commandant Robbins to let us dig as long as the quality remains above sixty percent or for sixty days, whichever permits us to work the longest amount of time. We'll offer partial pardons for digging partners willing to work twelve hour shifts, seven days a week. Lifers won't earn freedom, but Robbins' promises to reduce their hard labor by the number of days they continue to work."

A voice behind me asked, "Why should we trust him?"

The assembled men shifted restlessly and grumbled approval of the question.

Worth crossed his arms and scowled. "Robbins gave his word. He wants as much coal as we can pull out. Work hard now, and we'll keep it open. Refuse and you'll begin hard labor now."

"And if we work? How much credit do the rest of us earn?" a short man shouted. Men growled and nodded.

Worth held up his hand for quiet. "We'll reduce your time served by one quarter."

Another voice shouted, "Why not half?"

Foreman Worth looked out over the miners. "You're prisoners. Take what's offered, or we'll march you back to Port Arthur. You've got four days to decide."

"How can we trust you to record our totals and grant partial pardons?"

Worth's eyes narrowed. "I'll post the numbers on the tally board. Work teams will not change; you must sign up together. Each man, including the pickers, will receive one fourth credit for their efforts." He jumped down, retreated to the shift shed, and slammed the door closed behind him.

Over the following days, we continued our daily shifts. I watched Devon, deciding if I should ask him if he'd signed up. I hitched up my courage and approached him as he stood by the rain barrel, watching a group of men arm wrestle.

"Did you sign us up?" I asked.

His brow furrowed. "Do you take me for a fool, Ean? Of course I did. Don't you want to get out of here as quickly as possible?"

"Yes, but—"

Devon's eyes narrowed. "We'll bring down coal from the stalls. We'll have runners or pickers to load our hods and carry them to the trolleys so we can continue to dig. When coal tests come back as inferior, we'll mark those stalls with a painted red 'x' and haul 'em down."

"Sounds dangerous."

Devon smirked. "All mining is dangerous, Ean. When we yank down the pillars or they become unsteady, the only warning will be creaking sounds followed by a rumble. When you hear that, run. Don't stop for even one second. Understand?"

I nodded.

"After the dust settles, we'll return, load as much coal as possible, then back out."

I thought about the offer of a partial pardon. It meant I'd finish my time several months or maybe a year early. I renewed my energy, thinking about how soon I might be allowed to send and receive mail and, better yet, even be freed. Maudie Claire deserved my first letter. Hopefully, her family would write back.

Our expanded shifts turned our lives into an unending cycle of work and sleep. Devon and I increased our pace, averaging seventy-two trolleys a day, pushing our picker to his limit.

As weeks became months and December's summer heat arrived, the foreman's chart showed that I'd shortened my sentence by more than one year. If we kept our count high and the mine stayed open, I'd be free very soon—if I could keep up with Devon.

But each day, my strength faded. It took all my effort to lift a spoon to my mouth to eat before I dropped into bed. Even monster-strong Devon showed fatigue from the arduous pace.

❖

A strange groaning and sliding sound ricocheted through the stall as I stuck my pick into a large chunk of coal. I stopped, lifted my head, and listened. The space around me vibrated.

Devon dropped his pick and grabbed my shoulder. "Cave in!"

The wooden post beside me bent from the weight of the hill above and from our thrusts into the coal. Lantern light vanished. I coughed, choking on coal dust, as Devon dragged me through the darkness.

Suddenly, I tripped on a small pile of coal and fell hard, jolting my head back as though hit by a man's fist.

Before I lifted myself from the floor of the tunnel, timbers and coal dropped around me. I covered my head as I heard Devon's retreating voice yell, "Run!"

I breathed in my tiny pocket of air I'd trapped as more timbers fell.

My left leg lay pinned beneath a pile of coal. Luckily, my head and shoulders remained free of coal and timbers. I strained beneath the weight of timbers and coal to free myself.

Pain splintered through me as I staggered to my feet and made my way along the tunnel, dragging my injured leg.

Timbers groaned and shifted like ancient trees in a storm as I stumbled out of the small passage. I traced my path forward, using a wall as my guide. I coughed and inhaled coal dust. I blew out long breaths, trying to expel the thick film coating my mouth and lungs.

Coal continued to slough off and rain down like a torrential hail storm. Angry giant timbers moaned. One timber knocked me down, allowing the coal it held back to pour over me.

I wrapped my arms around my head to make an air pocket and arched my back against the pressure, coughing and choking. Though the blackness and pressure frightened me, I focused on slowing my breathing, waiting for rescue or for the coal to bury me for eternity.

The roaring river of coal diminished to a trickle. Could I withstand the pressure and keep breathing, or would my life end in this shaft? I closed my eyes and waited.

Blackness. Shifting coal. Distant moans and cries for help. Each moment that passed lessened my chance to survive. I allowed myself to doze.

Minutes passed like hours, but then—

Scrape. Scrape. Scrape.

"Hello? Hello? Anyone? Call out if you can hear us."

Few voices responded. I coughed and called out, "Here. Buried." My voice cracked as I struggled to inhale. "Here."

"Hang on. Keep talking to us. Call out which stalls."

Another voice called, "Last on left—Beside last pull down—Hurry."

"Last—on—right."

"Are others with you?"

"Don't know," I said, remembering shouts had stopped long ago.

The digging and scraping continued as I slipped in and out of consciousness. When a whoosh of fresh air arrived, I cried out, "Here!"

The digging slowed. A faint light penetrated the blackness. I heard clawing and voices approaching. Hands grabbed at me, lifting me from my heavy blanket of coal. I screamed as they dragged me out of the tunnel and placed me on a stretcher.

I awoke in pain but inhaling fresh air in a room filled with light. Lanterns hung around me. I lay flat on my back as a man washed my leg, then poked and prodded.

"Ah!" I screamed as he yanked on my leg.

"Had to be done. Yer bone was stickin' out through your skin, but we can save yer leg."

What? Save my leg? How bad was my injury? Would I walk again?

He patted my shoulder and wiped the sweat from my forehead. "You'll be good as new after yer bones mend."

He covered my lower leg with handfuls of minty-smelling leaves. Then he placed thin boards on either side and wrapped white rags from my shin to the bottom of my foot. "Keep the wound clean. Add the leaves to keep infection from settin' in."

The doctor's casual directness startled me. Did he mean I could lose my leg, or was he trying to scare me? And what did he mean about the minty leaves?

Before I could ask any questions, he left. His assistant helped me off the table and directed two exiles to carry me to my cell. Wordlessly, they covered me with a thin blanket and hurried away.

I lay on my cot, focusing on any small thing to ignore the throbbing in my leg. I revisited the cave-in, the darkness, and the pain as I drifted into and out of sleep.

Hours passed. All able-bodied miners rushed through the settlement in a steady stream, carrying injured and dead miners. Their voices remained hushed, or maybe I imagined the world around me. And what of Devon?

When I eventually drifted off to sleep, I entered into a dark world, where red-eyed people piled on top of me and threw coal snowballs at me. I heard their laughter, or was it miners outside my cell. I felt the weight of the coal bearing down on my body, pushing air from my lungs. I dreamt I stretched my hand up through the coal but couldn't find a way to escape. I'd awaken gasping and in a cold sweat, believing I'd keep these nightmares forever.

Theo brought food but hurried away, saying, "Glad ya made it out. Can't stop. I'm feedin' all the injured men. Keeps me goin' day 'n night."

Within four days word spread. The mine would reopen. Work schedules would be cut back to normal shifts as the condition of the mine was still being explored. Coal remained more important than miner safety.

❖

One dusk as crews returned from the mine, a familiar voice called in, "Ean, you mendin'?"

I lifted my head and shoulders from the bunk. Devon stood outside my window.

"I'll be fine. Were you injured? Did they find James and Martin?"

He leaned in, placing his elbow on the sill. "It doesn't look good for the rest of the men in our section. Been too many days. Coal must've crushed them." Devon hesitated, then walked away.

I was relieved to see Devon alive; his shoves had propelled me forward, saving me from certain death. In my old life, I'd have found a way to repay him. Here? I had more than enough time to think on it.

Theo stopped by that afternoon. "I hear you need a crutch."

"I do. Know anyone who'll make one for me?"

Theo returned with a long branch with a split end like a slingshot. He handed it to me. "Saw this branch in the woods. Got permission to cut it down and whittle the center where yer arm rests. Ask around ta see if you c'n git rags or old shirts to pad the crotch of the branch."

"I will. Thanks, Theo. This is—I appreciate your help. How might I repay you?"

"Nothin' needed. Jest git better."

❖

For a week of days into the next year, the doctor redressed my leg with fresh mint leaves and changed the bandages. On his final visit, he shared what he knew. "Follow your nose 'n you'll find the leaves by the river. Use them the way I've done. Wash the bandages every couple days."

"When can I go back to work?"

"Not certain you can. You've got one good leg and a crutch. Count yourself luckier than many."

The next day Worth, the shift foreman, came into my cell. "Doc says you'll be good as new, but I can't allow you back in the mine with a broken leg. I'll find a job you can do with your leg in that splint."

I grimaced and pushed myself to sit against the cell wall. "Do you remember that I read and write?"

"Yes."

He hesitated and shook his head. "Mine's closing soon. Be grateful they found ya and for whatever job ya might git."

The mine was a confusing and sad place. To date I'd earned a year off my sentence, leaving only a few months left to serve. Now if I couldn't work here what would happen to me? Port Arthur demanded hard labor. Where could I work?

That evening during meal hour, Theo arrived with mint leaves. "Here's yer stinky leaves, lad. Got laughed at for smellin' like a cup of lady's tea."

"Thanks, Theo." I took the leaves, shredded them with my hands, and mixed them in my food bowl with water to make a poultice.

"Them leaves work?" he asked.

"I guess. The redness is fading." I removed the old bandage, placed the poultice over the places where my bone had broken through the skin, and rewrapped my leg. "Thanks for bringing them, Theo."

He patted my shoulder. "I'll git more in a couple of days."

❖

Daily, the miners slowed at my doorway and looked in but never stopped to talk. I only got any news when they leaned against the wall outside my doorway.

"Saw 'em bring out three bodies. Didn't have a chance in that ole shaft."

"Heared they plan ta get the trolleys back inside. For sure, we ain't gettin' overtime."

"And them visitors jest keep showin' up and shakin' their heads. They think they know so much. Let 'em try to work down there. We'd see what they think then!"

"Cheap labor using exiles for diggin' and shippin' barges to New South Wales. Heared they're thinkin' of closin' the whole penitentiary."

"You always hear things, even when no one's talking."

The miners began to argue with each other as they moved on.

After a several crashes and wobbly attempts, I maneuvered the crutch well enough to hobble to the river to gather leaves. Two feet ahead in the marshy land, I spotted the mint bushes.

I edged into the marsh. My crutch sank into the soggy shore where men were washing clothes and bathing in the icy stream. As I struggled to free the crutch from the mud, laughter covered my back. I couldn't turn to glare down their comments, so I wriggled and twisted, attempting to back out of the muck.

Two men approached. I cowered, waiting for them to toss me further into the mud or worse. Behind them a dozen men laughed and hooted. I braced myself for the worst. But the two men lifted me out and settled me on solid ground. "What da ya need?" one asked.

I pointed to the bright green bushes. "Doc says to put the leaves on my leg."

They sloshed through the mud and tore off handfuls. "This enough?"

"Yes, much obliged." I started to hobble away. That's when I heard a miner say, "He smells like witch tea."

Another laughed. "We could use a witch to replace Robbins. Can't take much more of this place. Soon, I'll forget how to swing a pick and rush around in coal dust."

"Eh. You didn't know how to pick anyway," another said as their scuffle began and guards stepped in to break the men apart.

❖

Days, I hobbled outside; eyes followed my progress. Men who had avoided me in the past now dipped a nod. I'd heard that many believed cave-in survivors possessed special powers to be acknowledged in hope their powers of survival would rub off to protect others as they stepped back into the mine.

On my latest excursion, I searched out Devon. Because it was a humid summer day, many miners stayed inside their cells. Devon stood with a small group of men, tossing rocks into the empty rain barrel. He nodded as I approached.

I extended my hand to him. "Devon, thank you for rescuing me. Thank the others as well."

He tossed his head to one side in a nod. I saw the beginning of a smile before he looked away.

"What's the word on the mine?"

He shrugged. "Not good, Ean."

Nothing remained to be said, so I hobbled off.

❖

One week later, Worth, the foreman, called everyone to the main entrance. "We think the mine will stay open about two months' time. If the vein runs lean or there's another cave-in, that may change. We'll resume long shifts today. I'll reassign teams with missing partners."

Uncertainty overshadowed each shift. Day after day, I waited to be assigned a job. I was excited when Worth finally approached.

"While your leg heals, you'll work outside the entrance to the mine. Stand beside the work table, mark trolley tallies, collect old candles, and pass out new. Clean lanterns and check equipment."

"Will I earn time off my sentence?" I asked.

Worth stared at me. "You ain't picking or hauling or risking your life. Be grateful you're alive. Now git to work."

His explosive answer shocked me. I'd need to keep my head down. 'Twas not a time to anger the foreman.

My odd jobs required no reading or writing, leaving me with time enough to watch supervisors. They'd paw through chunks of coal from trolleys and take samples away. Finding dirt was a sure sign the vein was depleting, meaning future credit for early release depleted as well.

After the shifts changed, I posted the days' totals and read them out to each two-man team. A small satisfaction slipped over me when Devon's new partner failed to achieve any record-breaking totals. I imagined Devon's frustration and knew I'd helped him accomplish something special in the mine when we broke all tally records.

Every rumble of a trolley sliding back into the mine sent a shiver down my spine, causing me to relive the sound of thundering tons of coal falling around me. Most nights, a sooty terror filled my sleep. Cave-in after cave-in poured over me. I'd sit up screaming that I couldn't breathe.

Many nights, a guard entered my cell and rousted me. "Wake up. You're disturbing the others."

Those nights I'd stay awake, trying to picture Maudie Claire and Robert, the farm, anything that reminded me of happier times. Lately, the world of Maudie and her farm dimmed in much the same way the images of Fiona and Langstone and the printer faded. Had I imagined my earlier life? Was I a thief who'd stolen from Lord and Lady Colridge? Nothing made sense any more.

When Parkerson, the clark, earned his release the end of the month, I replaced him, selling the last coal through Port Arthur. He'd been a dishonored military officer who'd served as a guard at Point Puer before he became an inmate.

The day before he left, I asked him, "Do you know Edward Maddox, Barty Anders, Tom Marston, or Charley Stern?"

He eyed me as though I held a weapon. "I ain't no 'memberin' book." He handed me the tally log, showed me the procedure, then headed back to Port Arthur for his release.

Within a few days, I rechecked Parkerson's log books and discovered numerous errors. Satisfied with my findings, I mentioned them to Worth. Much to my surprise, he nodded and suggested I leave things as they appeared. I soon realized the two men were selling unrecorded coal by the dray load to a former inmate, who resold it to settlers near Launceston. And they said I was a thief.

One Sabbath afternoon as I stood by the stream, I heard my name called. Theo hurried over holding a crumpled paper. "It's a letter, for ya."

I took the paper and turned it over in my hands. It had been mailed six months ago from England, sent to Port Arthur and forwarded here.

My hands shook as I opened it. Theo stood next to me, anxious to hear my news. The clergy from Langstone wrote:

> Received your letters. Fiona's gone. Influenza took many, including Lord and Lady Colridge.
> God forgive your sins.

Theo waited, his eyes scanning my face while I soaked up the information. Fiona's gone? Had she died or left Langstone? And Lady Colridge, dead? Only her word could clear my name if I returned to Langstone.

Sadness drove through me like a knife. I reread the letter again and again, hoping and wishing what I read would change for the better with each reading. Finally, I crumbled the letter into a ball and threw it into the stream. It floated away like a dead leaf.

Theo cleared his throat and stood looking at me.

"No good news, Theo. I've no reason to return to England. The mistress of the manor house died, so I can no longer prove my innocence."

Theo reached up and patted my shoulder. "All them that matter know the truth already." He stayed next to me as we watched the latest arguments among inmates fester into fights.

When my shift ended the next morning, I asked permission to write a letter. I received one sheet of paper and considered my next decision. 'Twas not proper to write Maudie Claire because we weren't betrothed and because she couldn't read. But I could write to the O'Carroll farm.

> To Patrick and Galen O'Carroll
> Near Bicheno settlement, Tasmania
>
> Sirs, I am sorry for the grief I have placed on you. I expect to be freed soon and hope you will allow me to visit your family.
>
> Ean McClaud.

A problem arose: I had no money to send the letter north. But Theo gave me an idea as we stood by the rain barrel. He jabbed me in the ribs. "Watch that young guard on the end. He's 'bout to get a strippin' down."

Sure enough, as the guards changed duties, their lieutenant began an inspection. He stopped at the last man. "Sir, how many times do you think I'll remind you to polish your buttons and shine your boots?"

The young man stiffened his jaw and pulled back his chin. "Not many more, sir."

"Less than that. You disgrace this unit by your slovenly appearance."

"Yes, sir." The young guard stood stiffly at attention long after the lieutenant passed.

I asked Theo, "How did you know that would happen?"

He chuckled. "Been goin' on for weeks. There's yer money for postage. Drinks from his flask all day when he's on duty. He's much more interested in what goes down his gullet than in becomin' an officer. Pro'bly conscripted here."

I watched him set down his pack and bend down to brush off his boots. When he thought no one was looking, he pulled out his flask, took a swig, and returned it to his pack.

As he turned my way, I raised and waved my hand. "I'd be glad to help you. Sir, I'm an excellent boot cleaner."

"Help me? What makes you think I need help?" He crossed his arms and squinted.

"I overheard the mention that your boots needed polishing."

"And what do you want in exchange: my rum, I suppose?"

"No, sir. I want postage to send this letter north."

The young man shifted from foot to foot and rocked about, searching for an answer. He looked me over, eyed the crutch, and nodded. "All right, but all you'll get is postage, no rum and no meat."

"That's all I want, sir."

While I stood by my cell door, he left to gather up his boot black and a rag. He returned looking bleary-eyed. "I expect my boots done daily, without fail."

"Yes, sir, every day."

"And you will have them ready for me early each morning?"

"Yes, sir. I'll leave them inside my cell door. Place the next pair there for me to clean, sir."

With my first letter mailed, I impatiently waited for a reply. None came until the end of the following month. As I left the office, a soldier approached. "McClaud?"

I turned, ready for whatever punishment I'd earned.

"Letter."

Happiness slid through my body like a cool autumn breeze. "Thank you," I said as the letter touched my hand. I sat on the bottom step of the office and opened it, wondering if I'd soon feel happiness or disappointment.

> *Ean,*
> *We received your letter. All is well here. We harbor*
> *no ill thoughts toward you. You are welcome upon your*
> *release. M.C. sends greetings.*
> *Galen O'Carroll*

My heart raced. I read and reread the letter: 'We harbor no ill thoughts', 'You are welcome', and, the uplifting sentence, 'M.C. sends greetings.' I polished more boots and wrote another letter:

Galen,

I'm recovering from the coal mine cave in.
My left leg was broken. My time ends soon. I
look forward to seeing the farm and your family
once again.

   Ean McClaud

As March ended the news of the mine's closing caused a flurry of activity around Plunkett Point. Miners shoved empty coal cars into mine shafts and boarded up the office. Soldiers packed supplies and loaded their gear onto the trams that ran to Port Arthur. Worth gathered us in the common area.

"In two days' time, you'll be taken to Port Arthur for reassignment. Your hours earned toward a pardon have been forwarded. The Governor promises to honor them."

Every man nodded. The heavy weight of my years in Port Arthur lightened. Soon I'd be released. Freedom would arrive as surely as an approaching sunrise.

The last evening, I found Theo and Devon to say goodbye before we marched back to Port Arthur in the morning.

Theo patted my arm. "Ean, I wish ya luck."

"Thanks, Theo. Any news about your future?"

His brow furrowed. "Only what Worth mentioned earlier."

Devon tossed a handful of rocks into the barrel and watched the ripples spread across the surface. "Theo and I remain prisoners forever, Ean. There's no end for us; but you get out, you stay out!"

I reached my hand forward toward Devon. "I will. I'm sorry you'll not be freed."

Devon grabbed my shoulder and squeezed. "Don't ever forget."

How could he imagine I'd forget this place or him? "I promise. And I'll remember both of you and how you helped me. I wish I could help you."

"You can. Tell everyone about this horrid place. Someday, they'll close it down or learn to treat us like humans."

I entered my cell for the last night. Since the soldiers emptied one barracks, our barracks served as two-man cells.

The man with me was a tall, brutish fellow. I didn't know his name, but that changed in one horrific instance.

23

I woke before dawn the following morning, lying on the floor. My head ached. Blood dripped from my fingers. I gasped. A thin metal shaft lay near me; my new bunkmate lay on the floor, wide-eyed and dead.

"Guard! Help!" I scooted away from the body, dragging my heels through the red pool that spread across the floor. "Help!"

A handful of trustee exiles crowded the doorway. Guards pushed through. Two rushed me, grabbed my arms, and dragged me out of the cell. They threw me to the ground and shackled me face down in the mud.

"Call Robbins. Get this man in the choky. Now!"

Within seconds, they locked me in the mine gaol, a room below the barracks. I lay on the packed earth, unable to move. My broken leg throbbed in tandem with my head. I listened to the commotion and the shouting above me in the yard.

"Everyone. Back in your cells! Now! Shackle any man who resists."

I remembered getting into a shoving match with the burly man, but I gave as good as I got in the small space. Questions swirled around me like an angry wind off the ocean. Did his shove create the knot on the back of my head? How did someone get inside the locked door? Why did someone want him dead, or did they intend to kill me?

I recall my burly cellmate braiding a rope and swinging it menacingly toward me. Was that the rope I saw pulled taut around his neck as he lay dead on the floor?

In the late afternoon, I awoke when I heard a key in the gaol door. "You there, McClaud! Get up!" Commandant Robbins stood in my cell.

"I can't sir. My leg's broken. I—"

"Not as broken as it will be if the exiles get hold of you. Maybe we should let them punish you."

I struggled to my feet and hopped to lean against the wall. "I don't know what happened, sir. I woke up with—"

"No one cares how you woke. Padriac Jarvis is dead, and you're headed for Port Arthur's Tyburn Fair."

"But, I didn't kill him! I—"

He reached out and slapped my face so hard I dropped to the floor. "Stay down, McClaud. Stay down. Murder is a capital offense. Judge returns next spring to hold court. 'Til then, you'll be held in isolation within the silent prison."

Fear and shock crushed me like a trolley of coal. I grabbed my broken leg to brace it should he decide to kick me before he stormed from my cell. Six more months? I'd not have a chance to tell my story until next September, and then they'd most likely hang me.

In two days' time, I was taken to clark Glevins' office double shackled and cuffed, as if I'd be able to escape in my current condition. As Glevins entered, they held me upright against the wall.

"Ah, the bolter returns." He scanned my papers and glared at me. "Six months will give you time to repent before you're hanged. And to think I trusted you."

If time taught me anything, it taught me to keep my mouth closed. No amount of arguing for my innocence mattered.

His lips twisted into a snarl. "I assume you remember the rules."

I nodded. A bag went over my head before the soldiers dragged me out the door and up the hill. I moaned as my injured leg throbbed; they laughed. Inside the prison they dropped me in a windowless cell and locked the door.

When I pulled off the bag, it took a minute to adjust to the blackness of solitary. I reached around the small cell but found no crutch or blanket or bench. My dark days from my earlier imprisonment flooded back. I'd lost everything yet again. The trial lay six months hence. What chance did I have for justice? Who'd speak for me?

Life in isolation meant I returned to live in darkness. Days and nights, sunshine and storms, weeks and months held no meaning. Guards hauled me outside to the cage once a week, but I attended no Divine Service. My cell wasn't cleaned and I received no fresh clothes. I existed in my space only a hair's breadth better than the snails I brushed against when I entertained myself by running my hands along the walls.

Mornings, I exercised but had no need to force myself to gain strength. My leg continued to mend, but my ankle twisted inward, forcing me to use my heel to balance my weight. I staggered like a drunken beggar.

Days swirled into weeks, dragging me closer to my trial. I slept and waited with no reason to track time. Carving slashes in my arm required hope; none existed.

For weeks no person came to hear my story. When he did come, I might as well have spoken a fairy tale to the damp walls.

My cell door opened, and a small, chubby man entered. A soldier brought in a three-legged stool and handed him a candle. I shielded my eyes from the brightness of the candle. He covered his nose with a handkerchief and looked about.

"Yes. Uh, uh, um let's get started. Is your name Ean McClaud?"

"Yes."

"Were you found in a locked room with Padriac Jarvis?"

"Who?"

"The dead man, Padriac Jarvis."

"We were in the same cell, but I didn't kill him."

"Of course. Yes, but how do you explain his death?"

"I can't. We had a scuffle and—"

"About?"

"He wanted my bunk. I said no."

"Then what happened?"

"He hit me. The next thing I remember was waking up and—"

He stopped writing, stood, dusted off his breeches and yelled for the guard. In a few seconds' time, he left without comment.

For the rest of the day, I replayed what had happened with Padriac in the locked cell. Soldiers oversaw the cleaning out and closing of the second barracks. Each exile carried his bedroll into one of our cells to sleep the last night before Point Plunkett closed forever.

After dinner they locked the door. My bunkmate stood braiding a rope and grumbling. "Don't see why I'm sharing a space with the likes of you. You're that dumb root-grubbing Irishman who got hisself rescued from the mine collapse. Should've been you dead, not my mate, Martin. Now he was a true man."

I ignored his remark but couldn't erase the anger that swelled inside me. I lay down on my bunk, turned to the wall and closed my eyes to avoid him.

That's when he grabbed my shoulder and squeezed. "Don't turn away. I'm not done talking to you."

I pulled from his grasp.

He yanked me off my bunk. I landed on the floor with my broken leg twisted under me. I panted through the pain, not willing to give him the satisfaction of hearing me cry out.

He laughed and hopped onto my bunk. "Think I'll sleep here. You c'n sleep on the floor."

I remember scooting to the wall to pull myself to standing. His hand grabbed my shoulder again. I spun around just as his fist slammed into my chin. The next thing I knew, it was dawn and he lay dead on the floor.

Reason said I killed him, but I was innocent. The killer must have received help from a guard or he was a guard. Padriac said his friend Martin died in the mine collapse, and for some reason he blamed me. I didn't know the man. I could make no sense of anything that happened.

The day of my trial, a guard entered and handed me clean clothes and a bucket of water. "Get cleaned up. Trial begins in one hour's time."

I washed, changed clothes, and waited. The guard returned and handed me my crutch. "Sir, may I ask the month?"

"September. Why does it matter? You'll soon be hanged." He put a bag over my head and guided me down the corridor. We entered a space with a smooth floor; my crutch slid. I caught myself before I fell.

The soldier removed the bag covering my head.

I stood in a sparsely furnished room the size of Master John's print shop. A raised platform covered one end, where a judge in a black robe and a white wig watched me. A clark sat at a small desk near the judge, ready with a pen and paper. Two tables faced the judge. My visitor sat at one table, a stranger sat at the other. Except for two soldiers guarding the door, no other people were present.

A defendant's box, the dock, stood to the right of the judge. I hobbled into the box and was told to remain standing. My shackles were still attached, but my crutch taken away.

The judge called the trial to order.

The clark read the charges. "This man," he pointed to me, "Ean Mc-Claud, is accused of murdering Padriac Jarvis on the twenty-ninth day of March, in the year of our Lord, 1854."

The man who'd come to my cell rose. "Ean McClaud is present, Your Lordship." He sat down.

The man at the second table rose. "Adam Targill, magistrate for Governor Smarthe, Your Lordship. The government has conclusive evidence that Ean McClaud murdered Padriac Jarvis. The murdered man was strangled and stabbed. McClaud's hands were covered with blood. The blade used to stab the victim lay beside him. The lock on the cell showed no sign of tampering; it had to be unlocked by the guard who investigated the crime." He sat down.

My representative spoke. "We have no witnesses to refute the claims of the government." He sat down.

I gawked open-mouthed at him. Was that all he planned to say? I grabbed the wooden half walls of the dock to hold myself upright.

The judge turned to me. "Do you have anything to say?"

I swallowed hard. "Yes, sir. I did have a fight with Padriac, but he hit me and knocked me out. I walk with a crutch, sir. How could I kill a man twice my size?"

The judge looked at the men at both tables. "Anything more to add?"

"No, sir," answered both men.

The judge cleared his throat. "Ean McClaud, this court finds you guilty of murder. You are sentenced to hang on the sixteenth of November,

1854, by order of myself, Judge Garfield, signed the twenty-seventh of September, in the year of our Lord, 1854."

My knees gave way. I almost fainted.

My lawyer shuffled his papers into a valise and turned to me. "Not much else he could do. You were in a locked room."

"But I'm innocent!"

He shrugged. "You have a six-week reprieve. No hangings are scheduled until The Friends complete their visit." He signaled the guards forward.

"Friends?"

"The Quakers. They're here to investigate penitentiary conditions. Got patches of flowers planted in the assembly area 'cuz of them."

I shook my head. Flowers instead of a flogging platform? Who did they think they fooled?

"They'll rebuilt the scaffolding once those folks leave." He turned and left the room.

Before I had time to think, soldiers stepped forward, grabbed me, and returned me to my pitch-black cell.

I crumpled on the damp floor. Darkness covered my cell and my life.

Days would brightened as spring settled over Port Arthur. Summer heat would arrive, but I'd neither see nor feel those seasons.

My last days blurred into a foggy mist. A hollowness chilled every part of my body. I couldn't get warm. I ate but tasted nothing, moved but didn't feel the floor, slept but woke exhausted.

No person I valued knew I'd soon be hanged; no one would weep over my death. I wept realizing I'd never again feel the embrace of loving, caring arms.

24

Another wakening time. Another day or night to wonder if I'd soon be taken to the scaffold. If I'd been landed gentry, I could buy my freedom, even from the gallows. Commoners paid for their errors, real or imagined, and few noticed or remembered their sacrifice.

It was strange how my life whirled out of control. One small lie about my stealing a silk handkerchief changed me from an innocent to a convict, from being a rule follower to breaking any rule that stood in my path to freedom. I could only hope those I disappointed would forgive me.

When my cell door opened, a numbness held me in place. The guard placed a bag over my head, bound my hands, and shackled me. I quivered as I limped beside his stony silence; the only sound was the swish of my injured foot dragging through the straw-strewn hallway.

We stopped. The soldier removed the bag. I blinked. We stood at the entrance to the silent prison. The bright spring sunlight made it difficult to keep my eyes open. I straightened, preparing to meet the end of my life.

The soldier shoved me forward. "Hurry along now. Can't keep the gov'ner waitin'."

We descended the hill toward the harbor. November's sunlight painted the penitentiary walls rosy red. Tall grasses rustled. I trembled and tripped over my own feet. The soldier grabbed me and gruffly said, "Slow down."

I inhaled slowly, searching for one small thread of courage. Ma would expect her favorite son to conduct himself with respect, even on his way to the gallows.

I limped on, repeating the poem Maudie Claire had given me, stopping on the words, 'I rant against the coming of my death.'

That wasn't true. I no longer ranted. I'd done what I could to live my life respectably. I planned to die the same way.

We reached the gallows. I saw and smelled the new lumber used to make the steps, the platform, and the scaffolding. Nearby, exiles worked their regular tasks. None gathered to witness my execution. I stopped.

The soldier shoved me forward. "Keep movin'!"

I limped on. We passed the building where Barty made the special crate, passed the docks and the pillory, and continued up the hill. We entered the building where I'd worked in the clark's office, where I'd been sentenced earlier. At the clark's door, the soldier knocked.

"Enter," said a voice from inside the office.

I exhaled in relief. A different man had spoken. I'd not be forced to face Glevins today.

My shackles clunked across the polished wooden floor. I stood as upright as possible before the clark's desk. The man faced away from me. His thin body stood ramrod straight; he squared his shoulders like a young man. For a long moment, he ignored us.

The soldier called out to him. "Sir?"

The man turned.

I gasped. Edward!

The last time I'd seen him was a lifetime ago when we'd arrived on the prison ship. Soldiers had culled him away from Charley and me and taken him to Point Puer.

He faced the soldier. "Wait in the hallway."

"Yes, sir." The soldier exited.

Edward's face had lengthened; his chin sported a well-trimmed brown goatee. "Hello, Ean."

"Edward." My mind raced for what to say next.

"Call me Mister Maddox." His voice had dropped to a man's timbre. "I'm working here until a new clark arrives."

Seeing him increased my humiliation. A long-ago friend might be the one to speak the final words that sentenced me to death.

"Why was I brought here?"

Edward's face showed lack of interest in me; his body shared something different. "Smarthe requires a word with you. He's busy with Port Arthur business just now."

"You look well, Mr. Maddox. Tell me about you while we wait."

He snorted. "There's nothing to tell. Is there something else you'd like to discuss?"

"Do you know of the fate of my friends?"

Edward returned to his desk. "Your friends' names?"

"Charley Stern, you remember him, the thief we spent time with on the ship. Also, two convicts: Barty—no, uh, Bartlett Anders and Tom Marsdale, lifers."

Edward fingered through prisoner ledgers stored near the desk. He looked up. "Charley received his ticket of leave six months ago. Bartlett is dead, as is Tom."

A heaviness drew me down. I grabbed the edge of the desk. Both Tom and Barty dead. I'd be joining them soon. "What happened to them?"

He reopened their files and skimmed the information. "Tom died in an accident in the quarry. Bartlett died in his sleep." He closed the files. "Anything else, Ean?"

"What about you, Edward, ah, Mr. Maddox?"

"I don't want to discuss me."

He glared at me before he turned toward the window. He rocked back and forth a few times, then turned back toward me. "I've worked hard and done unsavory things to get this job, the one you threw away."

I lowered my gaze to the shiny surface of the desk that separated us. Edward stepped behind me. I cringed, expecting a blow for my insolence, but he closed the door to the hallway and returned to stand behind the desk. "What do you want to know?"

He'd changed. His voice held a sharp edge; he no longer trembled or cowered as he'd done on the ship. The hardness that spread across his face surprised me. "How were you treated at Point Puer?"

He clenched his teeth, then relaxed his jaw and squared his shoulders. "I survived until my sixteenth birthday. They couldn't wait to throw me into the penitentiary with murderers and thieves. But I stayed strong. I'm not the student of deceit like you've become."

His angry tone slapped against my face, but I withheld comment.

"I've worked long hours with Master Glevins to convince him I'm dependable. Now, my future is assured with a magistrate in Hobart Town or Launceston within the hour, thanks to the new Lieutenant Governor."

"I'm glad for you, Edward, ah, Mr. Maddox. Thank you for telling me about my friends."

He nodded and stepped to the door to recall the soldiers waiting in the hall. At that same moment, a Port Arthur officer entered and handed Edward a note.

"I see." he said. "Tell him I'll handle this. Dismissed." The officer turned and left.

"Ean McClaud," Edward said.

I straightened, dreading the finality of my conviction.

"There's a change in plans. Lieutenant Governor Smarthe is unable to speak with you today. You're to return tomorrow for sentencing."

I watched Edward's face for a word of encouragement or a flicker of remembrance about our friendship that started on the long voyage to Port Arthur. He didn't move or speak again. Our connection had shattered like glass tossed into a dust bin.

Back in my cell, I paced and reexamined my life one last time. Hangings in Port Arthur began after I'd escaped. Perhaps the new commandant didn't mind the loss of free laborers; he must have enough gathered here to fulfill his tasks without further transports arriving from England. Would the threat of hanging have deterred me from my escape more than three years ago? I doubted it.

The hours passed slowly. My second walk to the clark's office once again passed the gallows. Once again, no convicts stood waiting to watch the spectacle of my hanging.

I entered a different office. The soldier accompanying me snapped to attention as the Lieutenant Governor entered. Smarthe paid him no attention as he moved behind his desk. He took a long time scanning my paperwork, giving me time to observe his assistant.

The man reminded me of a nervous mouse with long legs. He wore small, wire-rimmed glasses on the end of his twitching nose. He hovered and fidgeted over the papers on Smarthe's desk. He'd not last a day in the penitentiary, the mine, or any other place outside the protection of this office.

Smarthe motioned to his assistant. "That will be all, Thompson."

The man backed away to the corner.

Lieutenant Governor Smarthe stood, opened a document, and cleared his throat. I straightened for the final reading of my conviction.

"Ean McClaud, by my order you've been granted a pardon."

Shock ricocheted through me. My knees buckled. "Released? I'm to be released? What about the trial, the hanging? I mean, did someone confess?"

Smarthe looked up. "Do you want to be hanged?"

"No," I stammered. Tears flooded my eyes as the words of my reprieve sank into my brain. I was to be freed. I wanted to cry and laugh. If only there was someone to rejoice with me.

Smarthe signed my pardon and handed it across his desk. "This colony has been too lenient. There'll never again be easy duty as you've served. Be grateful you're leaving now." He strutted to his window and turned to his assistant. "Thompson, notify the soldiers to take this man immediately to Eaglehawk Neck."

His mousy assistant scurried away. I shifted weight off my injured leg, waiting for a final lecture.

Smarthe stared at my worn, ragged clothes, then lifted his nose as if sniffing garbage. He turned away to emphasize his disgust. "The pardon remains conditional to your good behavior. You may not leave Tasmania without my permission, and I do not see myself granting it. Keep this pardon as your identification for the occasions you're stopped by a constable. I've written explicit directions to refuse your passage to England, even in death. Do you understand?"

I dipped my head. "Yes, sir." Inside I chanted, 'I'm free, I'm free.'

My knees wobbled. I straightened and looked straight ahead while inside I continued to silently chant, 'I'm free, I'm free.'

Smarthe continued, "As an escapee, you've lost any chance for a full pardon. One more crime, one more conviction and you'll return here for the rest of your life."

I clenched my teeth to keep from speaking. The anger I'd carried all these years for the injustices piled on me began to recede. A remnant of it refused to leave. I was *not* guilty of theft. I did *not* kill anyone. Yet those accusations would follow me through my life. I longed to shout my innocence, to remove this unfair blot from my family's name, but could not. Instead, I sighed. At least more years of my life wouldn't be spent in prison. I straightened as a final act of compliance, anything to end my ordeal as quickly as possible. I ventured to ask one last question. "Sir?"

"What is it?"

"May I know how my name was cleared?"

Smarthe's jaw tightened as if to hold back his opinion. "A soldier came forward last week. He came to your cell the night after the murder to pick up his boots. Overheard two exiles outside the window. They were laughing about how they'd stolen the key from the guard. Killed Jarvis because he murdered their friend from Macquarie Harbor prison."

A gasp of disbelief escaped my lips. If Theo and I hadn't overheard a young soldier scolded for his sloppy appearance. If Theo hadn't urged me to barter for postage to contact Maudie Claire. If that soldier hadn't returned for his polished boots at the exact moment to hear the convict admit the murder—I shook my head at all these happenings. The clergy shouted repeatedly that we had no hope, no possibility of redemption. My chin quivered. He was wrong. They were *all* wrong.

Smarthe handed my papers to the two soldiers entering his office. "See that he leaves Port Arthur within the hour. He's a bad influence on those who remain."

The soldiers whisked me to a waiting cart. One last time, I was shackled to an iron ring in the bed of the cart.

The ride should have been joyous, but I'd never be free in the way I anticipated, but what was freedom? Being a printer's devil, slaving for years for a bed and food? Working in a coal mine, never seeing daylight? And why did they continue to hold me when my name had been cleared a week ago?

As we neared Eaglehawk Neck, I brushed the dirt from the worn worker clothes I'd been given. My clothing and a piece of paper telling those I met that I'd been a criminal were my only possessions. I valued them above riches.

Soldiers checked my papers and held back the dogs as I was released from the cart. They kept their guns pointed at me as I limped away from the guard outpost.

I rounded the first bend in the road and stepped off to sit on a fallen tree. I inhaled deep draughts of the chilly air, closed my eyes, and dozed until a snap in the brush startled me to wakefulness. I stretched, and headed away from the Port Arthur peninsula forever.

My mind whirled with questions but no answers. Would the O'Carroll family accept me back on the farm? Did they know about the murder charges? Would the settlers living close to the O'Carroll's demand I move on? It was time to take my freedom and accept events as they arose.

The cold, salty air and the restless sea nearby surged with hope. I limped on and stopped when I wished. I slid down a low bank and waded in the icy ocean. No one watched me or waited with shackles or a cat-o-nines ready to strike me for breaking a rule.

I continued on. When my damaged leg tired, I slowed my pace and stopped to watch a breeze ruffle the nearby trees. Above me a white gull circled and dove into the sea. I started walking again. With each step I became lighter and freer.

The quiet was disturbed as a troop of soldiers marched south toward Port Arthur. Fear leapt through me. I stepped off the road to allow them to pass, but they stopped. Every man readied his gun.

"You! Raise your arms. Turn and put your hands on the tree trunk beside you."

I did as they ordered and swallowed down bile. What if they found reason to shoot me or take me back to Port Arthur? I'd heard stories of released exiles killed or wounded, then imprisoned and held for weeks because a soldier suspected the man to be a runner.

"Do you have papers?"

"In my breeches pocket."

"Remove them with one hand, then turn to face me with your hands in the air."

My pulse raced as I handed him my papers.

The soldier took his time checking each line and holding the Lieutenant Governor's seal up to the morning light. His hooded eyes scanned my clothing; then he handed me the papers and said, "Let him pass."

I stayed by the side of the road, shaking with relief until they'd marched on. When they were out of sight, I dropped down on the ground under a tree and wept.

After an hour's rest, I resumed walking. Just then, a wagon barreled toward me. I limped off the road, allowing it to pass. Dust clouds flew, obscuring the driver. The wagon pulled to a stop. I waited for the dust to settle, wondering if this was the constable come to imprison me or perhaps a farmer who thought I was an escaped convict and worth a small reward.

The small driver wore baggy trousers, a loose jacket, and a kerchief over his face. I raised my hands, prepared to surrender whatever was required to be allowed to continue north, everything except my pardon. I waited. The driver sat watching me.

"Ean?"

The voice was high-pitched. When the kerchief lowered, I saw Maudie Claire. Dust covered her clothing as well as the backs of the sweaty horses. She slid to one side. "It's you! Oh, Ean, I'm so sorry I'm late. It took me a long while to convince Galen to let me come alone."

My heart danced in relief as I watched her dust-covered, smiling face. "Late? How did you know?"

"Father's been tracking your arrest and sentence. He knows officers and clarks from his work for the government. A man named Mad something sent us a letter a few days ago."

Edward Maddox. I smiled and made a place inside my heart for his unexpected kindness.

"You know I was accused of murder?"

Her expression sobered. "Yes. Father and Galen wrote letters to the Lieutenant Governor on your behalf, but he refused to forward them to the judge."

I shrugged. "Thank them for me."

"Thank them yourself. Climb up. We need to head back."

"Maudie Claire, you drove all this way? Alone?"

A smile spread across her freckled face. "No, Galen's in Richmond. I promised we'd return quickly."

A shyness overpowered me. I limped toward the back of the cart.

"Ean? Where are you going?"

I slapped the side of the wagon and shrugged. "I've ridden in the back of so many carts over the last years it's—" I wiped away the tears gathering at the corners of my eyes.

I climbed up next to her. She smiled, then reached out and touched my face. I held her hand against my skin, drawing its coolness inside me and relaxing as she flicked the reins. We headed north.

She watched me, but she said nothing, perhaps sensing my need for quiet. My excitement blossomed. Maudie Claire sat next to me. Over the past years, I thought I'd never see her again. Now, sharing the wagon felt natural, like I belonged.

The evergreens along the coast road screened the ocean from view. Their branches spread lacy shadows across our path. The approaching summer created a calm inside me. I listened to the steady clop, clop of the horse hooves and swayed as each step carried us away from Port Arthur forever. I closed my eyes.

Suddenly, we stopped. My eyes shot open, expecting soldiers had surrounded the wagon, weapons drawn. I ducked down below the wagon seat.

"Ean? What is it?"

I exhaled and straightened when I saw no one approached. "Why did we stop?"

She held the reins in her lap. "I reserved a bath for you in the inn. I thought—"

I shook my head and chuckled.

"What's so funny?"

"It doesn't matter." I climbed down from the wagon. "Thank you for this kindness."

Maudie Claire smiled and handed me a basket. "I'll wait out here. We'll have lunch when you finish. Then we'll meet Galen and drive back to the farm."

I sat in the large copper tub, pouring pitchers of hot water onto my shoulders. I closed my eyes, absorbing the warmth. My breathing slowed.

A persistent knock woke me. "Sir, sir? Your hour is about ended. Do you desire more time?"

"No. I'll be out soon."

I finished scrubbing. The tub water darkened as my skin turned from dirty gray to sunless white. I stepped from the tub, noticing that the ends of my fingers and toes shriveled like dried leaves. I hadn't been this clean since I was a child.

My balance faltered as I stood on a braided rug to dry off. The twist of my broken leg was a permanent souvenir from my years in prison. Despite my fear in the mine, I'd done an honest day's work and helped Devon set new records. My limp lay witness to my courage.

As I dried my back, my fingers touched the lattice work of scars. Over time I'd had sixty lashes, enough to kill a less determined man. I vowed to never forget the pain of the cat across my back nor to stand idly by when one was raised in anger against any living thing.

When I stood in front of the oval mirror above the sink, I jerked back. A stranger stared back at me. His sallow skin belonged to a corpse. His brown hair, my hair, hung like frayed rope. I combed it back and continued staring into the mirror. Lines crowded the corners of my eyes. How old was I? Twenty? I appeared older than Master John, a man of thirty-five.

My beard covered my face except for two places by my ears where I'd plucked it out in moments of near insanity. I used the scissor from Maudie Claire's basket to trim my beard close to my skin. Then I scraped the remaining hair with a razor, shaving away any trace of the beard. The newly exposed skin was rough and blotchy. I dumped my shearings into a waste bin along with my exile clothes.

The basket Maudie Claire handed me smelled of freshly cleaned wool and cotton. New underwear and socks lay beneath the clothes. Did Maudie Claire pick out underwear and socks for me? A blush worked its way onto my face as I dressed.

The wool pants hung loose and the shirt bagged, but both stroked my skin like silk. I took the rope from my old breeches and tied up the new. The boy from Langstone had disappeared, replaced by a released criminal—no, a free man.

My insides churned as I returned to the wagon. Maudie Claire sat on the seat with her head back and her eyes closed. She looked like a dust-covered angel.

The gravel crunched as I approached. She opened her eyes and gasped. "My goodness! You look, ah, so-o different. How do you feel?"

I turned my face away, inhaled the chilly air, and swallowed hard before I faced her. "Free. I feel free."

Before she picked up the reins, she reached under the wagon seat and handed me a package wrapped in a small lap rug. Her fingers lingered on mine.

I opened the package. It was the green vest she'd made for me. "You'll want this. It's chilly today."

I slipped on the vest and stroked the raised pattern and oyster shell buttons down the front. We drove on in silence, heading back to the O'Carroll farm—heading home.

A Convict's Lament

When my whole life dims to its final days,

I'll trace each moment that I've spent with you.

Though clouds and rain obscure remembered views

And life is crowded with regret and pain;

My faults shall glare across my aging eyes,

Excusing not my sins nor absent faith.

I'd thought my life would be a bright'ning ray

Filled with your love, your face, your gentle grace,

But ne'er did I foresee our looming fate

That men would block our love at every chance.

As fear and pain become my daily life,

I rant against the coming of my death.

Remember me, hold fast onto our love,

For all's not lost until I cease to live

P. Eger

Reader Questions

What characteristics describe Ean at the beginning of the story?

Ean meets several people between his life in England and his stay at Port Arthur. Share your opinion on how each character affected his life.

the printer	Fiona	The O'Carroll's:
the giant prisoner	Edward	Maudie Claire
Mister Meed	Tom	Galen
Charley	Barty	Patrick
Devon Montross	Captian Woodwright	hired hand Robert
Theo	Lady Colridge	

What events in Ean's life caused him to modify his goals, change his direction?

Suggested Books and Research Information

Fatal Shore by Robert Hughes

The Bright Side of My Condition by Charlotte Randall

Patrick's Journey by Roy T. Humphreys

For the Term of His Natural Life by Marcus Clarke

Morgan's Run by Colleen McCullough

Kidd—A Naval Adventure by Julian Stockman

The Australians (book series) by William Stuart Long

Penal colony books by Franz Kafka

Life in Australia books by Kate Greenville

http://www.maritimetas.org/ The Maritime Museum of Tasmania

Chat, Comment, and Connect with the Author

Book clubs and schools are invited to participate in FREE virtual discussions with Paddy Eger.

Chat:
Invite Paddy to chat with your group via the web or phone.

Comment:
Ask thought-provoking questions or give Paddy feedback.

Connect:
Find Paddy at a local book talk or meet and greet. Visit her blog and website for dates, times, and locations or to set up your group's virtual discussion. For excerpts, author interviews, news, and future releases, visit *PaddyEger.com*

About the Author

Paddy Eger is a fiction author who lives in Washington state. Her love of story coupled with her years as an educator and a writer inspire her to provide glimpses into the lives of everyday people who are placed into extraordinary situations.

Her historical adventure novel is the product of a visit she made to the Port Arthur site on the southern coast of the island of Tasmania. Through a combination of research and imagination, she recreates the story of brutal prison life in the 1850s, where floggings, food deprivation, and hard labor were daily realities.

Eger's earlier novels include an award-winning trilogy about the lives of young, professional ballet dancers. She also publishes nonfiction materials in support of teachers, classroom adults, and parents. Visit her website: _paddyeger.com_ to learn more about Paddy and to follow her blogs.

Paddy Eger's Award Winning Trilogy

84 Ribbons

"A pure coming-of-age tale with moments of quiet drama *84 Ribbons* is about thriving despite the imperfections of life." YA Foresight, *Foreword Reviews,* Spring 2014. *DanceSpirit* Magazine's Pick of the Month, April 2014. "Any young dancer will find herself in Marta's story", Newbery Honor Author, Kirby Larson, *Hattie Big Sky.*

When the Music Stops—Dance On

Step into Marta's world. In the multi-award-winning second book, Marta struggles to regain her ability to dance and support herself at the same time stepping into adulthood amid unexpected challenges. Will she find a deep well of strength to meet her life-changing situations head-on?

Letters to Follow— A Dancers Adventure

Marta's best friend Lynne begins a grand adventure when she travels to Paris to join a dance troupe. Her move to a wacky boarding house is not a good fit for an outspoken American dancer but it creates humorous encounters with the tenants. At the end of the exchange, Lynne becomes the travel companion for her harebrained Uncle Leo. She sends postcards and letters to Marta to retell her madcap adventures.